"Duffy's Regiment"

This is the story of how one man's
half-century of service to his
community and country helped to develop
the Hastings & Prince Edward Regiment's
capacity for survival. After the testing
years of the 1930s it came through a
leadership crisis in 1940, found a new
spirit in the English countryside and
distinguished itself in fierce infantry
battles — but since then has had to
struggle against public indifference
to the old truth that
freedom isn't free.

By Kenneth B. Smith

"DUFFY'S REGIMENT"

A History of the Hastings and Prince Edward Regiment

Kenneth B. Smith

Toronto and Oxford
Dundurn Press
1987

Cover Design: Andy Tong
Design and Production: Nigel Smith
Printing and Binding: Gagné Printing Ltd., Louiseville, Quebec, Canada

The writing of this manuscript and the publication of this book were made possible by
support from several sources. The publisher wishes to acknowledge the generous
assistance and ongoing support of **The Canada Council, The Book Publishing
Industry Development Programme of the Department of
Communications** and **The Ontario Arts Council.**

Care has been taken to trace the ownership of copyright material used in the text
(including the illustrations). The author and publisher welcome any information enabling
them to rectify any reference or credit in subsequent editions.

J. Kirk Howard, Publisher

Dundurn Press Limited
1558 Queen Street East
Toronto, Canada
M4L 1E8

Dundurn Distribution Limited
Athol Brose, School Hill,
Wargrave, Reading
England RG10 8DY

Canadian Cataloguing in Publication Data
Smith, Kenneth B., 1921–
    Duffy's regiment

Bibliography: p.
ISBN 1-55002-022-6

1. Duffy, Angus, 1914 –   . 2. Canada. Canadian
Armed Forces. Hastings and Prince Edward Regiment –
History. 3. World War, 1939-1945 – Regimental
histories – Canada. I. Title.

UA602.H37S65 1987   356'.1'0971358   C87–094964–0

Contents

Foreword

By The Rt. Hon. Lord Tweedsmuir CBE

Ken Smith was the ideal man to write this book, coming as he does from a family long settled in rural Ontario. He joined the Canadian Infantry in the last war and went overseas as a lieutenant. He was in England in July, 1943, when the 1st Canadian Division landed in Sicily as part of the Eighth Army to begin the liberation of Europe. By late October he was on his way to Italy as a reinforcement officer. The ship was torpedoed in the Mediterranean — an experience he and all his comrades took in their stride. After a few weeks in Italy he found himself posted to the Hastings & Prince Edward Regiment, widely known as the Hasty Ps, and nine days later he was in the line. He commanded a platoon for the next 135 days until he stopped a burst of machine gun fire in the Liri Valley in the aftermath of the battle for Cassino.

To that same Regiment I had been posted some six months before his arrival. It was to be one of the most significant events in my whole life, as it was in his.

The people of the two counties of Hastings and Prince Edward have been hardy defenders of liberty since away back. Many are from United Empire Loyalist stock whose ancestors defended their own allegiance against George

Washington, and then moved further north to Canada to stay with that allegiance. These two counties are famous for their farmland, and men from the farmlands are natural soldiers.

Farmers know a lot about life, and a lot about death. They have what is so important for infantrymen — an eye for movement, for weather and for ground. And they grow up knowing how to use a rifle. It may be that they think slowly, but they think deeply. Not for them the flimsy delusion that evidence of peaceful intentions on the part of one's own peaceful country begets peaceful intentions on the part of a determined and heavily armed foreign aggressor. It is clearly a virtue to fight in the last ditch, but it is even more bitterly clear that it is not a virtue to find yourself in the last ditch, before you wake up to the danger. That is the reason why the Militia battalions of Canada, to whom the country owes a debt that is beyond calculation, have remained in being despite every discouragement.

This is not to lay undue blame at the door of those who formed any particular governments. It is one of the difficulties that all democracies face. The aggressor nation always has the same advantage that the burglar has over the house owner.

The author sets out the story of how men of these two counties became a famous fighting force in Canada's time of battle, in spite of neglect by a series of governments which reduced them at one time to drilling with wooden silhouettes of rifles. They set off for Europe in December, 1939, as a cheerful collection of Saturday night soldiers. They returned in 1945 having won 31 battle honours.

Anyone who ever had anything to do with the Hasty Ps had something to do with the making of the Regiment. In wartime it had, in turn, nine commanding officers, of which I had the honour to be one myself. I am not a Canadian citizen, but I am a Canadian soldier, and mightily proud of it. Under six of those commanding officers in wartime and four more in the postwar Militia, Angus Duffy served as

Regimental Sergeant-Major. Later he was to command the Regiment himself. He will always be regarded as representing the very spirit of the Regiment.

I was posted to the Regiment as Second in Command in the summer of 1943, just before we sailed for Sicily. When I met Angus Duffy I became instantly aware that I was meeting a man who was loved and respected to the highest degree by the whole of the Regiment, and so he remains today in retirement. At that time he was not quite 29 years old and he stood just under five feet, five inches high. For that reason he had always been called Shorty, until he became Mr. Duffy, which was always pronounced as if it were one word. He had a face that reminded me of several of the nicest characters from the Tales of Hans Andersen. Even then he was a father figure to the whole Regiment.

He was broad and strong, a formidable boxer and possessed of a delightful sense of humour which was a tonic to us when things were going badly. His origin was from two powerful strands of Canadian history — old United Empire stock, of New York Irish origin, and Acadian French from New Brunswick where he was born.

Duffy joined the Regiment as a private nine years before the war started and had risen to become a Company Sergeant-Major. Just before he embarked for Britain in December, 1939, he was promoted to Regimental Sergeant Major.

When they arrived in England the Hasty Ps found themselves in one of the worst British winters in decades, feeling homesick, miserable and out of their element. Angus realized that he had to capture their interest and their confidence before he could get their obedience. And he did so.

A stern regular army officer, with a distinguished career in the First War, replaced the first commanding officer. He was exactly what was needed. To him everything that was not perfect was disgraceful. Angus had to work like a Trojan to keep up with his demands. Lieutenant-Colonel Harry

Salmon was an ideal partner for Angus Duffy and together they set the battalion on its way to becoming a first class fighting machine.

Angus's devotion to his Regiment was absolute. He drove his men and himself to the ultimate. Behind a plain exterior he had a real streak of poetry in him. In insisting that all cap badges be polished until they shone, he would say: "That badge is not yours. It belongs to everyone who ever wore it in the past and will ever wear it in the future."

The war years dragged by on leaden feet, but the tide was steadily turning in the Allies' favour when we set out to land in Sicily. The Canadian Army with all its years of training and with the advantage of the lessons of other battlefields to profit by, and confidence in their methods of training, had changed from an amateur army to one more professional than any that had left the shores of Britain under Marlborough or Wellington.

On a burning July day in Sicily in 1943, Monty came to address us. Angus had paraded the battalion in a stubble field and Monty came into our midst in a Bren gun carrier and called us all around him. He gave the most impressive soldier's speech and quite the shortest we had ever heard. It lasted for less than four minutes. "Everything that I will give you to do will be difficult," he said, "but nothing that I will ever give you to do will be impossible." We never forgot that.

Our commanding officer, Bruce Sutcliffe, was killed on the day that we were ordered to seize a high point in the Sicilian hills at Assoro. It had been a vital defensive point for 800 years when Roger the Norman built his castle on the top of it, and it was just as strategically important that day as it had been when he built it. It was defended by some of the best troops in the German army, the 15th Panzer Grenadiers, whom Farley Mowat, then the battalion intelligence officer and now widely famous as a writer, once described as "old soldiers toughened in Africa and a fighting breed." That position had never been taken in all history.

But, as I will always believe, through direct intervention

of Providence, Angus and I were sitting on the peak next morning beside the ruin of the Norman castle. On the eastern side was a faint coral tinge in the sky which hung over the crater of Mount Etna. Inland medieval villages clung to tall peaks in the rising dawn. Below us was a German battery and a dusty road smoked with confusion.

Not many days later I ended up in a plaster cast. When I returned to the battalion it was in a rainy Italian autumn that found us among the oak woods in the foothills of the Apennines. There were many new faces, but Angus's was unchanged. All through Sicily and until half way up Italy men of the battalion had Angus still with them. By that time his sheer presence had come to mean a source of tremendous encouragement. Tired infantrymen were cheered to get a glimpse of him on a night march, to hear his voice or to get a slap on the back or a joking word or two — and then he would be gone.

But suddenly he was told that he was to go back to England and his great gifts were never properly used again. Wartime is a tremendously inefficient period in the use of resources, both human and otherwise, and no more striking example could be found than in the case of Angus. Eventually the war dragged to its end.

As I have written elsewhere: "Glib men have told us for the last six years we have been fighting to make it a better world. We had not. We had been fighting to prevent it from becoming a far worse one. That is a struggle as old as time. It is the never-ending fight for freedom." We had done our bit, as the men of the two counties always had done.

The story ends at last on a happier note when Angus's great service to his country is acknowledged by his being made a Member of the Order of Canada, to add to the recognition of a great Canadian that lives on in all our hearts.

Introduction

On a perfect morning in August, 1976, Sheila and I parked our rented Fiat in the village of San Tommaso, a few miles north of Ortona, overlooking the Adriatic. As we started walking toward the eastern edge of the village I said that we would soon come to a narrow track along a bank overlooking a vineyard. I hadn't walked there since 1944, but the track was still evident and 100 yards or so along it there was still a sharp right turn. The vines were heavy with grapes and the harvest had begun. There had been few vines when I was there before, because Canadian and German artillery and mortar fire had knocked down everything including most of the wires and supporting concrete posts. It was a nearly bare patch of sandy soil about 50 yards square, sloping away to the south and west.

On January 9, 1944, I came to that place with 11 platoon, 'B' Company of the Hastings & Prince Edward Regiment. We dug our slit trenches in the shelter of the banks along the two high sides of the vineyard. In the next seven days the village and my vineyard were shelled fiercely and often by the Germans who had been driven out of the area 10 days before by the 48th Highlanders. As we were having our midday meal on our second day, a Messerschmitt roared in at us out of the sun, just skimming the trees, but we saw it in time to dive into our trenches a second before machine gun bullets ripped across the sand about a foot away. A mortar bomb or a bullet had to be coming practically straight down to get you in a slit trench which could often be sited in such a way as to make that virtually impossible. Even under heavy shelling, an infantryman could soon develop a good sense of security there.

For some of my men, as for myself, this was the first time in the line, but NCOs like Irv Chambers, Ivan Ellis and Fred Forshee had landed in Sicily six months earlier. They soon taught us the difference between the sound of Jerry shells and our own, and hence the right time to take cover. They were able to work out immediately just where our Bren guns should be sited. A forward listening post was needed, a few yards up a very narrow path that branched off where the main track made its right-angle bend (and that little path was still there in 1976). Ivan Ellis went up the path to check a sentry about midnight and a rifle shot slammed into a tree trunk right above his head. He commended the rookie for being awake, in spite of his having forgotten to challenge properly. (If the challenge was "SWAN" and you didn't get the reply "EDGAR", or if it was "RUSSIAN" and you didn't get the reply "BEAR", then you might try shooting.)

The NCOs felt the Germans might try to send in night patrols when the shelling was keeping our heads down, and so we set up trip wires with tin cans strung on them, 25 or 30 yards in front of us. These marvellous NCOs made the youngest rookie feel confident, not to mention what they did for a young officer's morale. In the line it seemed only right that they should be on a first-name basis with me, a democratic practice that had long prevailed in that tightly knit small town and rural Regiment. They had seen lieutenants come and go, and there was good-natured chatter about who would get my watch or my boots when I was gone. I had been with the Regiment for nine days when we went into the line, and I was to last for 135 days more.

How did I happen to be in that Italian vineyard anyway, and not somewhere in Sussex preparing for the Normandy campaign? I had been at battle school at Crookham Cross-roads near Aldershot when the 1st Canadian Division landed in Sicily on July 10, 1943, but I was on the reinforcement list for the Royal Hamilton Light Infantry in the 2nd Division. Summer came and went and the RHLI was doing fine without me. The Canadian Government, however, felt that the 5th Canadian Armoured Division should join the 1st Division in Italy. The division was dispatched without any indication from General Bernard L. Montgomery that he needed or wanted any more Canadians for his Eighth Army.

Committing another division to the Mediterranean theatre required the rapid assembly of a large reinforcement pool. I was one of many hundreds brought together in the south of England in October and I was designated as a reinforcement officer for the Irish Regiment of Canada in the 11th Brigade, 5th Division. We embarked at Liverpool on October 26, and the next day joined other ships coming out of the Clyde. There were 1,800 of us aboard the S.S. Santa Elena, representing infantry, artillery, machine gunners, engineers, chaplains and even grave registration officers, and with us were all ranks of No. 14 Canadian General Hospital, including more than 100 nurses.

Convoy KMF 25A steamed a zigzag course for nine days through Atlantic swells, which weren't quite as rough as the Irish Sea. Being assigned as duty officer to the lowest deck was a traumatic experience for a not very good sailor. I was never so sick before or since. By Thursday, November 4, we were in pleasant waters, but as we passed Gibraltar about sundown, we had an inescapable feeling that Axis spies on the Moroccan coast had their glasses on us. The Allies had sea control in the Med, but the Luftwaffe was making an all-out effort to harass shipping.

Spitfires patrolled above the convoy as it moved along on November 5 and 6, past the flat headlands of North Africa. Sunset and darkness came on the 5th and nothing unusual happened. But the next day the Germans planned to end the suspense. Timed to reach the convoy just after the patrolling Spits were dismissed, two waves of torpedo bombers took off. At 6:05 p.m. the first Dornier 217 was spotted 8,000 yards off the port column and the escort commander gave the order to engage.

Aboard the Santa Elena some passengers were at dinner. Many others were strolling along the decks watching the sunset. I came out of the officers' dining room before 6 o'clock, chose a library book and headed for my cabin. I had just closed the door when "Action Stations" sounded. Out in the corridor again, I could hear the sound of distant firing and in a few seconds a burst of anti-aircraft fire from our own ship and then a mighty jolt. The ship lurched, the lights went out and smoke poured into passageways.

A single torpedo had hit near the waterline, putting the engine room out of commission and a bomb had hit the after deck. Emergency lighting came on in a moment, accompanied by the "Abandon Ship" on the blower.

For all but the nurses and ship's gunners "Action Stations" was an order to go below. The nurses' assembly point was on the sun deck. Tracers were still streaming in all directions, and the first boats were loaded and lowered before the firing died away. There was one scream, but no panic. On the horizon a Dutch ship, Marnix van St. Aldegonde, was burning, and the U.S. destroyer Beatty wallowed helplessly, its battles over. JU-88s roared in behind the Dorniers in the direction of the Matson liner Monterey. Bren gunners of the Perth Regiment, Irish Regiment and the Cape Breton Highlanders helped bring down at least one of the raiders.

That warm Saturday night was no ordinary bath night. As we waited at our boat stations it soon became obvious that the Santa Elena, although low in the stern, was not going down immediately. But skeptical soldiers were already in the water, paddling on rafts or swimming towards the anchored Monterey. Red lights on their life jackets made strange patterns as they bobbed up and down in the darkness. Shouts, songs and earthy jests echoed across the water. It became more of a picnic than a marine disaster for some of the raftsmen who had taken food with them from the ship.

At 11 o'clock John Bassett, adjutant of a reinforcement unit, ordered junior officers over the side. It was like a balmy September evening at home and the short swim to the Monterey seemed no great challenge. I had just entered the water when a lifeboat loomed out of the darkness. I avoided the bow, grabbed the stern, held on and gradually pulled myself aboard. Most of the others were Santa Elena crewmen who had given up on their ship.

Upon reaching the Monterey in tens and then hundreds, the swimmers, paddlers and lifeboat passengers all faced a 50-foot climb on scramble nets. Nurses accepted this challenge with amazing vitality, even after rowing all the way. As I reached the bottom of a scramble net, one nurse lost her grip near the top of the net and plummeted into the darkness. She landed in a small patch of open water between two lifeboats and immediately climbed to the top safely. It was nearly midnight when a submarine warning made it necessary for the Monterey to move. U.S. destroyers picked up the few Canadians still in the water. Every Canadian from the Santa Elena was safe.

All the next afternoon we watched a destroyer towing the Santa Elena towards Philippeville Harbour in the hope of salvaging all the equipment left behind. But this was not to be. Within a mile of shallow water an explosion shot the bow upward and the doomed ship slid back and almost straight down against the setting sun.

Instead of a reinforcement depot at Philippeville, our destination became Naples, because that was where the Monterey was directed to go. Most of us had only the clothing we stood in, but gradually we were outfitted. Former Italian barracks were our quarters for about two weeks in Caserta, and when our unit, officially called No. 2 Canadian Base Reinforcement Depot, moved to Avellino, we were closer to the front than the 1st Division's own reinforcement depot.

Just before Christmas some reinforcements from Philippeville passed through Avellino on their way to the 1st Division up the Adriatic coast. Since December 6, fighting had been fierce and officers were needed, according to friends of mine going up. "The 11th Brigade won't be in action for a while," they said. "Try to get a transfer to the 1st Div." I took their advice and in a few days I was on my way to the front by train. We reached Lucera that same afternoon.

It was Christmas Eve. Officers were quartered in the bishop's palace. I wanted to write some letters and I volunteered to stay part of the evening with an impatient officer who was under arrest awaiting trial for going absent without leave and joining an American unit. When the cathedral bells were ringing for the midnight mass I placed my bedroll in a long row on a marble floor and was soon dreaming of home. Late Christmas afternoon the train moved on toward Termoli.

It took until December 30 to get up through the various transit camps to 'B' Echelon of the Royal Canadian Regiment. Several other officers and I spent the night with a very nervous RCR quartermaster in a stone house at San Leonardo. I still had no idea which of the nine infantry battalions of the 1st Division I would be joining.

The next morning vehicles delivered officers and men to various units. I rode in a truck to battalion headquarters of the RCR. Everybody else went inside to report. An officer pointed to a large house half a mile away or so and said: "That's BHQ of the Hasty Ps. Off you go." I swung my kit bag over my shoulder and plodded across muddy fields to my new home. I knocked on a door of the big house. The officer who opened it said: "Come in. My name is Farley Mowat. I'm the I.O. Come and meet our padre, Fred Goforth." In a few minutes I also met the C.O., Bert Kennedy of Owen Sound, forty miles from my home town. He got on the phone to 'B' Company to let the company commander know that a new officer had arrived. Frank Hammond gave me a great welcome and we walked to his company headquarters. I would be taking over from Sandy Moffatt who was going back to England. Although I arrived knowing no one in the Regiment, the reception was so genuinely warm that I wondered how I could have been so lucky.

By the time we went into the line at San Tommaso I had learned much about my NCOs and men; how long they had been in the Regiment and where their homes were. The week in the line was a more concentrated period of learning than I had ever experienced. And I soon found that some events out of the line weren't covered by any training manuals either.

In a reserve company position for a couple of weeks, I was called to battalion headquarters one day to assist the adjutant. Returning to the platoon late in the afternoon I found that every man appeared to have had a very pleasant encounter with the local vino. One Saskatchewan lad was expressing his merriment in an unusual way — chasing another Westerner in circles near platoon headquarters with a Bren gun and firing at his feet. The only practical way to end that nonsense seemed to be to walk out there and ask him for the Bren. He handed it over, and it was amazing how quickly everybody sobered up.

The sunny Sunday afternoon of January 30 brought the Regiment the strange assignment of trying to push northward from the village of Villa Grande to seize positions beyond the Tollo Road. The middle of the afternoon hardly seemed the time to be trying it, for we had to cross half a mile of terrain that was as open and flat as a billiard table. We followed a barrage for several hundred yards, accompanied by tanks, but the Germans dropped a counter-barrage behind us. Our own barrage seemed to have stalled, so we had to withdraw with some casualties.

Ivan Ellis and I led the platoon in again in a dusk attack and we got close enough to hear the enemy talking behind a freshly laid smoke screen. Suddenly heavy weapons created a torrent of lead that would shred anything more than a foot above the ground. It was a long crawl back, shell hole by shell hole in a First World War scene complete with flares. One of my men died of wounds that night. Not exactly a Charge of the Light Brigade on a small scale, but not a masterpiece of planning either.

Later we learned that the idea had been to hold the interest of the German 1st Parachute Division which might otherwise have moved against the shaky Anzio bridgehead.

Ten days later the Regiment was out of the line for a rest in the dirty little village of San Vito atop eroded Adriatic cliffs. We debussed in sloppy mud in an orchard, a revolting tent site that made us wish we were still back in those comfortable San Tommaso trenches. But our luck soon changed when Ross Damude, the roly-poly second in command of 'B' Company met a British officer from the Allied Military Government. Friendly chaps like this Major had power to take over houses and send their civilian occupants to refugee camps. Within a few minutes he told Ross that the best villa in San Vito was ours. It seemed no time at all until we were in residence and Charlie Perry, our cook, was turning out his famous pies in the basement kitchen.

The most memorable feature of that rainy fortnight was the big spaghetti dinner laid on for 'B' Company with the aid of Joe, the only civilian allowed to remain in the villa, apparently because he was an American citizen. Our quartermaster supplied the flour, and women of the village spent most of the day making spaghetti which Joe cooked. He seemed worried all afternoon, but said nothing until our 110 men had all had seconds and thirds and were relaxing with beer and cigars. "We made only enough for 25 people," he told me. San Vito, for all its unattractiveness, seemed to have a capacity for miracles.

The days of March had a sameness about them. My platoon held various positions on the south bank of the Riccio valley, sometimes partly in view of the enemy, sometimes not. We lived in old farmhouses. A typical day began by preparing breakfast for a patrol of six or seven men who had been in a forward area for much of the night. There were weapons and equipment to clean. Ortona passes for 24-hours might be handed out, and occasionally a week's leave for someone at the Eighth Army Rest Camp in Bari.

In the afternoon a platoon commander would probably go to company headquarters to get mail or orders for that night's patrol. If wood could be scrounged, we could have a night fire in the big fireplace and the Jerries wouldn't notice the smoke. After the evening meal rum would be obtained from company headquarters and a section of about seven men would move out quietly at dusk part way along the route of that night's standing patrol, to prevent an ambush. After dark there would be card playing in the house and tea would be made. Water from the well would be safe when boiled, but there was always the danger that when you went outside a Jerry patrol might be lurking to catch you with your bucket down. About midnight, the platoon commander might put a bottle of rum in his pocket and go out alone to the section posts surrounding platoon headquarters, and down into the valley to visit the standing patrol or to await the return of a fighting patrol that had gone out further looking for prisoners. Nothing much to such a journey in the dark, but it could be a spine-tingler if a giveaway moon appeared.

Back at the house, there might be a phone message that the company on our right or left suspected the presence of a German patrol. Immediately warn the section posts. Heavy firing starts away off to the left. "The Van Doos have been in the vino," a corporal quips. The night passes without further incident.

April sunshine seemed to dry up all the mud in two or three days and it was soon clear that we would be moving. Indian troops moved in to bivouac in our area, in preparation for a takeover. On April 21 we were heading south in trucks through towns we had seen on the way up. Near Lucera we practiced attacks with tanks. A westward move brought us to Limatola, a village on the Volturno, for nine days under canvas with night marches and river crossings, and time off for jaunts to Naples and some great games of inter-company softball.

We were told on May 10 that an assault on the Gustav Line would begin the following night. A message from Field Marshal Alexander said that the drive for Rome would be the opening of the final phase of the war and "to us in Italy has been given the honour of striking the first blow." On Sunday the 14th we sat in the sun as Padre Goforth spoke quietly about the sustaining power of a deeply rooted faith. Our camouflaged tents came down in the afternoon and we moved out at dusk for the battle concentration area on the Gari River. Our convoy took narrow roads with no lights. The driver of the truck carrying 11 platoon got too close to the edge and we rolled into the ditch. Several NCOs and men were injured.

When committed on the 16th the Regiment's job for the next few days was to maintain pressure as the Germans fell back toward what the Allies called the Adolf Hitler Line. It was like Sicily, the old-timers said. March in burning sun; come under shell fire; dig in; move on again. Roadsides were heavily mined and we bypassed tempting souvenirs, for we expected them to be booby-trapped. We caught occasional glimpses of Monte Cassino on our right as we reclaimed the beautiful Liri Valley for the Italians, yard by yard.

By the morning of May 20 we were getting close to the positions from which we would advance to make the assault on the Hitler Line, a belt of formidable defences built over a period of many months. My platoon approached a pair of farmhouses about 400 yards to the right of our line of advance. All seemed quiet. With all Bren guns covering us, Irv Chambers and I moved to the back door of one of the houses and burst in. No Germans. Just about 25 Italian civilians. We occupied the houses for the next two days. Shelling was sporadic. Every time the Germans put one in our backyard, it seemed that all the 1st Division's artillery opened up in reply.

In the late afternoon of May 22 we got word that we were to move up in the evening. There was scarcely an hour's light left when we formed up at 'B' Company headquarters. We had only a quarter-mile to go before we reached 'C' Company positions. A troop of British tanks was with us. Although the crews seemed a little nervous, we pushed on through lush grain to a smaller house, where we wanted to set up 'B' Company headquarters before dark.

On our left, 10 platoon under Fred Lazier and Fred Forshee tried to advance toward a gap in the wire but were pinned down by machine gun fire. The rest of 'B' Company stayed out of sight behind the little house. About 200 yards ahead, well beyond the wire, was a large red farmhouse. Sporadic fire indicated that Germans were there. CSM Bill Nolan and I were about four feet apart at one corner of the small house when an armour-piercing shell whizzed between us and thudded into the ground. Our tank troop decided to call it a day.

After dark my platoon dug in within a few feet of the heavy belt of barbed wire and about 3 o'clock in the morning I sent a small party with automatic weapons out through a gap. They accompanied our pioneers who were clearing mines from a dirt road leading past the big house. They went nearly as far as the house and no one tried to stop them. When they came back about 4 o'clock the sky was brightening. We all moved back to company headquarters.

I'll never forget how that day dawned. A heavy mist lay over the warm, lush Liri Valley where the grain was waist-high. Before the guns began their prelude to the assault of the 2nd and 3rd Brigades, it was a quiet pastoral scene that must have appealed to the many countrymen in our battalion. But under the greenness lay heavily defended concrete bunkers and trenches.

The warm May morning must have reminded some of our men that the orchards of Prince Edward County would be in blossom.

Lance-Corporal Jim Gillan had often said to me that his main ambition was to get safely home to a Manitoba farm and behind a plough. That afternoon he died instantly right behind me as a long burst from a heavy machine gun cut us down together.

I fell with my right shoulder against the outside of my right ankle. After I managed to straighten out the leg, Corporal Carl Watson crawled over to me. I rolled onto his back and he crawled out of the line of fire. As stretcher-bearers carried me back towards the Regimental Aid Post we met tanks moving up for what was to be a furious assault on the big farmhouse. One of the many prisoners taken there was heard to say later that the fire was more intense than at Stalingrad.

Homer Eshoo, our medical officer, soon bandaged and splinted my leg and Padre Goforth gave me my first shot of rum. Corporal Joe Marin, who had suffered a chest wound, moved off with me across country. Our stretchers were on top of jeeps. We changed to an ambulance which brought us to No. 4 Casualty Clearing Station by early evening.

One of the strangest sensations of my life came when I was carried into a large tent, like a circus marquee, where rows of men on cots lay resting, bleeding, moaning and dying. Rain spattered softly on the canvas. It was a good feeling to be under cover. A forest of stands had quickly grown along the rows of cots. From each of them a bottle of blood or plasma was suspended. In a few minutes a bottle was right above me. I shivered as the refrigerated blood entered my veins. After a sedative came a warm drift into unconsciousness. It was two weeks before D-Day in Normandy and clearly the war was over for me, but the 144 days with the Hastings & Prince Edward Regiment had made me a Hasty P for life.

I left at a turning point. The British Eighth Army and the U.S. Fifth Army were moving relentlessly toward Rome. With the soldiers of many nations, the Canadians were reclaiming part of Europe from one of the most evil regimes in history. While no soldier can guarantee to make the world better, we most unmistakably helped to stop it from becoming unbelievably worse.

The intervening years have strengthened that sense of having shared a priceless comradeship. Attending Regimental reunions with lifetime friends, October after October, watching our young postwar successors on the march and joining them on special occasions have made familiar places in the Regimental area seem increasingly like hallowed ground. For 35 years after the war every gathering seemed to bring out stories about the Regiment that I had never heard before. These fragments of Regimental history were more numerous than memory can recall or prudence would attempt to compile, but they have inspired what follows here. It is a long look at a remarkable esprit de corps which carried the Regiment to great heights in wartime and kept it alive as a Militia battalion in an era of public apathy and government indifference.

Leadership will emerge as a vital factor in that survival. One man in particular who had much to do with shaping the Regiment in wartime continued to embody the Regimental spirit for decades afterwards. The year 1980 marked the 50th anniversary of the enlistment of Private Angus Bennett Duffy, legendary Regimental Sergeant-Major in the Second World War, commanding officer from 1958 to 1962 and Honorary Colonel from 1976 to 1981. We will see much of what happened through his eyes.

Men who are in their sixties, their seventies and even their eighties did great things for Canada as infantry soldiers in the Second World War. While generally they have said little about why they were able to do what they did, we will be able to identify some sources of inspiration. This account is based largely on relatively recent talks with many of them. It tells their story at a time when they can look back over most of a lifetime and set these experiences in a rich context.

They were part of great events. They brought to their battles the strengths of a largely rural people. The popular media in recent years have exaggerated the urbanization of Canada and too often have sought their heroes in that setting, as if our open spaces had ceased to be significant. Many urban Canadians have rural roots; some of them have been returning to the country since the 1960s; for others the longing is unfulfilled.

The story of this Regiment moves across a much larger landscape than most Canadian memories can encompass. The story really covers the whole 20th century. Men born just before 1900 went to the First World War as teenagers, helped found the Regiment in 1920 and answered the call in 1939. The very youngest to serve in the Second World War will see this century out. Today's Militiamen will carry the traditions into the next century.

This account is a story written with concern, not only that the military aspect of Canadian history is so unfamiliar to so many, but that the Canadians who would be called upon to bear the brunt of any war that might come in the near future seem so unprepared and unwilling to recognize that infantrymen will be needed in the future. Only a few are interested in preparing to do their duty, while the rest fall back on the highly questionable theory that after rearmament only nuclear holocaust lies ahead. Canadians of 1939–1945 displayed great inner resources. Is the same potential for heroism present today? That's a fair question in view of the uncertainties that have been surrounding us in Canada, especially about what is meant by Canadian identity.

The growing military might of the Soviet Union and demonstrations of how ruthlessly it can be used, send memories racing back to the 1930s when, despite the obvious menace of Nazi Germany, the prevailing view was that no harm would come to the world. Our armed forces are not large and only a small number in uniform have been trained for battle. Politicians responded to the material preoccupations of a pleasure-bent society by down-grading military preparedness in the 1960s and 1970s, and that sad situation was complicated by a troubled economy in the early 1980s.

Nations who have shared with us in defending our freedom-loving heritage in this century, and with whom we have continued to be allied, are entitled to expect that we still have some of our old spirit in reserve. Historically the Militia has embodied it, but nurturing it has not been an easy task.

We take up the story in Loyalist country around the Bay of Quinte just before the First World War.

Chapter One
A jeweller made it work

Non-professional soldiering has always involved informal arrangements that enabled men to fit their training into the day-to-day pursuits of civilian life. Jeweller Arthur E. Bywater in the pleasant Lake Ontario town of Trenton knew all about that. As Captain Bywater he commanded 'F' Company of the 49th Hastings Rifles when the Dominion of Canada wasn't much more than 40 years old.

The careful captain kept his company's rifles locked away in a room above his store, but they appeared on other occasions besides Militia parade nights. Trenton had an excellent High School Cadet Corps. Schoolboys came to the store after classes on parade days and he issued Ross rifles (without bolts) to these enthusiastic lads. They were proud to march through the streets with the rifles, wearing their smart khaki uniforms with red cuffs and red shoulder straps. The Corps was very impressive on the march and twice won the district championship at camp in Kingston.

Howard Douglas Graham, who lived on a small farm north of Trenton, was one cadet who treasured lifetime memories of parading with cadets from all over Eastern Ontario to be inspected by the Duke of Connaught on horseback. He was one of those who, still in their teens, witnessed far more stirring events in the trenches in France, and about 40 years later he was to become Chief of the General Staff.

Militiamen and cadets volunteered in great numbers when war came, but for some strange reason the government of the day gave little thought in its mobilization plans to long established Militia battalions like the 49th Hastings Rifles and the 16th Prince Edward Regiment whose predecessors had fought in the War of 1812. These Militia battalions bearing county names in the great old British tradition were generally ignored and brand new numbered battalions were created.

Capt. Bywater enlisted in the 39th Battalion in May, 1915. He joined the 4th Battalion from Western Ontario in the field and was wounded in action in August, 1916. Cadet Graham was 17 when he hitched a horse to a cutter and made the 12-mile journey to Belleville to enlist in the 155th Battalion. He left his uniform in the cutter in the driving shed that night until he had broken the news to his parents. He was soon overseas and he did not return until 1919.

The 49th Hastings Rifles and the 16th Prince Edward Regiment continued to exist throughout the war, but most of their strength was on paper because so many men of the two counties were on active service in nine different battalions — the 2nd, 21st, 39th, 59th, 80th, 155th, 235th, 254th and the 1st Forestry Battalion. The Town of Trenton was soon to support the war effort with more than its own manpower.

Trenton's population was about 4,500 in 1915 when the British Chemical Co. Ltd. and the Imperial Munitions Board chose a site on the east side of town for the large-scale manufacturing of artillery and small arms ammunition. Less than a year of round-the-clock construction produced a plant on a 250-acre site, served by road, rail and water transportation. More than 2,000 men of many nationalities worked there under strict security regulations. Soldiers with fixed bayonets patrolled the perimeter fences. A former departmental manager recalled in a 1932 speech to a veterans' gathering that at least one German spy had managed to penetrate the security screen and to work there long enough to become a senior man in one section, but he was detected and arrested, with a partner who worked in a Belleville hotel.

The plant was like a townsite itself with about 10 miles of rail lines, its own fire department and recreational facilities. Month by month, products from the Trenton plant contributed greatly to Allied firepower which by 1918 was finally grinding Germany down.

Monday October 14, 1918, was Thanksgiving Day, the first holiday that had been observed to any degree since the plant went into production. Canadians on the home front sat down to their turkey dinners that evening with a strong belief that peace was near. German forces were being hammered into submission by an Allied offensive launched in August, in which Canadians had been playing a leading part. October 14, 1918, was also the fourth anniversary of the arrival in England of the First Canadian Contingent and a special service was conducted in Saint Margaret's Church, Westminster. The Times of London that day commented on the notable record of the Canadian Expeditionary Force and presented these statistics:

Regular troops at the beginning of the war	3,000
Number in the First Contingent	33,000
Canadian soldiers overseas by Sept. 1, 1918	400,000
Troops in training	60,000
Canadians killed in action	50,000
Total casualties to that date over	175,000
Wounded and returned to the front	40,000
Returned to Canada	50,000
Canadians who received decorations	10,000
VC winners	40

The most recent action in which Canadians had distinguished themselves was the successful night attack on Cambrai which they had entered in the early hours of

October 9, climaxing a drive that began on September 27 when Canadian assault troops stormed across the Canal du Nord.

On October 12, General Arthur Currie, commanding the Canadian Corps, had received this cable from Ontario Premier Sir William Hearst: "The people of Ontario are rejoicing over the Canadians' glorious advance at Cambrai. The dogged determination, dauntless courage and heroic achievements of your wonderful troops inspire our deepest admiration and gratitude. God speed you to final victory."

The cease-fire was four weeks away, it turned out, but across Canada, in town and country, hopes were high on that Thanksgiving Day.

4

In Trenton at 6:40 p.m. about 600 men of the night shift had just reported in at the British Chemical plant. A small fire was discovered in the TNT building. The alarm sounded. The fire spread quickly. But men were clear of the buildings before the first of the night-long series of explosions began to rip the plant apart as the town shuddered. The sound was heard in Brighton, more than 10 miles to the west and dishes rattled in Belleville, more than 10 miles to the east. Chimneys and walls toppled and glass showered as the TNT building went first, then the gun cotton building.

The Daily Intelligencer in Belleville headlined its story the next day, The Miracle of Trenton.

"The miracle of Trenton is the one thought in the mind of everybody today after a night of terrifying explosions in the big munitions plant which rocked the town, broke almost every pane of glass, while masses of flame from burning chemicals leaped hundreds of feet straight up in the air. The plant . . . has been badly damaged, but officials state that as far as they know not one life was lost. . . . The principal reason for the absence of fatalities is the excellent organization and alarm system which gives every employee warning of impending danger.

"At intervals all night long explosions occurred, the last one being at 6:30 this morning, and the chemicals made a weird and wonderful conflagration with varied colors lighting up the sky and visible for many miles. As the town rocked from the force of the explosions and houses trembled and glass smashed, the residents became panic-stricken, and picking up whatever was handiest, fled to the open country. The explosion shattered every carbon in the street lights and soon the town was plunged into darkness, which added to the terror of the people. Soon every road leading out of town was crowded with hundreds of people, some only partly dressed, and among the throng were many mothers carrying their babies. Hundreds of motors also filled the roads hurrying people away from the unseen terror. Halifax and Morgantown disasters, in which TNT figured so prominently, were fresh in the memory of everyone who feared a repetition of those terrible events. Families were separated in the panic, and the night was one long to be remembered as a hideous nightmare."

Without deeds of personal heroism damage to the town could have been worse and there might have been a large toll in lives. Charles N. Barclay, a Scottish-born engineer and South African War veteran who was in charge of all operations at the plant, was one of those awarded an OBE. A train crew that took a locomotive into the plant area to pull two boxcars of TNT away from the danger area also prevented more devastation.

Trainman Ernest Duffy suffered severe hand burns in coupling cars, but never talked about it later outside of family circles. He had come from New Brunswick with his wife and young son, Angus. Trenton became home for the Duffys and in the early 1920s they lived across the street from Howard Graham who had returned from the war an acting sergeant, completed legal training at Osgoode Hall in Toronto in 1921 and established a law practice in 1922.

Capt. Bywater returned safely too and soon other former members of the 49th Hastings Rifles and the 16th Prince Edward Regiment wanted to resume their old identities as Militia soldiers of the counties they loved. In March, 1920, a merger of the two regiments was approved and the Hastings and Prince Edward Regiment was born, destined to produce Canada's finest rural and small town infantry battalion in the Second World War and probably the best of them all.

The first commanding officer was Lieutenant-Colonel Bywater and among his officers were the next six COs. They were: Major Darius Green, second in command, a farmer in the Bayside area; 'A' Company commander Major H.J. Smith, a lawyer originally from New Brunswick; Captain A.V. Yates, MC, a mining company executive in Deloro; Captain Arnold Adams, treasurer of Prince Edward County; Lieutenant B.C. Donnan, a lawyer who was to become Crown Attorney of Hastings County; and Lieutenant Sherman Young, a farmer who was a descendant of the first white settler in Prince Edward County.

Of the four company areas set out at the formation of the new regiment, three were in Hastings County — 'A' Company in Trenton, 'B' Company in Madoc and 'D' Company in Stirling. 'C' Company was in Picton, the principal town of Prince Edward County, named in honour of Sir Thomas Picton, one of Wellington's great generals. "Prince Edward was settled by a military race," said the H. Belden and Company Historical Atlas of the Counties of Hastings and Prince Edward, published in 1878. In 1922 'A' Company had a three-day camp on the Prince Edward shore. In 1923 and 1924 the four companies trained together at a nine-day camp in Picton with well over 300 men on strength. The beginning was good, but it was too much to expect that this or any other Militia regiment could go on increasing in numbers.

The loss of 60,000 Canadians on far-flung fronts between 1914 and 1918 was too fresh in public memory. Even if another war broke out, why would Canada have to be involved? Why should we become involved again in a conflict between nations overseas, some Canadians asked. Disarmament came to be regarded as a revered ideal, military activity as evil. In 1924 Canada's annual defence expenditure was less than $1.50 per person of the population, while the American commitment was four and a half times as great and Britain's outlay was nearly 15 times as great. The miracle was that the Militia still had any significant nucleus left when the late 1930s arrived. The reason seems to have been inspirational leadership.

Colonel Bywater attracted exceptionally good officers. Angus Mowat, a prewar member of the Trenton Cadet Corps, who had enlisted while a student at Queen's and was wounded overseas, was Trenton's librarian when he joined the Regiment as a lieutenant in 1921. The Colonel approached Howard Graham one day after a Rotary luncheon and suggested serving in the Regiment. The young lawyer joined as a provisional second lieutenant in 1923, was promoted to lieutenant in 1924 and posted to 'A' Company. Another young lieutenant who joined in 1923 was also destined to become a legend in the Regiment. Bruce Sutcliffe, who worked in the post office, had such a consuming interest in the military life that after his employment took him to Toronto, he remained an officer in the Regiment despite the distance, attending camp, mess dinners and other events faithfully. In Toronto he was Private Sutcliffe in the bugle band of the Queen's Own Rifles.

Chapter Two
"I suppose you're 16"

Angus Duffy had been born in Chipman, New Brunswick, on July 12, 1914, and he grew up with a sense of history. On his mother's side he could trace his ancestry to the French-speaking Acadians who left Nova Scotia at the time of the expulsion late in the 18th century. As a small boy he travelled on a railway pass with his mother to New Brunswick for summer holidays with grandfather Angus D'Aigle in the big white house beside a river where young Angus had been born. The house was a landmark in the community and Angus D'Aigle, shopkeeper and shoemaker, was known as the Squire.

Irish ancestors of the Duffys had come to New Brunswick from New York in the days of the Loyalist migrations that accompanied the Revolutionary War. Angus Duffy's Canadian roots were deep.

His uncle, Reuben Bennett D'Aigle, who went to the Klondike gold rush as a young man, became a legendary figure in Canadian mining. He had only moderate success in the Klondike, but beginning in 1902 he staked 30 gold claims in Alaska along tributaries of the Yukon River. He worked them until 1906, sold the best one at a good price and caught a river boat that connected with a steamer for Seattle. Not long after the young prospector's triumphant return, his sister left for private school in Toronto. At Loretto Abbey

Mary Agnes D'Aigle, sister of a famous brother, one day to be mother of a famous son, received the kind of education of which a young lady could be proud, developing a skill and lasting interest in watercolour painting.

After returning to Chipman, Mary D'Aigle was married to Ernest Duffy. They went to Ontario soon after the war began. After settling in Trenton they had six more children. The later Twenties and the Thirties were hardly prosperous times, but Ernie Duffy had steady employment with the CNR and in a big family everybody contributed.

Trenton is at the mouth of the Trent River on Lake Ontario, just over 100 miles east of Toronto. Young Angus Duffy was determined that no one should think shortness of stature meant a lack of initiative or daring. He felt he should be the first each summer to jump off the Dundas Street bridge into the river — with many repetitions during the season. One day when he was climbing ashore from one of these performances, the chief of police was there to meet him with a backhand blow that knocked him into the water and a promise to call at the Duffys' home that evening. The chief was as good as his word. His report was delivered after supper to Ernie Duffy who handed out appropriate corporal punishment to the young daredevil.

Angus Duffy read much about the First World War and this fostered a great pride in what Canadians had accomplished. He became a Boy Scout and because of Scouting he came to wear the King's uniform. It could have been Air Force blue, for in 1929 the Canadian Government chose 950 acres just east of Trenton as the location for what was to become one of the important air stations of the Commonwealth. But in 1930 his Scoutmaster, Howard Jarrett, an officer in the First World War and an officer in the Hastings and Prince Edward Regiment, invited a group of Scouts to join the newly formed signal platoon.

Militia training not only provided an opportunity to sharpen skills the Scouts already possessed, but as Duffy's contemporaries often pointed out, the $10 pay for attending a 10-day camp was enough to buy a good second-hand bicycle. Signalling, marching and camping were a cinch for those with Scouting backgrounds, but a trip to the rifle range was a painful experience for the young shooters. The First War Lee Enfields had quite a kick and shoulders were black and blue.

Militia service wasn't overwhelmingly popular in the community. First War veterans and schoolboys were the mainstays of the Regiment that was gradually becoming the best in Eastern Ontario. In an era when pacifists made governments edgy about military spending, training facilities, particularly outside the large urban areas, were limited indeed. Agnes McPhail, the first woman ever elected an M.P. in Canada was as ardent a pacifist as she was a socialist and regularly moved in the Commons that the defence budget be cut to $1. At the Regiment's annual banquet in 1927, an officer of the Argyll Light Infantry in Belleville called Miss McPhail a "protege of Soviet Russia."

In Trenton the Armoury wasn't really an Armoury at all. It was a shed, a lean-to structure along one side of the old Canadian Pearl Button Co. building just east of the Trent River. In addition to space for a miniature range there was a small storeroom with a stove. Here 'A' Company and the signal platoon did their training through the fall, winter and spring. It was always cold. Snow blew in through openings. Flooding was common in springtime. On a parade night Capt. Graham often brought along a basket of kindling with which RSM Ernest Almy would start a fire. At an appropriate time in the evening's training or lecture, there would be a break for the sandwiches and coffee Mrs. Graham had sent down.

Early in the summer of 1930 Private Duffy went to 'D' Company stores in Belleville to draw his uniform and in a few days was off to a 12-day camp at Barriefield, an army base on the edge of Kingston. His clearest memory of that camp was of marching up a hill in full kit, carrying a friend's rifle as well as his own. He hadn't mastered the seven-foot puttees that were supposed to be neatly wound around each leg. One came undone, an NCO stepped on the flapping end, Duffy stumbled and went down in a heap.

He was a few days short of the required 16 years of age when a muster parade was held on rough, ploughed ground. A sergeant advised him to stand on top of the furrow so that at least he would look tall enough for 16. When the pay-master came by and asked, "I suppose you're 16", Duffy had learned enough about the army just to answer "Sir" and all was well.

There was no Brigade camp in 1931. The Regiment carried out local training by companies, but 22 officers attended a four-day camp at Madoc that emphasized tacti- cal training. Officers of the Regiment were shocked at the suggestion from Military District 3 in Kingston that all rural units should adapt their training to this abbreviated style, leaving more money available for training urban units. The unfavorable reaction to this plan brought a decision to grant each unit some funds for local training in 1932 and the Regiment was allotted $1,100. About 150 officers from units in M.D. 3 converged on Trenton for training in the first week of July.

This still left funds for a Regimental field day and inspec- tion in September at Fireman's Park. The Officer Com- manding M.D. 3 carried out an inspection of the 200 men Lieut.-Col. A.V. Yates had on parade. Honorary Colonel Bywater led the Regiment in a march past. After lunch served by women of the Anglican Church, the officers carried out a tactical exercise on the role of an advance guard and a sports program rounded out a big day. Capt. Graham was commanding 'A' Company, Capt. Noel Broad of Madoc led 'B' Company while 'C' Company and 'D' Company from Picton were under the command of Majors Arnold Adams and Sherman Young.

It wasn't numbers that kept the Militia alive in the Thirties; it was spirit. The strength of the Regiment ranged from 140 to 180, but even those totals were above the official establishment. There was money available to pay the extra men because officers took no pay and NCOs drew only $10 each for camp.

For Duffy Militia service was a logical extension of Scouting and an even finer expression of the patriotism with which he was imbued. He worked hard at it. By 1933 he was a corporal. As a corporal he was so enthusiastic about soldiering that one summer he not only went to camp with his own Regiment but as a private with the Midland Regiment of Port Hope. Signallers had to pass annual tests of their ability to transmit messages with a heliograph, Lucas lamp, field telephone and flags. The equipment didn't always work.

On one occasion when the signallers were communicating by heliograph the C.O. ordered Duffy to send a message to battalion headquarters and the message was speedily sent. Fortunately there was a telephone link between that location and BHQ. After the C.O. moved on, the exact wording of the heliograph message was sent to the signaller on duty at BHQ. The C.O. wasn't surprised to find that his message had been transmitted with 100 per cent accuracy. He was heard remarking later to another officer that he "figured Duffy was smart enough to lay a line."

In those days when jobs were scarce one signaller named George who worked in a restaurant was told by his employer that if he turned out with the signal platoon on a certain Saturday instead of coming to work he would be fired. But if he hadn't been present in order to pass his tests, the platoon could not have gone on to inter-unit competitions. It was so successful that it was judged the second best signal platoon in Canada that year, but in making that possible one dedicated young signaller lost his civilian job. "To be without a job in those days was a very serious situation," Duffy said years later. "He stayed at our place for a while, but my Dad had seven of us to provide for. Shortly afterwards George left town. I don't know where he went and I can't remember his last name, but he was one of the heroes of the Regiment."

The hard work and self-sacrifice involved in achieving a

high standard of excellence was typical of the spirit that kept the Militia alive in the Thirties. Duffy summed it up once by saying: "We were patriotic. We had a tremendous pride in our little group and we said it was a good thing to love your country and to serve it. We said duty is very important. And a soldier had to be honourable; you never let your comrades down."

The signal platoon wasn't Duffy's whole life. He left high school early in the Thirties and worked for 20 cents a day plus meals when the airport was under construction. He also joined a boxing club at the airport. After winning a bout on a technical knockout after both he and his opponent had been floored in the first round, he became known as Battling Duffy.

On July 6, 1933, the Trenton Courier-Advocate reported that "Battling Duffy of Trenton earned the decision over Bob Schroeder of Belleville in the bloodiest fight of the night. This was the third straight win for Duffy who followed his usual tactics of not backing up a step, taking all the other fellow had to offer and then pounding him into submission." An account of a boxing evening some months later said that the draw between Battling Duffy and Art Angell was the best scrap on the program. The three rounds featured "heavy hitting with gory results."

Lieut.-Colonel A.V. (Tiny) Yates MC, 6 foot 6 of dauntless energy, became C.O. in 1932 and one of the best the Regiment ever had. His dynamic personality made him an ideal leader for those days when the country was in the depths of the Depression and government funds for the Militia were very restricted. He believed that there was no place in military service for pessimism and he did things in style.

The C.O. and Mrs. Yates entertained the officers at Crow Lake on an August Sunday in 1932 where they carried out a tactical exercise without troops (TEWT) on battalion defence. Prior to the annual meeting of the officers in Picton in October an exercise on battalion attack was conducted.

The ladies who had been attending a matinee joined the officers for dinner at the Royal Hotel. The evening ended with a ball arranged by 'D' Company officers. When the Regimental officers dined at the Belleville Club on a cold November day, again the gathering was preceded by a TEWT conducted by Major Donnan as part of a Canadian Infantry Association competition.

At dinner Colonel Yates raised the matter of affiliation with a British unit. He had found out that the Royal Sussex Regiment had no Canadian affiliate. What could be more appropriate than a link with a county where so many Canadians had trained during the First War? It was agreed that overtures should be made to the Royal Sussex.

The training allowance was raised to $1,400 for 1933, so a four-day camp was held in Madoc in early August. 'C' Company held a ball in Picton in May and 'B' Company made the social scene in Madoc in October. When 'D' Company officers entertained their men at a banquet in the Picton Armouries in December, Major Sherman Young noted in his speech that some "military experts" had launched what he called an agitation for the reorganization of the Militia, and what it might lead to was difficult to predict. His company could adapt to whatever role it might be given. Major Arnold Adams, commanding 'C' Company, said flatly that there was no better unit in Canada than the Hastings & Prince Edward Regiment. Certainly there was talent at the top. The second in command and all the company commanders had passed the Militia Staff Course.

When Major Donnan became second in command in 1932, the 34-year-old Captain Graham assumed command of 'A' Company. In 1933 he was Mayor Graham of Trenton after several years of service on the school board and town council. In June of that year he was named a King's Counsel, the first Trentonian to be so honoured. By the summer of 1934 he was Major Graham.

Most of the Militia Staff Course was taken in Ottawa, but

candidates also had to complete their qualifications by passing equitation in Kingston. The instructor there was Capt. (later Major-General) Churchill Mann. He wasn't the easiest man in the world to impress. He told Major Graham's class: "You have all passed. Each of you will get a certificate, but never show it to a horse."

Duffy was going up the ladder too. Before he could be promoted to sergeant he had to complete a four-week qualifying course in Barriefield. Parade ground skills were vitally important and candidates had to master all forms of arms drill instruction, whatever their specialties. They learned instructional technique by instructing one another. Duffy was out in front of the class one day giving rifle drill. He ordered the squad to slope arms and was checking the angle of each rifle and each forearm when the instructor urged more speed. A squad must not be kept in one position too long. For the life of him Duffy couldn't remember the command "Order Arms" to get the rifles from the shoulders back to the ground. He kept checking and stalling, hoping the right words would come to him and the instructor kept pushing. Finally he told the squad: "Take your rifles off your shoulders and put them on the ground." The instructor was enraged. He ordered two men to fall out, put Duffy under arrest on a charge of dumb insolence and ordered him to be marched to his tent. There Duffy sat on a stool for most of the day while the sun turned the Bell tent into an oven.

At the end of the afternoon, full of fear and foreboding, Duffy was paraded before Capt. Harry L. Salmon, sure that he was going to be sent back to his Regiment in disgrace. But Capt. Salmon, who was to be his colonel six years later, made a quick assessment of the situation. He was a good enough judge of men to know that the temporarily flustered young NCO wasn't insolent. The charge was dismissed. Duffy completed the course and returned to Trenton more dedicated than ever to the Regiment.

One aspect of being a sergeant took some getting used to. In the sergeants' mess there were free issues of beer on special occasions and the RSM insisted that teetotalling Sgt. Duffy should have a Coke for every free beer the other sergeants enjoyed. After one military funeral there were six free beers. Six Cokes in rapid succession put him off that stuff for life.

Times were getting a little better by 1934. There were three military balls and lots of soldiering too. The Regiment's training allowance was increased to $1,800 and this made possible a six-day camp at the Picton Fairgrounds, where about 200 all ranks attended. After the annual inspection the officers held a mess dinner under canvas with 60 guests. Old-timers always insisted that these prewar events were carried on with more panache and featured better food than post-war mess dinners, despite the somewhat rough-and-ready camp setting.

One year Major Graham had the job of running the officers' mess. At camp the Brigade commander was invited as a guest after church parade. The cook got drunk and Graham had to doff his jacket and carve the beef. On another occasion cocktails of gin with sweet and dry vermouth were to be served and the ingredients were in pails at the back of the mess tent. A waiter, needing a bucket for some purpose, threw out a pail of gin.

Although Colonel Yates announced at camp that he planned to retire early in 1935, his work was far from finished. He had been appealing to citizens of the two counties to help raise money for new Colours for the Regiment. Because of a delay in obtaining the King's approval of the design, the dedication and presentation could not take place at camp, but on Sunday, October 14, 1934, Lieutenant-General Sir Archibald Macdonell made the presentation in Picton. The Right Rev. John Lyons, Lord Bishop of Ontario, conducted the consecration. Less than a month later it was announced that the Regiment's affiliation with the Royal Sussex Regiment had been approved. The final flourish of the year was the acquisition of swords from Wilkinson's in Britain, made possible by putting all the officers' pay into Regimental funds, and properly accoutred, the officers gathered in Belleville on December 29 for a group photograph.

Lieut.-Col. E.A. Adams took command of the Regiment in March, 1935. In May the Regiment observed the Jubilee of King George V's accession to the throne. An increase to $2,200 in the year's training allowance made it possible for the companies to go to Barriefield to fire rifle and Lewis gun classifications, followed by a highly successful camp at Picton Fairgrounds with nearly 250 under canvas. The Royal Canadian Air Force took part in a tactical exercise, providing air-to-ground communications. An old Lysander with a hook between its wheels could be flown low enough to pick up a message attached to a cord slung between the butts of two rifles driven bayonet-first into the ground. The reply would be dropped with a handkerchief parachute.

In the fall of 1935 Capt. Christopher Nix of the 4th Battalion, Royal Sussex Regiment, visited the two counties. He met the Regiment at the Picton Armouries and had dinner at the Royal Hotel with the officers and their wives while the Regimental band played in the lobby.

Toasting the Royal Sussex, Colonel Yates expressed pride that the Hastings & Prince Edward Regiment had become the Canadian associate of an historic British Regiment which had troops on the right flank of General Wolfe's army in the battle for Quebec in 1759. Two battle honours won in the Seven Years War were Louisburg and Quebec. The regiment was raised in 1701 at Belfast and was first known as the 35th Foot. The succeeding years brought service in the American Revolutionary War, in Egypt and the Sudan. A total of 23 battalions of the Royal Sussex served in the First World War. In 1935 it had two battalions in the Regular Army, one in the United Kingdom and one in India, and two in the Territorial Army, comparable to Canada's Non-Permanent Active Militia.

The following year brought an opportunity for officers of the Regiment to visit the Royal Sussex. The Trenton Legion raffled off several cars and raised more than $15,000 which was enough to send about 20 First War veterans to France for the 1936 dedication of the Vimy Memorial. The group included Colonel Bywater, Major Graham and Major L.D. Foster who arranged to stop over in England. Officers of the Royal Sussex entertained them at the Royal Services Club and the Goodwood Races, and they stayed at Major Nix's spacious country home. He had told them that he was a farmer, but they found that his farming operation covered 3,000 acres.

The Sussex Daily News gave an account of a dinner in honour of the Canadian officers at Horsham Drill Hall. There were recollections of Capt. Nix's visit to the Canadian Militiamen in the previous year and of his returning "full of admiration for them, for they are enthusiastic, keen and efficient, in spite of the fact that they receive less government support, less pay and fewer facilities for collective training than do the Territorials of Great Britain."

Indeed, the Canadians who were now part of the Royal Sussex Regimental family had been achieving impressive results. Although the general public might not have been paying much attention to its achievements in the 1930s, the Regiment had been winning awards with regularity. In 1931 its record was good enough to win the 9th Infantry Brigade Progress Cup, followed by the Brigade Challenge Cup in 1932 and 1933. The Canadian Infantry Association Progress Cup was won in 1935, as the second best unit in the District.

A banner headline in the Trenton Courier-Advocate on Jan. 31, 1937, said HASTINGS & PRINCE EDWARD REGIMENT THE TOPS. Word had been received that the Regiment had won the Infantry Association Challenge Cup for general proficiency again in 1936 as the outstanding rural unit in M.D. 3. The signal platoon had won first place among all the rural and urban units in the District with 96 points out of 100. Fellow NCOs got so tired of Sgt. Duffy telling everybody how good the signal platoon was that they threw him in the shower.

In 1936 a Militia reorganization cut out or changed the

roles of nearly 40 infantry units, but the Hastings & Prince Edward Regiment survived, for it had managed to remain conspicuous by working hard. Numbers were small but quality was high. Officers had an inspirational role.

The Toronto Telegram reported that in the big city two officers of the Queen's Own Rifles had been decorated with the lifesaving medal of the Royal Canadian Humane Society, and perhaps no other Canadian regiment had been so honored even once.

Actually one Hastings & Prince Edward officer had won two of these medals within three years. Lieut. Gillis Ingram had gone out in a boat and had rescued two men from Lake Ontario, in spite of having a broken arm himself. On the second occasion he rescued two boys from an ice floe after their raft had drifted out into the lake.

The 1936 training allowance was raised to $2,400 and 31 officers and 250 other ranks had a one-week camp at the Sandbanks on Lake Ontario. Colonel Adams turned over command of the Regiment to Lieut.-Col. B.C. Donnan, but he didn't really retire. He loved the Regiment in which his father and grandfather had served. He requested and received an appointment as transport officer for the summer of 1937 and turned up at camp with lieutenant's pips on his shoulders. Shortly after camp he died of a heart attack and was buried with full military honours.

The year 1937 brought a young warrant officer a unique opportunity to widen his horizons. Angus Duffy was selected to represent the Regiment in the Coronation contingent. The Trenton Courier-Advocate wrote glowingly about "Sergeant Duffy" for his promotion to Company Sergeant-Major was too recent to be generally known.

"Sergeant Duffy is the senior NCO and member of the signals section . . . under Lieut. F.W. Sherbert and has served the unit faithfully and well for several years. His work during the past year was outstanding and he helped in a material way to advance the section to the high place it now occupies. Sergeant Duffy's work has been attracting the attention of senior officers for several seasons, and when the signals section topped a list of 11 during the season past to win high honour for itself and the unit, the selection of Sergeant Duffy was practically certain."

Duffy wrote to Lieut. Sherbert describing two weeks of strenuous training in Ottawa, delighting particularly in the fact that 60 per cent of the fine Canadian contingent were or had been signallers. A made-to-measure serge uniform and a complete set of new equipment added to the smartness. The Minister of Defence and Governor General Lord Tweedsmuir inspected the contingent which sailed on April 28 and landed at Southampton on May 7.

A special train took the Canadians to Brookwood and they marched two miles to Pirbright Camp where they were stationed with the Scots Guards, as were soldiers from Australia, New Zealand and Rhodesia. On May 9, three days before the Coronation, they mounted guard at Buckingham Palace and St. James's Palace. But later came an even greater thrill for a young soldier — receiving his first medal. The Canadians marched to Buckingham Palace where King George pinned Coronation Medals on half the contingent. Duffy was in the other half of the contingent whose medals were presented by Queen Elizabeth. The smile that charmed those soldiers was to capture North America on a Royal tour two years later.

There was time for a visit to the Royal Sussex. Duffy was shown around the Regimental depot, visited the Royal Sussex Chapel in Chichester Cathedral and saw on the wall the names of 7,000 men who had died in the First World War. A visit to the 2nd Battalion at Devonport the next day was made memorable by a meeting with members of the signal section. After visiting two companies that were camped on the Downs, Duffy enjoyed a band concert on Plymouth Hoe to round out the day. He presented a silver tray to the RSM of the 2nd Battalion from the sergeants' mess of the Hastings & Prince Edward Regiment as a token of good comradeship.

"The hospitality and good fellowship shown me by all ranks shall always remain a highlight of my life," he wrote to Colonel Donnan on his return. "My visit made me proud that my unit should be affiliated with such a splendid fighting regiment as the Royal Sussex."

Chapter Three
"It will be a long, tough war"

It took intense dedication to keep soldiering on through the Thirties with First War uniforms and little or no equipment, only guessing about what the future might hold. Veterans of the First War felt that there were serious times ahead and could detect no determination in the country to be prepared. But by the late Thirties international events forced upon military planners in Canada at least a trace of the realism that had been lacking for nearly two decades. After the First War the Permanent Force was given an establishment of 10,000 (but never came close to it) and the Militia was to provide a reserve force of 11 infantry divisions and four cavalry divisions! These objectives seem ludicrous now, and were, of course, totally beyond realization with widespread public objection to military spending. The defence budget was never over $11-million in the Twenties and little more than $2-million ever went to the Non-Permanent Active Militia in any year. Fewer men were trained than in the years before the First War. In the bottom of the Depression (1932-33) camp training was almost eliminated.

Major-General A.G.L. McNaughton, Chief of the General Staff, advocated restructuring the Militia as early as 1931, but the illusion of a 15-division reserve wasn't abandoned until 1936. It was cut to a still unrealistic seven divisions — six infantry and one cavalry. It began to seem possible by then that Canada might be called upon to participate in some form of military action, initiated either by Great Britain or by the League of Nations, in spite of having little military equipment and no real defence industries.

A mobilization plan was prepared, however, and it called for an overseas expeditionary force of two divisions, representing all parts of Canada.

Lists of likely units were prepared by officers commanding Military Districts. In M.D. 3, the Hastings & Prince Edward Regiment could hardly be ignored. Its men had made their mark in inter-unit competitions, usually performing with a certain flair, particularly in the days of Tiny Yates. At a Brigade camp in Barriefield in 1937, the Regiment came under the close scrutiny of two Permanent Force officers, Majors Harry L. Salmon and Chris Vokes, who would have much to do with shaping its course in the years ahead. It certainly didn't escape the notice of higher formations that all the Regiment's company commanders had passed the Militia Staff Course and in 1937 Major Graham was one of a select number of Canadian Militia officers to complete the Advanced M.S.C.

Official statements from Ottawa indicated in 1938 that development of the RCAF had much higher priority than the Militia, a policy nowhere more obvious than in Trenton. The Courier-Advocate urged construction of a suitable Armoury, for the ceiling in the old button factory drill shed was too low to permit soldiers to slope arms. The Militia had to be content with second place, but the Regiment was permitted to move its training to another old factory near the waterfront, west of the river, on the site of the present Royal Canadian Legion building. 'A' Company and the Signal platoon each had about 20 members at that stage, and in 1938 an anti-aircraft platoon was added. By this time Regimental headquarters were in Picton.

The drumbeat of European events was moving the world relentlessly toward conflict in 1938. After the German seizure of Austria in March the tempo increased. Munich appeared to slow it down, but Czechoslovakia was in the bag by March of 1939 and Hitler was on a course from which there was no turning back.

Nazi and Fascist equipment and tactics had been tested in Spain by the forces supporting General Franco, and that civil war was near an end when spring came to Eastern Ontario. The Picton Gazette reported in a front-page story on March 15, 1939, that enough willow wood had been shipped to Spain in 1938 to make 2,500 artificial legs, and added: "There is still sufficient willow in Prince Edward County for several years to come."

Although they didn't talk about it much, young Militiamen realized in the early months of 1939 that war was likely to come soon. On one occasion, Duffy was advised by a friend's father that if there was going to be a war he should get out of the Regiment. Duffy replied that he wanted to be prepared to help defend the country. "All I want to do in war is make money," was the older man's scornful reply.

On March 30, 1939, the Trenton company of the Regiment held its annual banquet. Honorary Colonel Bywater was the principal speaker and he said the calamity of war was likely. But while Britain might be assailed, she would never be beaten as long as she possessed the spirit that inspired the Canadians in the 1914-1918 war.

The next day Major Sherman Young was informed by National Defence Headquarters of his promotion to Lieutenant-Colonel to succeed Bryson Donnan as commanding officer of the Regiment. He had served continuously since the Regiment was formed in 1920. He had enlisted in the first week of the 1914 war and had gone overseas as a private in the 2nd Battalion in the 1st Division. At the second Battle of Ypres he was gassed, wounded and taken prisoner, exchanged at the end of 1915 and returned to Canada. He was commissioned in the 155th Battalion in 1916 and went overseas again for a period in 1918, retiring to his farm when the war ended.

The Belleville Intelligencer called the new C.O. "one of Prince Edward County's most distinguished military sons, possessor of a war record that compares favourably with any in the province." War was only five months away. The relentless pattern of events bringing it closer wasn't obvious in the delightful spring and summer to many Canadians clinging to a vain hope for peace.

Britain was about to make a pledge of mutual aid with Poland. The Italians were into Albania by early April, the British showing the flag in the Mediterranean and France rearming, but there was no plan to cancel the Canadian tour of King George VI and Queen Elizabeth.

By mid-April Britain was strengthening the defences of Gibraltar and President Roosevelt was urging Hitler and Mussolini to give assurances of peace for at least 10 years. Canadian authorities were concerned about guarding power lines and waterways after a cache of dynamite was discovered at Sault Ste. Marie. By the last week in April Britain had conscription. On May 15 Agnes McPhail, until then an unrelenting pacifist, supported a $63-million defence program in the Canadian House of Commons, her first affirmative vote on anything military since entering the House in 1921.

The King and Queen were in Ottawa a few days later. On May 20, in full uniform with bearskin head-dress, the King inspected the Governor General's Foot Guards of Ottawa and the Canadian Grenadier Guards of Montreal on Parliament Hill. The Regiment greeted the King and Queen in Kingston, the Royal train's only stop in the region. From crowds in towns and cities across the country came perhaps the most magnificent display of patriotism ever seen in Canada. Americans joined in with their accustomed fervour. Major Gordon Walmsley, clerk of Prince Edward County, wrote in a special Royal Visit edition of the Picton Times: "The loyalty of the citizens of the County of Prince Edward is not surpassed in the whole Empire."

On July 10 Britain warned Germany to keep its hands off Danzig. The July 14 Bastille Day parade in Paris drew a crowd of a million people to cheer a combined British and French military display and a fly-past of RAF aircraft. The British Parliament rose for the summer recess on August 3; the RAF had 120,000 officers and men in uniform by August 4 and the King reviewed the Fleet on August 9. Two nights later came the first blackout practice. By August 22 Anthony Eden was in camp with his regiment and the next day came the shattering surprise of the Russo-German non-aggression pact. On August 23 Hitler demanded Danzig and the Polish Corridor, but the British ambassador made it clear that Britain would stand by its pledge to Poland. Time had almost run out. RAF personnel, some with wives and families, arrived in Trenton during the following weekend, just as the first Canadian moves toward mobilization were taking place.

On Saturday, August 26, the Canadian Cabinet decided to invoke Section 63 of the Militia Act to put some Militiamen on duty on coastal defence or guarding public buildings, power plants, airports and ship channels. Section 64, covering a general mobilization could not be invoked without calling Parliament, and so units that actually weren't mobilized until later had volunteers on special duty for several days before war was declared. The Lincoln and Welland Regiment of St. Catharines had men guarding the Welland Canal and men of the Midland Regiment of Port Hope were on guard at Trenton Airport with fixed bayonets.

Leaves were cancelled for the 9,000-man Canadian Permanent Force (4,000 Army, 3,000 RCAF and 2,000 Navy). By Monday, August 28, recruiting in Britain amounted to mobilization. Children, mothers and invalids were being moved away from London. Britain's pledge to Poland was re-affirmed but by Friday, Sept. 1, Hitler's troops were over the border into Poland. Selected Canadian Militia units were ordered to mobilize. A telegram to Colonel Young reached Picton on Friday afternoon. The Regiment was about to go to war.

Colonel Young telephoned Major Graham at his law

office. Other officers were informed right away and instructed to be on duty early on Saturday in Picton, Trenton and Madoc Armouries, to organize recruiting and plan initial training. By the time Sunday radio broadcasts were telling of Britain's declaration of war on Germany, signs were already up in the two Counties inviting recruits to enlist. While Canadians made their way to church or stayed by their radios in homes and cottages, men were starting to report at the Armouries. Militiamen already had uniforms, but appropriate clothing for raw recruits was scarce. More tight-fitting First War tunics, trousers, puttees and peaked caps were already being collected by unmobilized units in M.D. 3 for cleaning, repair and reissue to the men who would sign up in Picton, Trenton and Madoc.

On the Saturday of that long Labour Day weekend, Duffy had just received a $6-a-week pay increase at the Benedict Proctor plant and was starting his annual holidays. He hadn't saved enough money for a car, but he had a boat with a new outboard motor and he was soon at a girl friend's cottage. Major Graham arrived there a few hours later with word that the Regiment was mobilizing and making it clear that he expected Duffy to return to Trenton with him right away. The young sergeant-major went home, put on his uniform and reported at Trenton Armoury. He was instantly appointed company sergeant-major of Headquarters Company.

Nearly all members of the Signal platoon and the anti-aircraft platoon volunteered and in a few days there were about 80 men on strength in Trenton, training with the 20 available rifles, probably none of which was safe to fire. Fred Burtt, a signaller, had completed a sergeant's course in the spring of 1939, but he was not quite 17. He was rejected as too young and told to go back to high school to complete his final year, but by 1940 he had a commission.

Signaller Tommy Cunnell was only 16, but prewar Militia records showed him to be 18 and no one at home objected. "Your father went through a war; you might as well go," his mother said.

Sergeant Gordon Way of nearby Wooler was one of those who reported in Trenton on Sunday, Sept. 3, but enlistment machinery wasn't ready and some of the potential recruits for the wartime battalion who sat around talking wondered aloud whether they would get overseas before the war ended. They were asked to return the next morning. On Monday morning men lined up early at the Armoury. Major Graham, who was making out forms, called any NCO he saw to the head of the line to be enrolled first and help with the paper work.

Sgt. Way was getting undressed for his medical examination when the medical officer said he had no one to help him with documentation. Sgt. Way said he could type and was given the job immediately, beginning his wartime career in the nude typing his own documents. The line of recruits was moving forward quickly, but he kept typing, putting on an item of clothing whenever there was a few seconds' break. The skill with which he pounded that typewriter all day every day for several weeks made the tall farmer indispensable to the Regiment. When a Medical Corps major downgraded his enlistment-day B category to C, Major Graham was concerned that the sergeant wouldn't qualify for overseas service. He suggested that Sgt. Way should see what could be done about having the B category restored. Some careful work on his records with ink remover solved the problem.

Practically every soldier expected to be going overseas soon, but enlistment actually covered only service in Canada. An additional form had to be signed, indicating willingness to serve anywhere.

Duffy urged the recruits to think that over carefully. It would be a long, tough war, he told them, and the chances were that only a few would survive. However, all but one signed. When Picton recruits had this Supplementary Declaration explained to them and were told they would have only a short time to consider it, one loud voice boomed: "I don't need any more time on mine. I'm all set to sign." This brought an outburst of cheering. 'D' Company signed to a man and the five in 'C' Company who declined were booed heartily.

More than 200 men had been enrolled by the time Canada declared war officially on Sept. 10. Although recruiting was progressing at all three Armouries, plans to concentrate everyone in Picton began the next day. But it took much work to convert the Picton Armoury basement and the old Miller Canning Co. plant to barrack space, enlarge and equip the quartermaster's stores and set up field kitchens. A Royal Canadian Army Service Corps officer arrived in Picton on Sept. 25 to discuss the purchase of provisions with local merchants whose cash registers were about to ring as they hadn't rung for years.

The Picton Fair on Sept. 28 and 29 provided an excellent opportunity to show the flag. The Lieutenant-Governor inspected an honour guard commanded by Ray Young and members of the official party said it was a better show than RCAF Trenton had put on.

October 11 was the first day of total concentration in Picton and a week later the officers moved into Rickerton Castle, a stone mansion in the easterly part of the town. By the end of October Regimental strength was about 800. Major Graham was second-in-command. Major E.W. Matthews of Stirling commanded Headquarters Company; Major Bruce Sutcliffe of Toronto, 'A' Company; Capt. C.L. Wallbridge of Madoc, 'B' Company; Capt. G.T. Ferguson of Consecon, 'C' Company; and Major Howard Reid of Milford, 'D' Company.

When the troops arrived in Picton from Trenton and Madoc accommodation was rough and ready. Duffy had been told that good quarters had been provided in the canning factory. Colonel Young showed him a shed attached to the factory with a big pile of straw in the middle of the room and about three inches of water on the floor. Duffy was appalled. "However, I got used to sleeping on straw and in the wet and so did everybody," he recalled later. "They were a very keen bunch in those days and not afraid of work. They were prepared to do anything."

Recruits had come from the towns and villages and farms and other widely scattered points, hitch-hiking or riding the rods. A telephone caller from Carolina wanted to know if he could join up and he was told to come as soon as possible. Private Truax turned out to be a well-spoken good looking man, a little older than many of those enlisting at the same time. His desire to be an infantry private seemed strange, but he was welcomed. A few months later in the depths of an English winter, he turned out to be a good man to have in a flu-ridden barracks. He finally admitted that he was a medical doctor and accepted a commission.

As the Regiment took shape, key people were given special jobs because their qualifications seemed uniquely suitable. First War veteran Lieut. Ray Young was musketry officer right from the start. Capt. Reg Abraham, a customs officer, became quartermaster. Cab driver Art Storms became transport sergeant, mechanic George Hamilton was technical sergeant and Bill Gibb who tinkered with weapons, armourer sergeant.

Kippy McAlpin hadn't been in the Militia. After 13 years in the grocery trade in Picton he decided to enlist for a change of scene. The first person he met was Capt. Abraham who immediately assigned him to the stores. Procedures for ordering and paying for food for the troops had to be learned on the job.

With entitlement to draw one pound of meat per day per man and one pound of bread, bountiful quantities of food appeared for every meal.

Getting the men into adequate boots was a serious problem in the early stages. Many weren't well enough shod to go on route marches, but they went anyway and came back with bleeding feet. Some managed to solve the problem by buying civilian work boots in Picton stores.

Nobody could remember such perfect fall weather and it was ideal for outdoor training well into November. RSM "Daddy" Dadds of the Royal Canadian Regiment was the chief instructor, responsible for making 800 individuals into a regiment fit to go overseas. Although equipment was scarce and even uniforms slow in arriving, officers and NCOs could sense the growth of something greater than the sum of its parts. A sense of pride, a spirit of adventure and encouragement from the surrounding community all prevented boredom. But parade after parade after parade couldn't make them soldiers.

"We were a pretty bobtailed outfit in those early weeks, but the spirit was there," Duffy said 40 years later. "Although we couldn't always keep in step, we weren't afraid to get out in the cold. It was getting cold in late November when we learned there was a big shot coming to inspect us and we didn't know at first that it would be General McNaughton, commanding the 1st Division.

"We formed up and waited patiently, and then impatiently, for two hours and he finally showed up, and I believe he was happy with us. At any rate it was firmly established then that we were going to be part of the 1st Brigade and moved to England quickly. Needless to say that suited us."

Duffy kept telling his men in Headquarters Company that they were the servants of the rifle companies and were going to be responsible for seeing that they had everything they needed in battle.

By the time December had come, Sgt. Way was concerned about the fact that men were shivering on parade because they had no greatcoats. He mentioned this to his brother who had just graduated from RMC and had been posted to the Royal Canadian Ordnance Corps. Lieutenant Way said there were lots of greatcoats in Kingston, so the sergeant took a truck to Kingston and returned with enough greatcoats for all and many suits of battle dress.

Fifteen weeks' training were completed by December 6, but few men were familiar with the key weapon — the Bren light machine gun which had replaced the Lewis gun. The Regiment received three Brens that night and "Daddy" Dadds called Duffy in at 6 o'clock. He could have the Brens until 6 o'clock the next morning and would have those 12 hours to qualify all 180 men of his company. Duffy spent one hour memorizing the first three lessons, the next eight hours giving all his men the first three tests on the weapon and was back on parade at 5:00 a.m.

The Regiment's last week in Canada began on December 10 with a church parade that featured fervent hymn singing. Everyone sensed that departure was imminent. Orders demanded disposal of personal effects such as cars and motorcycles. Wednesday brought medical examinations in chilly quarters in Kingston and the results meant remaining in Canada for some who were very keen to go overseas. Advance pay came on Thursday, but training continued, even at night.

Duffy was conducting weapons training on the Armoury floor that evening when he was called upstairs to the C.O.'s office. Colonel Young and Major Graham were there. The C.O.'s message was brief. "From now on you are Mr. Duffy. Mr. Birkett won't be going with us. You are now Regimental Sergeant-Major."

"Sir, I can't be the RSM," Duffy replied. "I don't know anything about the job. I've just been CSM of Headquarters Company. I've never formed up a battalion parade."

"Get back down there and straighten out your Regiment," was the Colonel's blunt reply. He had just made one of the best decisions he had ever made in his life. It was a decision that had much to do with the making of the Hastings & Prince Edward Regiment and spreading its fame throughout the 1st Canadian Division.

Chapter Four
"A very good show, Mr. Duffy"

By Friday, December 15, Colonel Young and the adjutant, Capt Art Norrington, had left for Halifax. The troops were confined to Picton, but all knew that they would be boarding trains soon on short notice. Two trains pulled into Picton station on Sunday night, an hour and a half apart.

Civilians were crowded along all sides of the Armoury floor when Duffy called the Regiment on parade. Then briefly it was "Stand easy" and the civilians began to mingle with their men again. When the time came to move, Duffy ordered the civilians off the floor, but nothing happened. He walked half way up the stairs toward the officers' mess so that everyone could see him and tried again. "You bloody people, get off my parade square!" he bellowed at the top of his voice, "and for those who are supposed to be soldiers . . . First Battalion, Hastings & Prince Edward Regiment . . . ATTEN---SHUN!" Duffy long remembered the look he got from the startled civilians. "Parents, particularly mothers, were looking at me strangely. They must have been wondering what kind of a monster was now in charge of their sons," he told a friend. It was an emotional moment.

Major Graham and some of the others had grim expressions. They were going off to war for a second time. Some of the keenest to go were being left behind because their medical categories were not high enough or because they were too young. A few of the latter managed to get on the trains, but careful checking at Halifax prevented them from stowing away aboard H.M.T. Ormonde which moved out of the harbour early on December 20 to join a convoy.

Colonel Young was C.O. of the ship and Duffy was ship's RSM. It wasn't a pleasure cruise for anybody. The ship had usually sailed in southern waters. There were cooling fans in abundance, but no source of heat.

The food was strange. A kipper for breakfast on Christmas morning was hardly a treat. The crossing was rough. Seasickness made the regimental routine of mounting guards and assigning other duties chaotic at best. No soldier had anticipated manning any of the ship's weapons, but there was a big naval gun in the stern. A senior petty officer was in charge of the gun and members of the signal platoon made up the gun crews. It was extremely wet and windy. A greatcoat was quickly soaked by spray. At the end of a shift a soldier would be coated with ice and there was no way to get clothing dry again. Colonel Young had asked the ship's captain for waterproof clothing, but it was refused.

Later, at Duffy's request, the Colonel again asked that the men be given protective clothing, and it was refused again. He told Duffy: "Take the men off the gun. To hell with the bloody ship. Let it sink."

"But we're on it too."

"Take the men off the gun, Mr. Duffy."

After two hours without a gun crew the captain relented and issued waterproof gear.

Maintenance of discipline was made difficult by the fact that the NCOs had a posh mess in the second class lounge with plenty to drink and stewards to serve them. The men had no drinks in their canteen at all. Duffy ordered the NCOs to confine their drinking to the mess and to do nothing that would create friction with the men. That night Duffy heard a great noise, saw water flowing down a corridor and found a merry group of senior NCOs giving a sergeant a seawater bath. He put five of them on charge immediately, including two company sergeant-majors.

The brand new RSM didn't know how to write out a

charge and spent all night in the orderly room, checking manuals in order to document the allegation that these five were guilty of "conduct to the prejudice of good order and military discipline." He went to the Colonel the first thing in the morning and asked to have the charges dealt with immediately. If he couldn't exert his authority over the senior NCOs, how could an effective chain of command be established to maintain discipline in the Regiment? The Colonel saw the point.

One after another the five were paraded in and reprimanded. Afterwards Duffy saw them standing in a group, and as he walked by CSM Edwards of 'B' Company said: "Just a minute, Shorty." They had been friends for years and Edwards had always greeted his friend this way, but Duffy turned abruptly and told him: "Don't ever call me Shorty again." Edwards replied: "I'm just telling these guys that the RSM wants us to be soldiers, and the first one who doesn't support that little guy is going to get his ears bashed in." Edwards was very influential and there was little trouble from any NCO from then on.

Patrolling aircraft met the convoy on the morning of December 29 off Northern Ireland and the year ended with the ship anchored off Greenock. The troops wanted to go ashore in lifeboats to celebrate New Year's Eve and Duffy had to mount a special guard to see that everyone stayed on board.

On New Year's Day the Regiment went ashore by tender, was welcomed to Greenoch, marched two miles to the railway station, boarded a train at noon and was seen off by a good crowd. After a bacon-and-egg breakfast near the end of the journey the next morning, a welcome from General McNaughton and a brisk march to Maida Barracks, an eager but very green Regiment was ready to start big league soldiering in Aldershot.

A battalion of the Gordon Highlanders was leaving for France. The Hasty Ps wondered when their turn for action would come. None could have guessed how very far away it really was.

In the deep and damp midwinter of early 1940, Aldershot was a grim introduction to the Old World for the men of Picton, Bloomfield, Cherry Valley, Waupoos Island, Salmon Point, Glenora, Greenbush, Demorestville, Consecon, Schoharie and Northport. There was nothing like it back in Havelock, Frankford or Bancroft. In due course they were at home in Fleet and Farnborough and Frimley, in Ash Vale or on Pirbright Common, in Bisley, Bagshot, Woking or Worplesdon. But that didn't come until after the trauma of adjusting to life in a Crimean War barracks with practically no heat, antiquated plumbing, unaccustomed rations, a strange currency, a rigidly enforced blackout and more beer than they were used to.

The Regiment was slow in finding its feet, as homesickness and disorientation, or what we would call today culture shock, took their toll among men who had never been far from home before.

The few First War soldiers in each company provided an invaluable steadying influence, but in that coldest English winter for many years they couldn't prevent their young comrades from coming down with influenza or worse. Pipes outside the buildings meant frozen plumbing to add to everyone's discomfort.

At one point during the early weeks there were about 300 men sick. Everyone was cold all the time, food was less than wonderful, mail was scarce and morale was slipping badly. All battalion commanders were called to a meeting with General McNaughton. The next day Colonel Young made it clear to his officers that he wasn't satisfied with the standard of discipline, and five days later he relayed the message that Brigadier Armand Smith, commanding the 1st Brigade, wanted to see greater progress.

The Brigadier was displeased because the Regiment tended to straggle on a church parade. Not knowing how soon the 1st Division might be in action, senior officers couldn't wait indefinitely for the Hasty Ps to shape up.

A lieutenant and a sergeant of the Royal Canadian Regiment appeared at Maida Barracks one day and Duffy soon concluded that they were looking the situation over on behalf of the higher formation. They questioned him at length about his own training and experience and how he proposed to instill discipline.

At 9 o'clock on Monday, February 5 a phone message from Brigadier Smith directed Colonel Young to report to General McNaughton at 11.45 a.m. He wasn't away for more than 20 minutes and when he returned he was no longer C.O. Major Harry L. Salmon of the RCR would be taking over quickly. He was a 1st Division staff officer who had been wounded twice and had won the Military Cross twice in the First World War. Brigadier Smith and Major Salmon met the officers in the mess shortly after noon. It would be a pleasure and an honour to command the Regiment he had known so well in Canada, Major Salmon said. There was no doubt a standard of training second to none could be reached with a united effort, but officers who would not co-operate would be severely dealt with and might be returned to Canada. Colonel Young was on his way shortly and others were soon to follow.

The next day written confirmation of the change in command arrived at the orderly room with the notice of Major Salmon's promotion to Lieutenant-Colonel. Before the day was out an unexpected chain of events began that would encourage Colonel Salmon in his demanding task. He would soon see that the tottering Regiment still had a potential for greatness.

Pte. Lee Keech, a transport driver, was desperately ill with meningitis in Cambridge Military Hospital in Aldershot. Padre Walter Gilling went to the hospital and found that Pte. Keech had died and reported this to the new C.O. Colonel Salmon called Duffy in and ordered a full military funeral, for Keech was the first Hasty P to die on active service. That meant a gun carriage, drums draped in black, an escort and firing party. And the whole Regiment would have to learn to march in slow time. Duffy had commanded a firing party as a corporal in Militia days, but he was flabbergasted, having to co-ordinate all the parts of a difficult ceremonial that would require perfect marching, and changes from quick time to slow time and back to quick time again, all on icy roads.

Since arriving at Maida Barracks, Duffy had already had several occasions to seek the advice of a barrack warden on the camp staff, an ex-RSM of a Scottish unit. "There's no way you can do it, wee mon," said the old warden, "your outfit can hardly march." Duffy insisted that the Regiment could master all the ceremonial of a full military funeral if he could only get a gun carriage. The warden was apparently impressed by Duffy's determination. For three bottles of Scotch he would find a gun carriage. He was as good as his word, returning with two good drums and black covers for three drums as well.

Then Duffy approached RSM Frank Darton of the RCR, who assigned CSM Peter Bingham to train the escort and firing party. Duffy drilled the Regiment. Capt. Winston Hicks, an undertaker in civilian life, and Adjutant Art Norrington arranged for a plot in a rolling section of the Aldershot Military Cemetery, full of winding paths and surrounded on all sides by hedges.

On the cold and foggy Friday afternoon of February 9, the Regiment rose to the challenge of honouring a comrade and Duffy could sense their determination to do it well. At 2 o'clock the parade moved off behind Colonel Salmon to the chapel where the flag-draped coffin was transferred to the gun carriage. The cortege then proceded up a hill in slow time, led by the escort, firing party and eight bearers. After 200 yards they changed to quick time and on approaching the cemetery returned to slow time. At the gate the gun carriage was halted and the coffin was moved to a bier on which it was wheeled to the graveside. With the firing party just inside the gate in two lines facing inward, the cortege moved slowly into the cemetery, while the bearers, coffin and escort approached the graveside by a shorter route.

41

Maida Barracks, Cambridge Hospital and the Military Cemetery are shown on
this detailed 1940 map of Aldershot. (British Crown Copyright Reserved)

After prayers the body was lowered, three volleys were fired, Last Post and Reveille sounded and the companies filed out in excellent order and marched past.

On the return to barracks they changed from slow time to quick time flawlessly and halted with precision. Back on the parade square, the officers fell out and were dismissed by the C.O. Duffy dismissed the parade and reported to Colonel Salmon near the square.

"That was a very good show, Mr. Duffy," he said. "Those men are the best in the world. If this Regiment doesn't become the outstanding Regiment in the Canadian Army, it will be nobody's fault but yours and mine. The RSM bridled at that, for he was already working himself to the limit of his endurance. But the Colonel explained what he meant. The men were good, but they must be given first-class leadership by the officers and NCOs.

Duffy felt that for the first time the Regiment had really accomplished something and had finally started to take form. He sensed that everyone felt good about that. The young RSM could see that the Salmon regime was going to be memorable for exacting discipline. He wondered how long he would last himself. He was likely to be as troubled by the C.O.'s harsh measures as he was by the slackness that had brought the period of crisis.

But his beloved Regiment was being saved from extinction because it discovered inner resources in honouring a comrade. He was determined to see the situation through, although there were moments in which he wondered if the RSM shouldn't be someone with Permanent Force experience who could write up orders and perform many duties he had still to master. Fortunately Colonel Salmon could see that in Duffy he already had the ideal RSM, a conviction that grew steadily over the next six months.

Chapter Five
Canadians at centre-stage

Although he had been RSM for only two months, Duffy understood enough about the job to know that the maintenance of high morale was vital to the Regiment's survival. The men had to feel not only confident but comfortable in their still strange environment. Duffy was convinced that the senior NCOs' role was crucial.

The sergeants' mess should be more than a place for heavy drinking, he declared, and then he backed up this opinion with a plan that hard-bitten sergeants refused to believe at first. Duffy introduced afternoon tea. The barracks were very old, but the sergeants' mess was relatively new and well furnished. Every Wednesday, after the sports program finished late in the afternoon, the mess was open to female guests. Members of the Auxiliary for Territorial Service (ATS) and nurses' aides quartered nearby readily accepted Duffy's invitation to tea — and dancing. Jack Armstrong entertained at the piano. The event became popular, attracting visitors from elsewhere in Aldershot Command.

The tea-dancing RSM was tougher than any of his sergeants. He stood 5 feet 4¾ inches, but he had played most team sports and he was a good boxer. He used his authority with great forcefulness, for he believed that meticulous attention to duty was vital to the development of excellence. Uniforms, weapons, deportment and quarters were under his constant surveillance.

The barracks were far from clean enough one day and Duffy felt the sergeants weren't bearing down on the problem. He collected some fire buckets, cancelled lunch in the mess, got down on his knees to show how a floor should be scrubbed and set the sergeants at it. He believed that sergeants should know everyone else's jobs as well as their own and first-class NCOs meant a first-class regiment, in his opinion.

You couldn't just command the men of this Regiment, you had to show them, and this lesson was impressed on the sergeants that day in a way they wouldn't forget. Colonel Salmon had already adopted this policy with the officers, turning them over regularly to a company sergeant-major for rifle drill and marching. The Colonel continually reminded Duffy that small details were important and excellence came from making sure that no details were overlooked. If he saw a scrap of paper on the parade square, he would send for the RSM and say: "Mr. Duffy, there is a piece of paper on your parade square. Get it off."

Salmon's barrack-room inspections on Saturday mornings are still remembered for the fierce intensity with which he sought out imperfections. Followed by the second-in-command, the RSM, the quartermaster and the regimental quartermaster-sergeant, he would go from room to room. A lieutenant would call his men to attention as the C.O. entered. Everything might seem to be spotless, stovepipes would be gleaming and the beds would be lined up perfectly. But he could still find a bit of ash on a poker. Not good enough.

He would say to the platoon commander: "How many men have you? How many sick?" Then he would stop in front of one man and ask the officer: "What is this man's age? What is his religion? What did he do in civilian life? How well can he shoot?" The platoon commander, who might have just arrived the week before, would be left speechless and probably trembling.

One morning he came to a man with a broken bootlace.

When asked for an explanation, the platoon commander could merely say: "I'm sorry, sir, I didn't know."

"What do you mean, you didn't know? You must know everything about your men. You expect them to support you in battle."

Then the soldier was asked why he had a broken bootlace.

"I went to the RQMS, sir, and he didn't have any."

"Is that right, RQMS?"

"Yes sir, we are out."

Then Capt. Abraham, the quartermaster, felt the lash.

"What do you mean, we have no bootlaces?"

"I have indented for them, sir."

"I don't give a damn about whether you indented for them. The men have to have bootlaces. Now listen — we will require a new captain quartermaster, a new RQMS, a new platoon commander, a new company commander and a new 2 l/c in this Regiment if I find one more man without a bootlace."

Duffy must have been relieved at being omitted from that list of endangered species.

Needless to say, the worst never happened. Salmon got the lesson across. Most important in the Regiment are the men. Every officer and every NCO must know their men thoroughly, how to look after them and show real concern for them, and try to be worthy of their loyalty. The spirit that made impossible things possible began to develop in that uncomfortable winter in Aldershot, where it often seemed that the first task was physical survival.

There were tiny fireplaces and sometimes stoves in those ancient barracks. The Regiment had been there for only a short time when Duffy noticed that coal was disappearing quickly from a big pile inside a brick enclosure. He put a guard on it at night, but coal kept disappearing. Sergeants were put on guard and the result was no better. Company sergeant-majors were put on guard and still the coal supply dwindled. One night Duffy saw a CSM carrying a scuttle of coal to a nearby barracks occupied by British women of the ATS. He could hardly make chivalry an offence, so he turned his mind to other matters.

Although the Regiment was surviving, it was far from battle-ready and there was no time to lose. Divisional headquarters asked for a report listing all unfit to serve in France, which was taken to mean that the 1st Division was slated to join the British Expeditionary Force. Every phase of training was intensified. NCOs just back from a course with the Welsh Guards put the rifle companies through their paces on the parade square. Night marches and tactical exercises were begun. Nearly every day for many weeks, a company would march several miles to the ranges in all weathers, fire all day and march back. Duffy often marched with them.

The early days of March brought the first decent weather since the arrival in England. Soccer, softball and boxing teams were training hard for inter-unit competition. General McNaughton inspected the Regiment and all went well. Generally morale was high, although the introduction of mutton was not well received. The cooks didn't seem to know how to handle it and the troops refused to eat it. Colonel Salmon went to the mess hall and stood on a table. "If I can eat it, will you?" he asked. "Yes, sir," was the reply. He took two forkfuls and said there would be no more mutton.

Brigadier Smith dropped in one day in March to warn the Regiment of possible raids by I.R.A. men seeking weapons. A special guard of 14 men was mounted, but defences were never tested. Shortly afterwards one NCO and one man got a bit closer to action when they were assigned for a week to a fishing trawler to provide protection against enemy aircraft with a Lewis gun.

By April everyone was convinced that a move to France was imminent. Trucks were dispatched to a railway siding to move 160,000 rounds of ammunition into the quartermaster's stores, to be kept intact until a move to a theatre of action.

Everyone seemed to assume that the pattern would be similar to that of the First World War. General McNaughton learned from Canada that the 2nd Division would be coming over in July and should be ready to go to France in

November. In the early weeks of 1940 senior Canadian officers in London had begun planning not only moving the 1st Division to France, but the establishment of reinforcement depots near British bases in the Rouen area, in tents at first and then huts. Canadian hospitals were being planned for another area, as if this war was to cover no more ground than the 1914-1918 struggle. Key Canadian officers went to France for a week in March. Lieut.-Col. E.L.M. Burns, who was to become a general later in the war, saw his friend Mike Pearson at Canada House after his return and predicted that the Germans would easily outflank the Maginot Line.

But before that happened, Canadian infantrymen in the Aldershot and Pirbright areas were training as if to refight the First World War. All the 1st Division battalions occupied trench systems just like those inhabited by Canadian troops in France 25 years before, seeking to master the old rituals of patrols and raiding parties, putting up and crawling through barbed wire in darkness. Unreality was present on the Continent as well. For six months men of the B.E.F. had been fortifying a line facing the frontier of neutral Belgium which they wouldn't even be occupying, for they were to move forward into Belgium to counter any German offensive, and in any case this line wouldn't have stopped the kind of attack that ravaged Poland.

No one seemed to question the training that went on in England. If that was what was demanded at the top, regimental commanders couldn't change the system. Confidence in top British leadership was less than complete, however.

When Sir Edmund Ironside, Chief of the Imperial General Staff, addressed Canadian battalion commanders and 2 i/cs in the Aldershot Garrison Theatre, he held forth on the theme that the war would soon be over. The Germans had no chance, he said, because they had no generals who had been more than captains in the First War. Ex-sergeant Howard Graham could make no sense of this theory and Colonel Salmon thought it was stupid.

The German invasion of Norway and Denmark on April 9 made it appear that the time to commit the Canadians had arrived. The 2nd Brigade was slated for Norway. Sniper rifles, grenades and mortars were requisitioned from the Hasty Ps, ostensibly for the Princess Patricias, but the 2nd Brigade show didn't come off. Night training in the trenches on Hankley Common continued.

In May the B.E.F. in France at the Belgian border consisted of 10 divisions in three Corps. A fourth Corps slated to go over in the summer was to include the 1st Canadian Division. There were stocks of food and ammunition for the Canadians in storage on the Continent in April, and even spare vehicles.

As if to continue the First War theme, preparations were made for the 1st Brigade to move to Tilshead on Salisbury Plain where Canadians had wintered before going to France in 1915. On the day before the move, the blitzkreig roared into Belgium and the Netherlands and the nature of warfare was changed forever. But for 10 days the RCR, the Hastings and the 48th were in tents on the plain, spending the daylight hours digging in the chalk and most of the night acting out the ghostly trench warfare routines of 25 years before. "All we acquired were a few more muscles," Duffy said. Colonel Salmon used the time to good advantage, weeding out inadequate leaders. Three company sergeant-majors were demoted and some officers departed on short notice. The C.O. told the officers to stop addressing their subordinates by their first names, for in a life-or-death situation the person in command must hold to a standard that allows no informality. That Salmon edict was soon forgotten.

The Canadians knew that the situation on the Continent was bad and they crowded around radios to hear the news whenever they could. Nazi forces were in control of the Netherlands by May 15 and the situation rapidly became worse. Instead of heading for Paris, the Germans had driven a wedge westward by May 20 to take Amiens and Abbeville and reach the Channel. On May 21 civilian lorries returned the Regiment to Aldershot.

"The amount of secret mail pouring into the orderly room seems to indicate some plan for an early move of the Division to an active theatre," the writer of the war diary speculated. By May 22 the British had pulled back to the Franco-Belgian frontier. The German pincer swung north to besiege Boulogne and Calais. With Gravelines and Dunkirk threatened, about 60 British, French and Belgian divisions seemed trapped. British reinforcements were sent to Boulogne and Calais on May 22.

General McNaughton had been in constant touch with the War Office and was asked to report as early as possible on May 23 to get the details of an awesome assignment. He was to restore road and rail links between the Channel and the B.E.F. through Hazebrouck and Armentieres, about 30 miles inland, although Boulogne was completely encircled. He would take in at least a Canadian brigade and assume command of all troops in Calais. The operation was code-named Angel.

A 1st Brigade field day was cancelled and everyone was put on two hours' notice to move. The day before about 175 reinforcements from Canada had arrived at Maida Barracks and about the same number of men had gone on leave. At a meeting of senior 1st Brigade officers it was noted that the Regiment's whole signal platoon was on leave. If these men could not get back in time to move, signallers from another unit would replace them.

McNaughton ordered the 1st Division battle headquarters to be on a train for Dover by 3 o'clock. He and a small party were to leave Dover that night by destroyer to reconnoitre the situation in Calais and Dunkirk, while a 1st Brigade Group including artillery, engineers and field ambulance personnel were preparing to entrain for the Channel and to cross on May 24. Their vehicles would follow from Southampton.*

Although none of his own troops had been committed,

---

* For more on the story of how Canadians briefly held centre stage at a critical point in the war, see Chapters 5 and 6 in Vol. II of John Swettenham's *McNaughton*, and Chapter IX of Colonel C.P. Stacey's *Six Years of War*, Vol. I of the Official History of the Canadian Army in the Second World War.

the commander of the 1st Canadian Division had authority to report directly to Ironside on the feasibility of reinforcing the B.E.F., and thereby power to influence to some extent the course of the war. He reached Calais by midnight aboard a destroyer, concluded that the situation there was still reasonably stable, and despite intensive dive-bomber attacks, went on to Dunkirk. French reinforcements expected at Dunkirk could get there sooner than the Canadians, so McNaughton decided that if any of his own troops were to be committed they should go to Calais.

McNaughton telephoned this message to Guy Simonds in Dover for relay to Ironside. Later however, Simonds learned that the War Office had already approved in principle the evacuation of Calais. The troops in Aldershot knew little or nothing about what had been transpiring since the morning of May 23. At 4 o'clock the Regiment was ready to move, but later learned there would be no departure until the next morning. Certainly the 24th of May was to be no holiday.

'B' and 'C' Companies were up at 2.45 and on the parade ground at 4.45 and moving out by train at 6.00 on what came to be known as the Dover Dash. The second train left at 7.00, but neither made it to Dover. The RCR, the 48th and 1st Brigade Headquarters got on board ship but never sailed. McNaughton was back in England by late afternoon and present at a conference attended by Prime Minister Churchill, senior cabinet ministers and the defence chiefs of staff. Angel was off, although Churchill told McNaughton to consider himself still on two hours' notice.

For the Regiment, it was a day of tension, boredom and frustration, sitting in railway carriages. Was there going to be action or not? Those who got out of the trains were ordered to stay close by, but that was too much to hope.

Later in the day a pub owner came to the train to complain that two kegs of cider were missing. Duffy was convinced that they had been hidden for the return journey. A coach-by-coach search finally located the cider behind a ceiling panel in a toilet. Duffy seized the kegs and put them under guard in the baggage coach. When he checked a little later, all members of the guard were drunk. The Regimental provost section was ordered to take over. On his next visit Duffy found a provost corporal roaring drunk and threatening to knock any challenger's head off. Since boyhood Duffy had known this corporal as a boxer with a powerful punch.

A foot shorter and 30 pounds lighter, Duffy decided that his job as RSM was to subdue the corporal. His approach was direct and friendly. "We've been friends for years, but I must place you under arrest," he said. He ducked away from a punch and instantly floored the corporal who got up and surrendered.

Duffy glanced over his shoulder. Colonel Salmon was in the doorway of the coach watching. "Perhaps he decided right there to keep me as RSM," he said later.

Back in Aldershot the uncertainty continued. By May 26 the scheme was on again and then cancelled again. But Lord Gort, commanding the B.E.F., kept urging that the Canadians be sent until the War Office turned him down finally on May 27. By that time the Dunkirk evacuation was underway and the intervention of a Canadian Brigade could hardly have delayed that. McNaughton had decided that an anti-invasion role was best for his division. Each of the nine infantry battalions would be the main component of a mobile group. An advance party from the Regiment moved off for Northamptonshire on May 29 and the main body followed in civilian buses on the night of May 31. Progress was slow because all road signs were down.

Major Graham and Capt. Abraham were riding in an old Austin car at the rear of the convoy led by Colonel Salmon. Although the general direction was supposed to be north, they concluded at dawn that if the sun was about to come up on the left, the column must be off course. The road came to a dead end. Turning the convoy around in a confined space was a slow job and it was mid-morning before the Regiment was at its destination.

On Saturday and Sunday, the first two days of June, the

drama of the Dunkirk evacuation was at its peak and by June 4 it was over. Canadian 1st Division troops were in a position to counter any German seaborne or airborne landing in eastern England. The Regiment was based in and around the pleasant town of Finedon. It took six miles of telephone wire to link the scattered company headquarters. The bugler had to be driven around in a truck to make his Reveille heard in all the billets. The Bell was a popular pub. Local tradition claimed that there had been licensed premises on that spot since 1062.

This was the first contact with life in the English villages and countryside that these Canadians soon learned to love. It was a pleasant change from Aldershot, but all too brief. The Canadians were among the best equipped troops in Britain, but even at that, odds and ends of civilian vehicles supplemented unit transport. Padre Walter Gilling had no vehicle, but the medical officer had a hearse. The few days in Finedon were quiet and by June 6 the Canadians were all back in Aldershot, little suspecting that decisions already taken in Whitehall would involve them in a bizarre series of events that could have ended the war for the 1st Brigade.

Something was in the wind, the diary writer concluded, for some nearby gunners and engineers were moving. A visit by the King and Queen on June 8 was another reason to expect something, and Sunday, June 9, confirmed it.

At 8.30 a.m. all Regimental transport — 55 trucks, 14 motorcycles and now including a car for the padre, formed up in convoy and moved off to reach Exeter by nightfall. A church parade at 9.30 was followed by a pay parade at 10.30. Colonel Salmon was back at 1.30 from a conference at 1st Division headquarters with word that there would be a move in a few hours. Bren gun carriers were to be at Farnborough station ready to move off by train the next morning.

The troops didn't know that about two weeks earlier, when the withdrawal from Dunkirk was just starting, Prime Minister Churchill had decided that, to keep France in the war a little longer, a new British Expeditionary Force would go to France and link up with British divisions still there. The 1st Canadian Division would be part of this new force that would try to hold a bridgehead in the Brittany peninsula.

The Regiment received a warning order at noon on June 12 for a move late that night. No destination was mentioned, although by that time 1st Brigade transport that had moved by road to southwest England had begun arriving at Brest by ship.

Duffy was worried as he watched the sections, platoons and companies march to the railway station after midnight. Two men in each section carried the unexpended portion of the day's ration in buckets on a pole and each man carried some bully beef and biscuits. He wondered how they would perform if they ran up against the Germans. Although the Regiment had its full issue of ammunition, that wouldn't be much more than 250 rounds per man. Would they just keep on firing or pull back when it was wise to do so?

Colonel Salmon took charge of the first train carrying Headquarters Company, 'A' Company and the 1st Field Company Royal Canadian Engineers. Major Graham commanded the second train carrying battalion head-quarters, as well as 'B', 'C' and 'D' Companies. It was nearly noon when the first train reached the quayside in Plymouth. Much confusion surrounded the embarkation for France and it was 9.00 pm. before the Regiment sailed aboard the French ship Ville d'Angier, with the rest of the Brigade aboard another. Major Graham saw a message on a ship notice board indicating that the French had quit fighting. Although safely anchored in Brest harbour at dawn on June 14 it was another five hours before the ship brought the Regiment to the dockside. The troops disembarked quickly and marched to a park at the top of a hill. Duffy and the paymaster went across town by streetcar to locate the men of the carrier platoon and pay them in French money.

When they stopped at a French barracks to get directions, Duffy was appalled to see a scruffy French soldier at the gate with a wine bottle in his pocket, a cigarette in his mouth and his rifle leaning against the wall.

Soldiers inside were sitting around with their rifles on the ground. They have never had any intention of fighting, Duffy thought, and they are just fat slobs. Are the men of my Regiment going to lay down their lives for them? His apprehension about the whole expedition mounted.

Air raids added to the general confusion in Brest. Although McNaughton had expected the 1st Brigade to assemble somewhere in the Brest area, near the western tip of Brittany before pushing inland, British Movement Control officers had been instructed to move the units inland by train as they had in the fall of 1939. And so units of the 1st Brigade Group

were headed for destinations even further inland than the base of the Brittany peninsula which was supposed to be approximately the line the new B.E.F. would hold. General Sir Alan Brooke had set up headquarters near Le Mans and had already learned from senior French officers that the French Army was incapable of real resistance. But the 1st Canadian Brigade was soon rolling inland aboard three trains, while McNaughton and the most of his troops were still in southwest England.

By midnight the train commanded by Colonel Salmon had passed through Rennes, well beyond the base of the Brittany peninsula. At Laval, about 140 miles from encircled Paris, a British major appeared alone at the station and gave the order to turn around. Colonel Salmon questioned him closely and satisfied himself that this really was a British officer. The train headed back towards Brest, from the brink of disaster.

Along the return route columns of refugees were thickening. Mounds of bicycles were stacked on station platforms. Some of the people waiting in the hope of catching trains held their hands out for food. Many soldiers gave away their rations. "It was very sad," Padre Gilling said later, "for we were witnessing the disintegration of France."

The train reached Brest harbour late in the afternoon of

June 15 and each company was assigned an area along the waterfront. Some men found several huge vats which they ventilated with bullet holes and then lined up with mess tins to catch the wine. During the evening the Regiment and the RCR went aboard the S.S. Canterbury. They were joined by remnants from many British units, wounded French and Belgian soldiers, some British Army nurses, a banker from Nice and a British brigadier with no troops. The 48th were well on their way home, for their train took a short route to the Channel and they found a ship waiting at St. Malo.

A Sunday morning departure was expected, but most of the day went by with nothing to do but sit and wait. Stories that circulated on deck became grimmer and grimmer as the troops watched truckloads of equipment being dumped into the harbour. No one would escape, one rumour held, because Hilter had ordered all Channel ports closed. If any vessels tried to leave, French battleships would blow them out of the water. But late in the afternoon the ship sailed and anchored in Plymouth Harbour just after dawn.

Lady Astor was at the dockside late in the morning, and when she offered bully beef sandwiches, which was about all the men had had to eat for days, she received a rather rude response. "You aren't anything like the nice Canadians who left here a few days ago," she said.

It was a long rail journey back to Aldershot. The Colonel and the RSM were thankful that the Regiment had got out of France. Salmon knew that the men were frustrated and disspirited because they had missed a chance to show what they could do against the Germans, but at least they could be soldierly.

And so he insisted that the march back to the barracks in full equipment should be of parade ground standard — heads up, arms swinging — and at a brisk pace. A good Regiment had survived a strange assignment with potential for disaster all the way. There would be time now to make it a great Regiment.

Chapter Six
Surrey, Sussex and Scotland

A safe return to Aldershot was no reason for relaxation.
Colonel Salmon demanded stricter discipline than ever.
While intensified training might have been resented briefly
at first, men of the Regiment did sense that it was a great
honour to be standing with the British people in defiance of
Hitler whose troops were just across the Channel. In fact, on
June 29 General McNaughton predicted flatly in a message
to the Minister of Defence in Ottawa that the Canadians
would be fighting in England. Being in the front line brought
a sense of elation.

Sgt. Art Storms' safe return with the C.O.'s station wagon
on June 19 and the arrival of all but three men who had
travelled inland by road from Brest were exploits to cheer,
in spite of the loss of vehicles, equipment and records, and
worst of all, abandonment of the 500-pound Little Chief, the
sheet zinc Indian mascot, liberated from the roof of a Picton
cannery.

By June 20 the Regiment had received notice to draw 40
new vehicles and was soon ready to roll again. Salmon's
recovery plan was already featuring long marches in the
countryside to overnight bivouacs, and it was now time to
forget barrack life. In fact the Maida Barracks parade
square was being covered with steel standards to discourage
enemy landings.

Most of the next three months — the whole gorgeous summer — was spent under canvas on the 3,000-acre Lyne House estate of the Broadwood family, owner of two villages, including Rusper. The name was derived from the fact that the line between Surrey and West Sussex ran right through the manor house. The setting was marvellous, but it was no rest camp.

In Aldershot Colonel Salmon's training program had been so intensive that Duffy used to say that his own day began about 11 o'clock the night before, because planning for the next day took hours and hours. Basically the same routine was followed under canvas.

When awakened by the orderly sergeant while the camp was still asleep, Duffy was always outside in 90 seconds to report to the C.O. and signal to the bugler to sound Reveille. He would then receive an oral report from the orderly sergeant, usually criticizing something that could have been done better; the orderly sergeant would chew out the orderly corporals from each company; the orderly corporals would go back to their lines, and in a few minutes 800 men would be on their feet, snapping and snarling. Duffy would also visit the signal platoon and the provost section to find out what had happened during the night.

After breakfast he would accompany the C.O. or some other officer to inspect whatever training was in progress, paying particular attention to how the NCOs were performing, or he might conduct a class for junior officers. He was present in the late morning to parade soldiers charged with various offences before the C.O. and at noon there would well be some matter to take up with the senior NCOs at the sergeants' mess. As well as accompanying platoons on afternoon training, the RSM would be out again with platoons or companies doing night exercises.

Duffy believed that firmly enforced discipline and a strong command structure was better for morale than laxity, and even brought a charge against his brother that reduced him from sergeant to private.

The Salmon regime, then in its final weeks, showed no relenting either. Inspections were as rigorous as ever. Lieut. Bill Seamark, newly arrived from Canada, and assigned to the signal platoon, soon saw the logic of his colleagues' preparations for these inspections. If everything in every tent was perfect, some officer would then be quizzed on his military competence, which could be embarrassing.

It was better to leave some tiny imperfection for the eagle-eyed C.O. to pounce upon, roar about and then go away. And so on the eve of an inspection Seamark would meet with Bernie Madden, John Stevenson, Harold Ruttan and Jack Morgan to decide who would perpetrate tomorrow's dastardly misdeeds. Someone would leave the metal tip of a shoe lace on a tent floorboard, or leave one button undone on one greatcoat hanging in one tent, or leave the safety catch off one rifle in another tent, thus guaranteeing a fierce but brief uproar, and then peace.

Seamark also learned quickly that sergeants usually had the best ideas. On the evening before his first battalion exercise, the brand new signals officer learned from his sergeant, John Cote, that none of the company commanders ever sent any messages. Couldn't they be given the idea that messages were important? To help the companies put on a good show, Cote asked, why not write out in advance the messages that they should be sending on reaching various objectives? Seamark agreed. The next day signallers with messages in their pockets accompanied each company in the attack exercise. They aimed their Lucas lamps at a pre-arranged spot near battalion headquarters where Seamark and some other signallers were waiting. At the appropriate time, signallers with the companies would start sending their messages. If the first two or three words were the same as pre-arranged, the signallers at BHQ would quit reading and take a copy of the message to Major Graham.

With Salmon, following the companies, was Cote, carrying a field telephone and a long line back to Graham. The messages at BHQ were read to Salmon. "'A' Company on intermediate objective" or "'B' Company on final objective" or "'C' Company needs ammunition," etc. Salmon didn't think much of the infantry tactics displayed, but he praised the company commanders for using their communications. They hadn't sent any messages, of course, but when the technique was explained to them by Seamark, they all saw the wisdom of it, and the signal platoon's morale went up.

Colonel Salmon's period of command ended in August. One gift he received on his departure was a silver inkstand. About 35 years later, Ken Willcocks, a postwar C.O., found it in mint condition in a Toronto antique shop. It was purchased and placed in the sergeants' mess in Belleville.

Higher formation chose a strange successor. Lt.-Col. James Edgar of the Princess Patricia's Canadian Light Infantry was indiscreet enough to turn up the first day wearing PPCLI badges. He stayed only four weeks, apparently the required period for confirmation of rank. He certainly wasn't there for disciplinary purposes, so it wasn't a case of sending another Permanent Force officer in to show Militiamen how to be soldiers. The Hasty Ps were as good as anybody in the 1st Division at this point. Ironically, in 1941 the Patricias were not performing satisfactorily and they were taken over by outsiders. Chris Vokes and Rod Keller, both future generals, each took command of the Patricias for a period to smarten them up.

Training emphasized anti-invasion measures, particularly infantry and tank co-operation in attacking enemy forces. There was enough aerial activity over the south of England, day and night, to suggest that there might be a real enemy on the ground some day soon. Emergency assembly points were designated and commandeered civilian buses with Royal Army Service Corps drivers were attached to infantry units to rush them into action. There could be armed parachutists to deal with, not just German aircrew floating down after their aircraft had been destroyed. Some of the latter seemed to believe that an invasion had started and even asked to be taken to the nearest German officer.

A few days after Colonel Edgar's arrival, Brigade sent the duty company out to round up parachutists and everybody else wanted to join in the hunt. But the "parachutists" found in a pub were just two Londoners on a country walk.

Two weeks later both 'A' and 'B' Companies were ordered to capture parachutists seen coming down about 1,200 yards away. One turned out to be a German and the other a New Zealander who had dived at the German aircraft which crashed near the 48th Highlanders. The German surrendered to one of the Regiment's British bus drivers, but was claimed by a 48th patrol before anybody else arrived.

Men of the Regiment were becoming known to the other units as the Plough Jockeys, a name they soon cherished as a mark of distinction. In the rural environment where they were so much at home, they were determined to show the urban regiments in particular that they could march farther and dig in faster and patrol more effectively than anyone else. Their physical strength and high morale showed on the playing field. Beating the 48th Highlanders for the Brigade softball championship capped a summer of growing confidence. In the fall they dominated in soccer, taking the Brigade championship handily.

The chance to show who would be the toughest opposition for invading Germans didn't come, although a warning of imminent invasion was sounded one September evening with the ringing of church bells. For eight days the Regiment was on stand-to and one hour's notice to move, but it had been a false alarm.

(Writing after the war, Churchill explained that reconnaissance information had convinced the Chiefs of Staff that an invasion was about to be launched against southeast England. The code word Cromwell was issued to Home Forces and repeated for information to other commands. Home Guard commanders in some areas, acting on their own initiative, ordered church bells rung. A new set of ground rules made clear that no Home Guard commander was to take that action in future unless he had actually seen 25 or more parachutists landing.)

Weekend leaves in London could be more adventurous or even more dangerous than life in camp, as Ray Young had found out. He checked into a hotel near Marble Arch, had dinner, went to a show and returned in the blackout about midnight. There was a bomb crater outside the hotel, but he made his way around it and went inside. He climbed several flights of stairs in the darkness. Looking for his room, he occasionally flicked his cigarette lighter. When he thought he was near the right door, he flicked the lighter again and found himself standing on the brink of an open elevator shaft. One more step would have been fatal. He reached his room safely and when he got up he found that he had been the only guest in the abandoned building all night.

Howard Graham, who had been second in command since early 1939 and declared fit to command in an inspecting officer's report before war began, finally took command as the war was entering its second year. The Regiment, hammered into shape by Salmon, was now ready for the polish Graham's more relaxed hand could give it, in the friendly surroundings of the English countryside.

Predominantly rural Surrey and Sussex remained the Regiment's home for the next two and a half years. For the first 12 months of that period scattered billets in the Betchworth area between Reigate and Dorking made these Canadian countrymen a real part of a rural community.

The signal platoon's telephone circuit linking the companies was about 18 miles long. Headquarters Company was in a large mansion called Mynthurst Manor about three and a half miles from battalion headquarters, a large country home called Ravenleigh. 'A' Company occupied a property called Betchworth Manor.

Half of 'C' Company was in a golf clubhouse on Reigate Heath and half in six rooms of J. Arthur Rank's home nearby. 'D' Company was comfortably situated on another large property at Buckland Corners. 'B' Company was in Wanham Manor, a very large house with several bathrooms.

In carrying out his special responsibility for maintaining not only discipline but security at battalion headquarters, Duffy managed to avoid calling a roll. A man who might be a few minutes late in returning to camp a couple of times could face a charge of being absent without leave. Duffy's attitude was that these men were responsible enough to know when they must be on duty at BHQ and as long as they were doing their jobs well, he did find it possible to turn a blind eye occasionally. But every man must be in shape to do his job and all BHQ troops — the provost section, the intelligence section, stretcher bearers and the rest — all had to turn out for PT early in the morning. Right after Reveille they had to be out running and sometimes the course was five miles long. The last man in had to move all the sandbags from in front of the big windows on one side of the big manor house to the other side. That task alone was good for keeping in shape.

Duffy stayed overnight occasionally with friends at Coulsdon and getting back in time in the morning required perfect train connections. One morning he didn't make the connection at Reigate Station and had to run three miles at top speed to camp. By the time he reached BHQ it was raining hard, so he ran down the middle of the road shouting "No PT today". But the provost sergeant had already taken everyone out for a run. For months, men seeing Duffy passing their quarters would open a window and shout: "No PT today" to remind him that nobody was perfect.

After about three months in these quarters, the Regiment moved briefly to the Brighton area to take over coastal defence duties from the Seaforth Highlanders. Billets were larger, but the weather was colder. 'A' Company was lucky with both billets and battle stations in the Dyke Hotel. Aerial activity was greater than at Betchworth, but possible enemy intrusion from the sea was the main concern. Near the coast 'B' Company challenged and fired on a private motor vehicle that failed to stop. Shortly after celebrating its first Christmas overseas the Regiment turned its quarters over to the Royal Hamilton Light Infantry and returned to Betchworth.

The sky often glowed on those long winter nights as bombers pounded London. In February bombs fell near 'D' Company, blowing up a gasmain, killing and injuring civilians and severely damaging buildings. A few nights later 30 incendiaries were dropped along the Dorking-Brighton railway line.

As the days of preparation for action stretched into weeks and months, it took patience and ingenuity on a battalion, company and even platoon basis to keep daily programs interesting and flexible enough to prevent boredom. There were limits to how many gas lectures, how much grenade practice, how much equipment cleaning or vehicle maintenance, kit inspection or squad drill anyone could take, even though it was broken up by sports on Wednesday afternoons and the occasional dance or concert in an evening. For most men, obviously the joys of time off in the rural surroundings they came to cherish made it all worthwhile. There were many marriages. In the Betchworth days one man in the pioneer platoon who had married a girl in Reigate was prepared to show during a three-day exercise how much home life meant to him.

He went the first day's 20 miles, but instead of staying with his platoon, he walked about 20 miles back to Reigate, saw his wife and returned in time to rejoin the exercise in the morning. The second night's stop after another 20-mile march during the day was too far from Reigate for a return on foot, but he made it home and back by bus during the night. The third day's march of about 20 miles back to Betchworth was child's play.

Providing guards for 1st Brigade headquarters or 1st Division headquarters became a soon forgotten routine task, but not guarding Chartwell in Kent, Winston Churchill's country home. 'B' Company under Stan Ketcheson and 'C' Company under Ron Church each performed this duty for short periods during 1941. The Prime Minister came down to Chartwell for weekends.

Robert Morrison of 'B' Company often recalled that it rained so much that tents the troops occupied in a wooded area near the house were flooded most of the time. Entrenching tools were lacking and it was difficult to drain the water away from the site. K.K. Kenny put a sign on his tent: GIVE US THE TOOLS AND WE'LL FINISH THE JOB, but Ketcheson, unimpressed by his plagiarism, made him take it down.

Morrison was on roving picket duty in the grounds one evening when Churchill approached. He saluted.

"Why didn't you challenge me, Canada?" Churchill growled.

"I know who you are, sir."

"Oh, how do you know me?"

"By your cigar, bald head, double chin, short neck and fat belly, sir."

"But don't forget the Germans have bald men with short necks and fat bellies who smoke cigars."

"You're right, sir, but they would do up the bottom button on their vests.

The Hasty Ps weren't exactly guardian angels. A large pond on the property contained ducks and trout. According to Morrison, both helped to supplement his platoon's rations. A camouflage net from a steel helmet made an excellent fishing net.

During 'C' Company's tour of duty, Ron Church was appalled to see a civilian fishing in the pond early one morning. He rushed from his quarters and ordered the man to leave immediately. "I'm the next-door neighbour," the fisherman replied. "Winston said that I could fish here." That settled that. Church was soon in friendly conversation with the neighbour who had been to Canada and knew the Bay of Quinte well — but insisted that the correct pronunciation was "Kantay".

In the cause of maintaining Regimental spirit and pride in

its traditions Duffy was prepared to adopt unusual measures for which there really was no official authority. A spotless and gleaming cap badge was absolutely imperative. "That badge isn't yours," he would say. "It belongs to everyone who ever wore it in the past and will ever wear it in the future. Keep it shiny or I'll see that you are transferred to some other outfit."

He often stopped men with dull badges and ordered them back into camp. And for those who were properly dressed but still managed to act in a manner unfavourable to the Regiment's reputation were dealt with quickly and directly as well. On Duffy's orders, the provost section kept potential bad actors under scrutiny when they were in pubs in such towns as Horsham. Those who consumed too much found themselves suddenly whisked out the door and into a truck and taken back to camp. If an inveterate absentee ever received mail, the return address was noted and this made it much easier to pick him up.

If all the rules and regulations were followed, everybody would be locked up, including me," Duffy often said. An RSM from the Algonquin Regiment who was attached to the Hastings for a period couldn't understand why Duffy didn't go by the book at all times. As far as being RSM was concerned, Duffy was really writing the book as he went along.

Perhaps his most unconventional decision in England was to involve men in detention in a major training exercise. He saw no reason why these essentially good men who were in custody because of absences or drunkenness or insubordination should miss tough and important training. He decided that on an important three-day exercise he would take a dozen men from detention and patrol far out in front of the Regiment to detect the presence of the "enemy".

Officers warned Duffy that he would be risking a court martial that could end his career, if any men escaped. He recognized that, he said, but he would be carrying live ammunition in his tommy gun and the men would be told that the first one attempting to escape would be shot.

During the first day's advance toward contact with opposing forces, Duffy and his screen of scouts were about five miles out in front of the Regiment. At noon Duffy took his men into a pub for a beer — the last thing they ever expected to happen. It rained during the whole three days of the exercise, but these men worked day and night and did their jobs superbly. Naturally Duffy covered more ground that he might have done in other circumstances, and so he became so exhausted that he could hardly walk, but two of them encouraged him to keep going on the final few miles. He had expressed his confidence in them dramatically for he believed that they were in custody because someone had failed to give them proper leadership. Events were to prove later that hellers in England were among the best men in real action.

Tactical training schemes were tough, but the Hasty Ps loved to end them with a flourish, particularly if it meant marching past some other unit. Whenever it was possible, Duffy arranged for the band to meet the troops and play them back to quarters. The band came out in pouring rain at the end of one long scheme on the Downs and played the Regiment home. All the drumheads broke, but the rhythm was maintained. The bass drummer's wrist was bleeding where the drumstick thong cut into it as he pounded away.

When making his rounds of the companies Duffy often approached from an unexpected direction, and on a back route into Headquarters Company one day he saw a great cloud of dust in a nearby field. Some men were cultivating it for the farmer, pulling harrows with a Bren gun carrier. He felt he had to stop them, for they were using War Department petrol, but he was aware of their disappointment and the scorn of the farmer who understood why these farm boys wanted to work the soil.

Helping farmers received official approval shortly afterwards and units in rural areas were encouraged to grow some of their own food. A 20-acre field behind Mynthurst Manor was made available to the Regiment and Gordon Way was put in charge of the operation. He borrowed a plough and harrows and towed them behind a Bren carrier and planted a very large potato patch which thrived. A smaller area planted with other vegetables didn't provide anything for the table, for it was constantly raided by hungry soldiers.

In September, 1941, two years after mobilization, Major Sutcliffe was acting C.O. while Graham, obviously marked for a higher command, was doing a senior staff job at 1st Division headquarters. It was a relatively quiet period with emphasis on weapons training rather than prodigious feats of marching. Officers were being encouraged to teach their men about the organization of enemy forces using a series of pamphlets entitled A Popular Guide to the German Army.

A fierce-looking recruit arrived directly from the 2nd Battalion in Canada — Chief Petawawa-much, a wooden Indian carved at Pembroke and shipped over aboard a destroyer. He is still with the Regiment and after the war a light-hearted Militiaman got him a Social Insurance Number, 460-917-321.

When Bill Graydon arrived in Bognor Regis as a reinforcement officer just before Christmas, 1941, a friend had expressed the hope that he wouldn't join 'A' Company, and certainly not 7 platoon. They were the tough guys whom the company commander, Major Cyril Osmond O'Conor-Fenton delighted in taming.

Graydon got 7 platoon. One lance-sergeant was so skilled with dynamite that the men wondered in just what line of after-hours activity his talents had been so finely honed. With a little explosive he could cut down a tree as neatly as if it had been sawn. His pistol practice was just as spectacular. When he was bragging about what he could do and was offering to bet on his own prowess, many in the platoon were eager to bet against him. Graydon covered all the bets on the sergeant's behalf, walked 10 paces out in front of the platoon and held a pencil at arm's length. The sergeant cut it in two with the first shot. Graydon gathered up the money and the platoon went to the nearest pub. This act wasn't pursued as a way to get free drinks from strangers, however. Graydon decided to quit while he was ahead.

For the first seven months of 1942 the Regiment was based at Middleton-on-Sea, just east of Bognor Regis. Some battalion exercises dealt with repelling enemy landings. Beach patrols at night watched for the real thing. Fog sometimes distorted vision and occasionally the sound of wind and rolling surf registered on some ears as the sounds of boats and men.

Battalion headquarters officers lived near the sea in a large house owned by the editor of the Daily Express. Late one night Graham, Sutcliffe and Padre Gilling were all sure they could hear movement on the beach.

Sutcliffe telephoned 'A' and 'C' Companies to get their patrols into the area quickly. A few minutes later shots were heard. One patrol had fired on the other, approaching from the opposite direction. No one was hit, but the results could have been tragic.

After 3 o'clock one cold wet morning, Duffy came back to battalion headquarters from a long beach patrol with one of the companies. He was tired and troubled at the prospect of having to demote a company sergeant-major that day. He was fed up and ready to quit. He went inside BHQ where Graham was working and on the spur of the moment Duffy entered the C.O.'s office. He asked to be relieved and to be reduced to the rank of corporal. Graham spoke quietly but firmly: "You know, Mr. Duffy, you're just the same as me. You're going to do as you're damn well told. Now get out!" He followed Duffy to the door. "Angus," he said, "come back in. You're to go on leave tomorrow."

During the stay on the coast there were many opportunities to strengthen the Regiment's affiliation with the Royal Sussex Regiment, with parades, training the Home Guard, participation in community events and even a cricket match.

On one occasion Graham ordered Duffy to prepare for a ceremonial parade in order to present a contribution to the Royal Sussex P.O.W. Fund, a day's pay from every man in the Regiment. Graham insisted that the very highest standards of smartness must prevail. Each company must have the same number of men on parade and all the drill must be perfect. Duffy spent many hours rehearsing — standing in front of the Regiment with his back to the companies, giving the commands which the C.O. would give . . .

First Battalion, Hastings and Prince Edward Regiment will present arms . . . PRESENT . . . ARMS!

The rifles seemed to move from 800 shoulders in perfect rhythm, accompanied by slapping sounds on the slings at just the right second, but Duffy didn't want anyone to become overly confident. "Keep still, you men on the left," he roared at one rehearsal. "Rashotte, what are you moving for?" Mitch Rashotte, who was in the rear rank, wondered for years how Duffy, with his back to him, knew that he had moved. Long after the war he asked Duffy how he did it. "I knew you always moved after you presented arms," he replied.

The parade was a great success. Senior officers present were greatly impressed, including Brigadier Harry Salmon. Brigadier Rod Keller said the Regiment's drill was the smartest he had ever seen.

When the whole 1st Brigade went on parade, Duffy acted as Brigade RSM. One of these occasions was the visit of Prime Minister Mackenzie King, who had been booed in Aldershot three days earlier. McNaughton and other dignitaries accompanied the Prime Minister. Duffy was determined that no Hasty P would insult the Prime Minister and he took up a position behind the Regiment so that the men could hear his growling reminder of what unpleasant things would happen to anyone who was so foolish. Mr. King's remarks about how proud Canadians were of their armed forces were followed by three cheers for the PM.

Duffy made a point of never going to the headquarters of any higher formation. He would arrange to meet a Brigade staff officer at the location where a parade was to be assembled. He knew he was good at his job and he wanted no other. He stayed well away from any senior officer who might become interested in taking him away from the Regiment he loved.

Platoon and company training featured unarmed combat, bayonet fighting, cross-country running, river crossings, map reading, aircraft recognition and camouflage. On a battalion level, training schemes might involve attacking the 48th or the RCR in the role of paratroop invaders, or acting defensively in a night attack from either of those units. The 1st Brigade might attack another brigade or the 1st Division might take on a British division. In all weathers the troops moved across flat countryside or the steep rolling terrain of the Downs on schemes lasting a day or a week. They swam or forded rivers, climbed steep embankments carrying more equipment than they ever would in real action, slept in the open and sometimes walked until their feet bled.

Chaplain, paymaster and dentist all went along with the fighting men on Exercise Beaver III in April, 1942. The 1st Division, under Major-General George Pearkes, was moving north toward Horsham from the Channel. The 2nd Division was the enemy. To confuse the 2nd Division, Pearkes mixed up his three brigades, so the Regiment was brigaded with the Patricias and the West Novas. When their patrols made contact with any 1st Division battalion, 2nd Division units couldn't be sure what other battalions were in the vicinity.

The 2nd Div. defenders of Horsham put up strong re-sistance, however, and it took unusual tactics to penetrate the town's defences. Alex Campbell put a whole platoon aboard a double-decker bus on its ordinary run. By lying on the floor while the civilian passengers remained in their seats, the platoon escaped detection until it was in the heart of Horsham. It was a hard-fought battle. Maurice H. 'Battle' Cockin, intelligence officer of the Regiment, was a cool, well educated Englishman. Men who didn't take to him very enthusiastically at first had occasion to change their minds. In the course of an argument with the I.O. of the Essex Scottish, Cockin got into a fist fight and was hailed as a real Canadian from then on.

Exercise Tiger in May, 1942, had six participating divisions. Sussex and Kent were two countries at war, with Surrey neutral. The Sussex force was mainly the 1st Canadian Corps and the Kent force was mainly the 12th British Army Corps. The two armies made contact and the Regiment, in a pursuit role, found itself deep in Kent, a long way from its base in Middleton, when the scheme ended. General Bernard L. Montgomery, directing the scheme, ordered the Canadians to return to camp on foot. It took four days. Just over 500 men were on the march — more than any other battalion — and few fell out. Graham led the column all the way home. Exercise Tiger showed that the Regiment had an excellent supply system. Food was always on hand when needed and battalion transport stood up better than any other unit's.

In September, 1942, Graham was promoted to Brigadier to command the 7th Brigade in the 3rd Division and Bruce Sutcliffe succeeded him as C.O. About the same time Guy Simonds took command of the 1st Brigade and Harry Salmon became a Major General to command the 1st Division.

Having been overlooked for Dieppe had been a blessing in disguise for the 1st Division. With three years of training under their belts, the men wearing the red patch on their shoulders were close to combat readiness.

The final two weeks of December saw the Regiment on the Duke of Argyll's estate at Inveraray, Scotland — learning how to do assault landings on an enemy coast, moving from ships to landing craft in the dark, constantly drenched with rain. All ranks were ready to admit that they had never been so tired and cold in their lives, but they knew they were marked for great things and Regimental spirit kept them going.

Assault craft on a Christmas Eve exercise didn't get the troops as close to shore as usual and many had to swim for it. Then came a 20-mile march into the mountains in single file, led by 'A' Company, with Bill Graydon's platoon near the front. A figure loomed in the blackness. "Close up, close up," he ordered. "If you're so smart, carry the Bren and see if you can keep up," one man snarled. The stranger took the Bren until the next break. Graydon knew it was Simonds. "Didn't you know who you were talking to?" he asked the soldier later. The man replied: "Of course I knew, but I knew he didn't know I knew."

Bog holes with a covering layer of floating moss were the main perils of the route. Men kept dropping into them right up to their armpits. Duffy kept getting water in his ears. On reaching the designated objective, the column was ordered to return to Inveraray. On the way back, Bert Kennedy and his company sang snatches of Christmas carols, interrupted by splashes, gurgles and time for retrieving floating helmets. But no men fell out on those punishing 40 miles that even the toughest wanted to forget. Morale was even strong enough to stand a breakfast of nothing more than gobs of lumpy porridge. Heroes were men of the transport section who drove through the night to bring in a huge load of Christmas mail, including parcels.

The fierce pace of training continued for six more days. Most of December 31 was spent travelling by sea to Greenoch where the Regiment landed from Canada three years before. A southbound train was boarded after tea and 1943 was greeted just over the border, at Carlisle.

Chapter Seven
Safe shall be my going

Except for a delayed Christmas celebration on January 6, 1943, being back in Sussex by the Sea meant no relaxation for the men of the Regiment. From Possingworth Park, a camp they had helped to build, they were soon ranging widely across the Downs after a 1st Brigade concentration at Rottingdean, on the coast east of Brighton. Mortar, carrier and anti-tank platoons had opportunities to do field firing and the rifle companies' exercises featured co-operation with tanks. The most interested spectator at a company attack demonstration was Brigadier Graham, who had been given command of the 1st Brigade in mid-January.

A 1st Brigade move to Eastbourne saw the companies in excellent billets in a fine residential area. Big training schemes started right away. The Regiment was in the vanguard of a 1st Division sweep inland from Herstmonceux, remembered for the Monkey Puzzle pub and the girls of the War Office staff who were based in Herstmonceux Castle.

By March the Regiment was in Steyning, inland from Worthing, and a few days later at Newhaven, about half way between Eastbourne and Brighton, for coastal duty. Then it was back to Steyning. At Possingworth Park again, an inspection by General Salmon was followed by a tactical exercise featuring patrol action against the Black Watch.

Duffy estimated that since January his men had marched 800 miles on schemes. At a muster parade on Easter Monday, April 26, Sutcliffe warned all ranks to maintain tight security, for a move to an area of special training was near.

The men didn't know it yet, but the 1st Division and the 1st Canadian Army Tank Brigade were about to join Monty's Eighth Army, then in Tunisia after the final sweep of the North African campaign.

On Churchill's instructions General Sir Alan Brooke, Chief of the Imperial General Staff, met with McNaughton to inquire if a Canadian infantry division and a tank brigade could participate in operations to follow, and a favorable reply came back from Ottawa quickly.

Churchill's determination to strengthen the Allies' hold on the Mediterranean and to strike at the under-belly of Hitler's empire prevailed. Sicily was the closest new target for victorious forces in North Africa and so the planning of Operation Husky began. On April 29, the day the Regiment left the south of England for Scotland for final training, General Salmon and other senior officers took off for Cairo to meet Montgomery, but their aircraft crashed and all were killed. Major-General Guy Simonds, who had been commanding the 2nd Division for only a few days, replaced Salmon.

Seven days of combined operations training at Inveraray turned out to be even tougher than the session four months earlier, although it featured mostly the same activities — climbing scramble nets, running up and down difficult hill terrain and carrying out landings in assault craft. This time aircraft and naval guns were giving real covering fire or laying smoke screens. Methods of dealing with pillboxes and barbed wire were rehearsed in detail. Everybody — quartermaster's staff, cooks, mess staff, and orderly room clerks — had to learn and practice the drills for embarking from a ship in landing craft.

Exercise Dalmally, near the end of this intensive training

period, featured an island landing by the 1st Division and the Tank Brigade, with supporting fire from a cruiser and a destroyer. The enemy was the British 41st Commando.

The last exercise at Inveraray ended in miserable weather with snow on the hills and driving rain on the beaches, but by the next day the Regiment was in comfortable billets around the town of Darvel, south of Glasgow and about 10 miles east of Kilmarnock.

Clearly real action was near. More than 50 new vehicles arrived, seven new Bren carriers and six new 6-pounder guns for the anti-tank platoon. As the pace of preparations was stepped up, the C.O., second-in-command, or adjutant, as well as the company commanders might be called away at any time for conferences. Duffy's role then was really acting company commander for battalion headquarters. At the same time he was deeply involved in the day and night training program.

Each platoon had to go into the hills on a fighting patrol and Duffy was out with them night after night, because it was his policy to accompany the men in all tough situations. One of his jobs was to site a Bren gun that would be fired on a fixed line, a few feet over the heads of each night's patrol. The sited gun had to be wired into position, with a guard posted, to make sure that no one moved it. The situation a platoon was likely to meet in action was thus presented with great realism and there were no accidents. Platoon commanders and sergeants developed confidence, and while tension could develop on these night exercises, Duffy was aware that morale was steadily growing.

These first Canadians to be stationed in Darvel enjoyed an active social life over the next five weeks. The local Red Cross sponsored a supper dance, a long remembered example of Scottish hospitality. In an old theatre that served as a mess hall there were dances three nights a week. Duffy and Padre Reg Lane arranged for young women from nearby factories, with supervisor-chaperones, to be transported to and from the dances in eight regimental trucks. Scottish country dancing and Ontario hoedown went together beautifully.

The Regiment went aboard the 14,000-ton H.M.T. Derbyshire for Exercise Wetshod, the closest thing possible to a real assult landing. During the night of 21-22 May all ranks entered assault landing craft off the Island of Arran for a seven-mile run to the beaches of Troon, a short distance north of Prestwick. It was wetshod indeed. Some men waded ashore from water that was up to their necks. The next day Sutcliffe left for a conference of 1st Division C.O.s in London.

Back in Darvel May 24 brought no holiday — but tropical kit was distributed, which at least made it clear that the real landing wouldn't be in Norway. Three days later the identification bureau of Canadian Military Headquarters in London photographed and fingerprinted everybody. Major Alex Campbell, who had returned from a period with the Guards in Tunisia, was clearly anticipating a resumption of action. He took 'A' Company on a night exercise emphasizing compass and map reading, while the mortar platoon carried their mortars four miles on handcarts and made a river crossing. On June 1 vehicles began leaving for the port of embarkation.

In the crowded early days of June the Regiment was without a second-in-command after Major O'Conor-Fenton suffered severe injuries in a motorcycle accident. Major the Lord Tweedsmuir, son of a Governor-General, arrived to be the new 2 i/c. He had been a 1st Division staff officer and a company commander with the Seaforth Highlanders.

An important addition to platoon firepower was introduced at this stage in the form of the PIAT (Projector, Infantry, Anti-tank), replacing the heavier and more unwieldy Boys anti-tank rifle. The British had found it useless against the 1940 blitzkreig, but it had been lugged by thousands of cursing, angry men through training schemes ever since.

In Darvel, Duffy got a few days' leave on short notice.

He wanted to go to the south of England which had been home territory for more than three years. Ash Kirkey, the orderly room sergeant, said he could book a seat on a train. Duffy came in at the end of a day's training, changed quickly and grabbed his travel warrant. A waiting jeep roared to the station and Duffy was aboard the waiting train in seconds. He found the right compartment, occupied by two brigadiers and a high ranking naval officer. The fourth seat was reserved for "Brigadier" Duffy, who sat down, said nothing and disappeared as quickly as possible into his sleeping berth. On reaching his destination the next morning he dashed from the train and got out of sight immediately.

On his return he started to berate Kirkey, who was ready.

"Did you get to England and back?"

"Yes."

"Did you get a good seat on that crowded train?"

"Yes."

"Well, what are you complaining about?"

On Sunday, June 13, the Regiment left friendly Darvel by train for Gourock, where 'A' Company went aboard H.M.T. Derbyshire with the 48th, and the rest of the battalion, with Brigade Headquarters, found places aboard H.M.S. Glengyle. Lord Louis Mountbatten visited the Glengyle the next day. The war diary quoted him as saying that, unlike the beaches of Dieppe, the shores to be assaulted this time would be softened up by heavy bombing.

By this time, after three and a half years, company sergeant-majors were used to receiving unusual orders from Duffy, but they were puzzled by his insistence that at least one man in every section carry a soft white brick on going aboard.

As soon as all the troops were aboard Glengyle, Duffy ordered the CSMs to get the men with the bricks busy scrubbing the mess tables, top and bottom. Somehow he knew that this would bleach the wood white, as the Royal Navy men liked to see it. Usually the senior service wasn't easily impressed, but to the Glengyle crew it seemed that these Canadians did know a thing or two. They impressed the officers too.

The captain had a sailmaker produce a replica of the Regimental battle flag, about 15 feet by 20, to fly from the masthead, but according to Howard Graham, General Simonds wouldn't recognize this as an official regimental colour because it hadn't been blessed.

Daily shipboard routine included strenuous PT, inspections, roll calls and trips ashore for long route marches. At night the men practised boarding landing craft in the dark, but blindfolds were needed on deck, for it was light until half an hour before midnight. Lord Tweedsmuir ordered the armourer sergeant to check all weapons to make sure that the many salt water baths of recent weeks had not damaged them.

On June 28, late in the day, Glengyle was one of 10 troopships that began moving down the Clyde towards the open sea. A message from the admiral in charge of the convoy was heard on loudspeakers. About 26,000 Canadians were told that they were embarking on one of the largest combined operations ever carried out.

On July 1 came the official revelation that the convoy's destination was Sicily and the Regiment would be landing in the southeast corner, near Pachino. While Montgomery's Eighth Army would be concentrating on eastern Sicily, George Patton's U.S. Seventh Army would strike in the west. Sealed bags with maps, photographs and detailed orders for all units were opened, and the information was passed quickly to all ranks. Pat Amoore, an Italian-speaking British intelligence officer attached to the Hastings, described the terrain and the kind of troops likely to be encountered.

There was a large-scale model of the invasion beach to study. A British submarine discovered a complicating factor. A false beach, less than 100 yards off shore, might prevent assault craft from getting right in.

Duffy watched the reaction of the men as they heard the news that they would be landing on an enemy coast in nine days, as they listened to lectures or practised their boat drills again and again. Their morale was high, but approaching a great moment in their lives, they were sometimes subdued. All members of one platoon, however, shaved all their hair off, except for a few tufts, as if to impress the enemy with their fierceness.

In the nearly four years since mobilization Duffy had become something of a father figure to many men, although he hadn't quite reached his 29th birthday. Realizing that this could be his last opportunity to tell two younger brothers at home what he thought about the war and about life generally, he wrote a long letter to Armand and Arnold on July 5. They would be just starting their summer holidays.

"I do hope that you fellows spend all the time you can in the open, boating, hiking and camping out," he began. "These things teach you to appreciate good companionship and the beauty of the great outdoors . . . .

In just a few days you will turn the radio on to hear of one of the biggest and most important battles of the war — they will be broadcasting from the battlefield. That's why I can tell you about it now. The Hasty Ps will be there — in time you will hear about just how important and difficult a job we had to do. But the lads are keen, fit and anxious to get at the job, come what may. If it is humanly possible we will do our part because we know there are millions of people waiting to be freed from the bonds of slavery which bind mostly all Europe. We'll do the job because it is a hard one . . . because we have all the traditions of those men of the Hastings & Prince Edward Regiment who have fought in all the wars for freedom on our shoulder. We will not let them down . . . .

We offer our lives without any stipulation to you who will reap the benefit of our sacrifice, except that you keep the world for all the years to come, a free, clean and good place.

I wish you could see the fellows now — they are as happy as lads on a holiday. As for me, I have never felt better in my life, both physically and mentally. True we are confident and

prepared to do our job no matter what the cost, but we realize we require courage and endurance more than men normally possess, so we turn to God and with the prayers that we learned so long ago as boys we ask him to give us courage, endurance and generosity that we may face whatever the fates have in store for us as men should, unflinchingly . . . .
I often think of St. Peter's Church in Trenton, its great coolness, the sun streaming in through the coloured windows, the old maples gently rustling just outside. It seems so very far away — so very peaceful. I want both of you to make a trip to Trenton, make a visit and light a light at the altar for me, and offer it that I may have the courage to do all those things that I may be called upon to do, worthy of my home, my family, my country and my God . . . . I am well and happy and face the future unafraid, determined to do my job to the best of my ability. I could ask no greater honour in this life than to be the RSM of the Hasty Ps. I could ask no greater honour in death than to die serving my country in the ranks of this Regiment."

The poetic letter gave powerful expression to Duffy's quiet faith. It must have drawn floods of tears when it appeared in a hometown newspaper that summer. It is still a moving message today, reminiscent of the words of the First War poet, Rupert Brooke, so often quoted in Remembrance Day services:

War knows no power. Safe shall be my going
Secretly armed against all death's endeavour;
Safe though all safety's lost, safe where men fall;
And if these poor limbs die, safest of all.

Roaring winds and tremendous waves lashed the convoy as evening came on July 9, with only hours to go until the landing. Toward midnight the wind died down, but a heavy swell remained. By midnight the ships carrying the 1st Division were anchored so that transfers to landing craft could begin. At 1 o'clock 'A' Company left Derbyshire in three landing craft and literally bounced around for hours. Departure of the other companies from Glengyle was delayed by the swell and by a long wait for an alternative type of landing craft that might be better for crossing the sandbar near the beach. Duffy remembered it this way:

"We were packed below deck two hours before we were to embark in our small assault landing craft. The lights were all out, of course, and the idea was to get used to the dark before having to move. There had been a great burning of papers that shouldn't be taken ashore for security reasons and we had rubbed the residue from the burning on our faces to darken them. All equipment was tied down so there would be no squeaking.

"Despite all our training, things started to go haywire. The very high waves forced us to change our landing craft loads, and in the shuffle the mortars got lost, and then something else got lost, and then two of the craft in the process of being put into the water were destroyed by the high waves, and finally the ship's captain ordered all the lights on. We had been training for months to go in very quietly with absolutely no lights, and sitting below deck to accustom our eyes to darkness, but all of a sudden the lights were on and there was the greatest din you ever heard. Of course we were still about six miles out."

Duffy was concerned about getting away on time because Colonel Sutcliffe had ordered him to bring two 3-inch mortars to him soon after reaching the beach, in case an attack had to be made quickly on Pachino airdrome.

Just getting into the landing craft was tricky. Duffy was assigned to the same one as the adjutant, Capt. Jim Bird, Padre Reg Lane and assorted people attached to battalion headquarters. One means of transfer was to climb down a scramble net and wait for the waves to carry the landing craft close enough to jump in. After he got aboard, Duffy speeded the process by plucking other men off the scramble net. Grabbing them by their equipment he told each man when to let go and flung them one by one into the huge metal box that was to carry them ashore. Getting a few bruises was better than being crushed between the landing craft and the mother ship.

It was after 3 o'clock when 'B' and 'C' Companies started to move toward the shore. British commandos landed and naval gunfire tore the fleeting night apart. Duffy couldn't locate the craft bearing the C.O. and others from battalion headquarters, and Bird and the Royal Navy man aboard the landing craft seemed to be disagreeing about what to do next. "I will land you anywhere you wish," Bird was told. "It's your responsibility to land us on the right beach and we will do our job," the unhappy adjutant replied. Duffy broke in: "Gentlemen, this discussion is very interesting, but we are being fired on. It's nearly daylight and we will be caught out here in the open. Wait till you see three assault craft heading in. That will be a rifle company. We should be about 300 yards behind."

Following 'A' Company, the BHQ craft got right in, over the dreaded sandbar, and like 'A' Company it missed its objective by only a few thousand yards. 'C' Company missed its beach by a mile, but with islands and most of a continent to liberate, it didn't matter much where anybody started. Only one company hit the right beach, thanks to the navigating skill of its commander. Bert Kennedy of Owen Sound, whose family firm made ship propellors, brought his 'D' Company in right on target.

Opposition in the vicinity of the beaches was dealt with. Duffy got the mortars to the C.O. two hours late, but no attack on the Pachino airdrome was required. The RCR pretty well took care of that.

News stories published in Canada on July 10 said Canadians were part of the invading forces that hit the Sicilian beaches that morning, but the 1st Division was not identified until July 13 and the regiments in the division were not named officially in any communique until July 30, although Canadians back home with men in 1st Division units had it figured out long before that.

Lord Tweedsmuir and others not in the initial assault caught up to the Regiment on high ground overlooking the

Pachino airdrome.* He found battalion headquarters in a vineyard full of olive and almond trees with a good well nearby, but early the next morning the site had to be given up to 1st Brigade Headquarters, and the push inland continued.

Pursuit was the operative word for most of the next two days, in constant clouds of dust and for long hours under a merciless sun. In the afternoon of July 11 the almost unbearable heat caught the men at what the war diary called the lowest physical ebb of the campaign. It was nearly midnight before they covered the 20 miles to Rosolini. After a rest until about 4 a.m., they slogged on again.

There was a shortage of transport because 500 vehicles had been lost when enemy action destroyed three ships off North Africa. The RCRs were well out in front of the Brigade, riding on tanks and wheeled vehicles while the Hastings and 48th followed on foot, but their turn was coming.

A stop at noon when rations came up stretched into the early evening and then the rifle companies advanced — one on tanks, one on field guns, one in regular transport, some on mules and one company marching. It was after midnight when the column reached the hilltop village of Giarratana, went through without trouble and occupied a position more than 50 miles from the invasion beaches. Trucks went back for the exhausted marching men of 'C' Company and they fell asleep as soon as they got aboard.

The advance was halted for 48 hours, but patrols were active out in front. Word came round in the evening that Monty would be visiting the 1st Brigade the next morning. Everyone thought this meant a ceremonial occasion and so, as usual, it was Duffy's job to form up the parade. He was

* From this point until well into the Italian campaign, a major source of information is an unpublished account by Lord Tweedsmuir in the possession of the Directorate of History, National Defence Headquarters, Ottawa.

preparing to call out markers from each of the three battalions half an hour before Monty's scheduled arrival time when Brigadier Graham sent for him and said 15 minutes would be sufficient. Everyone remained in the shade of olive trees. At the agreed moment Duffy called them on parade, forming perfectly straight lines along three sides of a stubble field, but when Monty arrived he stood up in his vehicle and called the men around him. So much for a sergeant-major's formality!

The Brigade resumed its pursuit of the enemy that evening with the Hastings leading. Tweedsmuir was in command of an advance guard of tanks, carriers, anti-tank guns and machine guns that moved off at dusk on July 14 with 'B' Company men riding tanks. The main body followed aboard tanks and in vehicles an hour later, heading for Vizzini. The British 51st Highland Division, moving generally the same direction, actually had men in Vizzini, Tweedsmuir learned when his column met some Highlanders in a broad moonlit valley. The main body of the Hastings caught up with Tweedsmuir's force, the whole battalion settled in for the remainder of the night and both Graham and Simonds came up to discuss the situation with Sutcliffe.

The advance resumed at 4 a.m. on July 15. Vizinni, set on top of a high hill, was full of debris and dead horses, but no enemy. The Highlanders had things under control, Tweedsmuir found:

> "The C.O. of the Black Watch stopped us and we pored over the maps, but so little was known of the country in front that we shook hands with the cheery assurance that we might meet the enemy anywhere. We pushed on . . . and five minutes later passed the outposts with the glorious feeling that we were now on our own. It was a beautiful day and the Sicilians harvesting in the fields made it hard to believe that we were now in enemy country, headed for the enemy, and in fact the spearhead of the whole Eighth Army . . . . The atmosphere grew more electric with every mile we went. Suddenly the narrow valley gave way to a broad open plateau with the

town of Grammichele perched like all Sicilian towns on a hilltop."

The leading carriers and tanks were in or approaching the town and wheeled vehicles had to stop for a crater in a level crossing when suddenly fire poured down from hills on both sides of the road. Tweedsmuir quickly moved to a ditch with a radio set. It was possible to get some trucks out of the way, but accurate mortar fire crashing down on the column soon had other trucks burning and their ammunition exploding. 'B' Company had gone into the town, and as the other companies reached the area they were soon engaged in an intense fire-fight with the enemy on the hills. They had come a long way for a good scrap and were more confident of success than their commanding general.

After Sutcliffe had deployed his rifle companies as in countless schemes back in England, Simonds drove up to battalion headquarters where Duffy was putting up the battle flag. He asked for the C.O. Duffy escorted the general to where Sutcliffe and Graham were watching the battle. Duffy heard Simonds say: "I want this battle stopped. I don't like the plan." Graham replied that Sutcliffe had made the plans, which he approved, and with the companies committed, the battle couldn't be stopped. Duffy decided this was no place for an RSM. He didn't want to hear or see a senior officer reprimanded.

The plan of attack was a good one. All the companies did a good job, particularly 'B' Company in the town, forcing Germans of the Herman Goering Division to abandon a fight they might have won. The chance to capture badly needed vehicles and stores of food was a bonus. And for the future good of the 1st Division, Monty, who had learned of Simonds' clash with Graham, told the young general plainly that in future he should let brigadiers run their own battles.

About sunset on July 16 the Regiment moved up the main Syracuse-Palermo highway in captured transport. Progress was slow until the column had passed heavily bombed Caltagirone. After another 20 miles in moonlight the ride ended in an orchard near Piazza Amerina. After noon the next day the advance resumed along the same road. The 2nd Brigade, in the lead, encountered strong opposition. Sutcliffe returned from a Brigade conference with orders to undertake a night march across to Valguarnera, 10 miles away. He sent a dispatch rider to the rear to get Tweedsmuir.

"I returned with him, riding pillion, weaving in and out of the jammed traffic. We got orders as I got there to move up a road to the right. We moved up about a mile and debussed. Dusk had fallen and it was too dark to read a map.... We had no recce, no time to read maps and we resorted to our good old principle — go there and think of something when you get there."

The advance resumed at about 9.30 p.m. along a trail through a pine woods and onto open sandy uplands. The moonlight was bright enough to make tracks of the carriers easy to follow. They disappeared on some hard ground, and suddenly tracks appeared again. But the column didn't follow — for they were quickly recognized as the tracks of a Tiger tank. Tweedsmuir was to be left out of battle again, as was common for the second-in-command, and in a few minutes the tank on which he was riding reached the edge of an escarpment. It was foot soldiers only from there.

Sutcliffe sent Bert Kennedy and Duffy ahead to find the best approach routes. The moon was gone and they soon got separated in the darkness. It was nearly two hours before Duffy got back to lead Roly Cleaworth's 'C' Company over the first mountain ridge and down into a deep ravine. There was noise ahead. A runner was sent back to warn Cleaworth to deploy the company and be ready for action. Duffy crawled forward and was about to throw a grenade when he recognized an approaching hulk as Alex Campbell. He had brought 'A' Company around the other side of the same feaure. The two companies pushed on in the blackness across more ridges and gullies.

Approaching a feature that seemed to be their objective they awakened a group of civilians who had been sleeping under the trees. As daylight came the two companies took up positions on a hillside overlooking a road, aware that they were well behind enemy lines after eight hours on the move. Radio sets had little range in this terrain, so the surest way to re-establish communication with battalion headquarters was by runner. Duffy volunteered to go and asked George Ponsford, CSM of 'C' Company, to go with him — back over eight miles of mountains with gullies 3,000 feet deep.

They took one map and set out. On their way they could hear heavy firing on the area they had left, and later learned that six truckloads of German soldiers had been gunned to a halt and between 80 and 90 had died. Alex Campbell, rushing forward, firing a Bren from the hip, had accounted for 18 of them.

'B' and 'D' Companies had wrought considerable havoc closer to the town, but were unable to take it. The RCR got within half a mile of Valguarnera and their second-in-command, Major J.H.W.T. Pope, died heroically, trying to stop tanks with a PIAT.

Duffy and Ponsford were fired on once by the Germans, but they got back to Tweedsmuir in three hours. Taking all the ammunition they could carry, they set off for Valguarnera once again, hoping to get into the fight before it was over. On reaching their early morning position again at about 3 o'clock in the afternoon they found 'A' and 'C' Companies had moved. A few civilians still in the area seemed friendly and offered food. Ponsford refused it and kept watch on the road. A few minutes later he yelled to Duffy that Germans were coming. Ponsford wanted to take them on, but Duffy ordered him to follow him into cactus at top speed. They completed their fourth eight-mile journey across Death Valley after most of the rest of the Regiment had returned. The Hastings and the RCR had harassed the Germans for most of the day and when the 48th entered Valguarnera at night they found it unoccupied.

Sutcliffe was still missing. Graham ordered Tweedsmuir to move Support Company toward Valguarnera by the very crowded main road. During a halt in a traffic jam, Sutcliffe appeared in a jeep, tired but exultant. He had had to lie low for three hours in an orchard within 10 yards of a German machine gun post. Worst of all, Canadian machine guns had fired on him, he told Tweedsmuir, and disappeared to get some rest.

German shelling was heavy as the convoy neared Valguarnera, and Tweedsmuir led the way into the courtyard of a 16th century mansion in a hillside orchard. By mid-day on July 19 the whole battalion had found this place of shade and rest and relatively comfortable dining. Sutcliffe went to Brigade in the evening and just after midnight he sent back an order to start marching toward Assoro, principal objective of the 1st Brigade, while the 2nd Brigade headed for a similarly imposing mountain strong point, Leonforte.

It took some time to get the weary battalion moving. The column moved through Valguarnera where the smell of death lingered. Just beyond the town a huge convoy of tanks and guns had formed up. The infantrymen made their way past, covered another two miles or so, but were halted then by Graham and told to rest. There was no need to repeat the order. Men hit the ground near the edge of the road and were almost instantly asleep. Passing tanks and artillery vehicles soon coated the sleepers with a fine dust. By dawn all were up and moving again.

The approach to Assoro, through the Dittaino River valley, was easy for the Germans to keep under observation from their mountain strongholds, but at ground level the route through the valley seemed wildly different from the map. As the valley broadened out the road and a rail line kept criss-crossing. In another mile or so the companies halted and took up positions, two on low features on the left and two in the valley.

"BHQ was under a cork tree by a deserted barn: the largest tree we had yet seen in Sicily. We had breakfast and the day grew hotter and hotter. On the bare hillsides it was like a furnace. At mid-day the C.O. went off on a recce. It was the last time we saw him alive. We could hear the distant crump of shells ahead where the enemy were ranging on the road. The news came through quite bluntly. The C.O. had been killed by a shell which had mortally injured the I.O., Capt. Cockin. A jeep brought Cockin back on a stretcher. He was lying on his face and could hardly speak. He asked for me feebly. He had just one sentence to say: 'For God's sake, don't go down that road.'"

Tweedsmuir, now in command, went to Brigade head-quarters to get the orders Sutcliffe had been preparing to follow. Take Assoro. The plan he inherited was to get behind the Germans and assault the undefended side of the 3,000-foot peak that rose so steeply and menacingly from the valley.

It was late in the day before Graham had completed his orders to his battalion commanders and Tweedsmuir was able to meet his company commanders. The sun was going down as they stared northward at the great Assoro peak six miles away. Tweedsmuir took a rifle and held it at arm's length, as he had often seen Scottish shepherds do with a crook. Tilting the rifle at an angle parallel with the Assoro slope, he saw that it could scarcely be any steeper.

An assault company to carry only its own weapons and ammunition had already been formed from 20 picked men of each company. Alex Campbell was company com-mander with Les Yates as 2 i/c. George Baldwin, Farley Mowat, Fred Burtt and Cliff Broad were platoon com-manders.

At 9 o'clock the entire 1st Divisional field artillery unleashed intense fire on road junctions just beyond Assoro, and barrage after barrage hammered approaches on the enemy's side of the town periodically for the next four hours. At 9.30 the companies moved toward the start line in vehicles on a road that had been heavily shelled during the day. The troops dismounted near a burning railway station and moved on. In single file they covered more than a mile of road, but soon they cut northeastward across pasture land and dry rocky stream beds. A bright moon was riding high, and so was determination — to avenge a fallen commander and support his already promising successor.

Chapter Eight
Fame in the morning

For Lord Tweedsmuir the route to that decisive night had been as unconventional as the tactics chosen to fit the brutal terrain. His being in Canadian uniform at all had been made possible by the kind of unexpected events his father might have woven into a novel. After Eton and Oxford, the young John Buchan had gone to Uganda in the Colonial Service, but desperate illness sent him home to England. A dramatic change of climate was prescribed. His father's residence in Canada as Governor General suggested a visit there. Northern forests and rivers captured the hunter and fisherman in him. He travelled 3,000 miles by dog team in a year as a Hudson's Bay Trader in Baffin Land. The world was on the brink of war when he came south again. Tommy Waitt, a trail rider in the Peace River country, where he stopped on his way to Ottawa, was to join him in Aldershot a few months later as his batman for the rest of the war. John and Alastair Buchan both joined the Canadian Army in Ottawa. To qualify as lieutenants, John and others had to pass an examination in Kingston. He sometimes jokingly reminisced about the limited scope of the candidates' military knowledge: "We had to use strange instruments that involved telling time by the stars. The clever ones focused on the Kingston City Hall clock and got that one right."

The day just ending was only the eleventh in Sicily and the 1st Brigade was facing its toughest challenge of the campaign. Brigadier Graham had given his old Regiment the task of taking Assoro, and anything but success was unthinkable. The plan's best feature was its sheer audacity — marching all night to get behind the enemy and scale a mountain on its undefended side. Sutcliffe could have done it well, but Tweedsmuir, with his eye for terrain and movement, a countryman who had hunted big game on the plains of East Africa and had stalked game on Scottish moors and mountains and in the forests of northern Saskatchewan, was made for the hour. So were many of his men from Canadian farms and villages. Later he was often to say of them thankfully that they knew where to put their feet in the dark.

Alex Campbell's assault company was in the lead, followed by Tweedsmuir and Duffy and the signals officer, and then the other companies — a long snake of men moving slowly and steadily onto ever higher ground. Detection seemed only to be expected — but a barn was empty, an enemy outpost unmanned. A fire was burning ahead. A dog was barking. Both were given a very wide berth. About 4 o'clock the climbers halted on a ridge near where the last 1,000 feet to the peak began.

First a formidable ravine with sheer sides had to be crossed. Caught there, the Regiment would have been destroyed — but a goat track provided a route to the boulder-strewn bottom from where the wickedly steep last section of the climb began. The assault company went to the left and 'B' Company, BHQ and 'C' Company to the right, with 'D' Company following closely.

For the last leg Tweedsmuir was up with the front section urging them on and Duffy was right with him. The climbers had more than stamina left. A certain fury bore them upward too. Three Germans at the crest scarcely knew what was happening before they were dispatched. Just after 5:30 the Regiment was on its objective.

Enemy action to dislodge the Canadians seemed slow to begin, but it did come with shattering intensity. After rather ineffective sniping, machine guns, light and heavy mortars and 88 mm guns took over. Then airburst shells rained shrapnel into hastily contrived slit trenches. Two of the platoons most exposed to enemy fire were commanded by young lieutenants from Trenton — Fred Burtt and Jack McKibbon who had both been signallers before the war. Duffy was proud to see them performing so well under intense fire.

"The Huns were milling around the town and our men shot up truckloads of them when they tried to clear out the narrow streets," Tweedsmuir told Ross Munro of the Canadian Press when he came up two days later. "There was sniping such as I had never seen before. It was guerrilla and mountain warfare rolled into one."

Deadly accurate artillery fire came down on and around the great Norman castle, but the men on the peak were able to pinpoint many of the German gun positions and call down enough Canadian fire on them to reduce their effectiveness. Still men were wounded, and for the first time since the landing, they weren't able to get the attention they needed right away. They were placed in a cave and given morphine. In spite of everything, as the day wore on, it was hard to keep awake, Tweedsmuir wrote later. At 4 o'clock a runner brought word that a German counter-attack was coming from the town of Assoro:

"We were very short of ammunition. We put a call through to Brigade and asked for immediate artillery fire on the town. The first salvo hit the castle and we gave the correction 300 yards west. The next was dead on the edge of the town, on the slope below. . . . The shells shrieked into the tightly packed houses. . . . Our guns pounded the town intermittently . . . and the long night began with the battalion standing to. We were expecting relief. At midday Captain Stockloser and the RSM (the incomparable Mr. Duffy) had climbed down the hill into the ravine with the object of working down it and reaching Brigade headquarters to get supplies and ammunition."

Stockloser and Duffy made it to Brigade by mid-afternoon in spite of having at one point to cross 500 yards of ground covered by enemy machine guns. "We ran like hell,"

Duffy later told war correspondents. They quickly outlined the situation to Graham. Lt.-Col. Ralph Crowe of the RCR was there. He had been a Hastings company commander in England and immediately volunteered the services of two of his companies to carry up whatever the Regiment required. Stockloser and Duffy guided the carrying party of 100.

Just before dawn on July 22 the vital supplies reached the top. Italian prisoners of war were forced to help the weary soldiers on the final part of the ascent. An artillery forward observation officer (FOO) and two signallers brought up a wireless set. The Germans were still shelling the peak and Tweedsmuir's apparent disregard for his own life worried Duffy. As the shelling got heavier the most obvious place to take shelter seemed to be on the other side of a stone wall. Tweedsmuir had started back towards the wireless set when Duffy grabbed him by the foot and pulled him down. But soon every Canadian on Assoro could breathe more easily.

> "We were now well fed and well enough armed to deal with anything. At midday the road was cleared. Reinforcements came up as the Huns had now drawn back from the ground immediately overlooking the town. The wounded were evacuated and the Brig came up to see us. He was lyrical with excitement. The Huns started to shell the road below, shooting just over the castle. The Brig continued his conversation lying on his face. The rest of the day we took it easy. We were very cheerful. Assoro was to be made a battle honour. We asked permission to move off the hill to a more restful area, but it was refused. We slept well that night."

One soldier told Tweedsmuir that he now believed in God. Tweedsmuir would go further. He said afterwards that the miracle of Assoro was "a clear sign that God wanted us to win."

After a night climb to positions west of Assoro, the 48th Highlanders drove the Germans from heights where they had been able to control the road to the top. The enemy had withdrawn from the town by the afternoon of July 22. By the next morning Canadian control of Assoro was unchallenged. Fierce artillery fire, directed from the peak, had pounded the message home to the Germans miles away that they had lost a major battle. With a captured map showing distant enemy strong points and a captured 16-power periscope, Hastings officers had been able to supply the gunners with all the target information they could handle.

A German withdrawal from the town permitted the Canadians to move about more confidently. On its edge an empty barber shop was taken over by a soldier who had been a barber in Picton. A well in a courtyard nearby was the only source of drinking water and Duffy had placed a guard there to protect it. During the afternoon he had visited the guard when he noticed some men moving further into the town. They were actually out looking for more barbering equipment. Duffy ordered them back to the courtyard where there was shade, for the temperature was well over 100 degrees Fahrenheit. Duffy was following them back towards the well when suddenly two shells screamed down into the courtyard, followed by a third right on the well. Three men of the Regiment and an artillery signaller died instantly. Five others were wounded. Duffy never forgot the sight of the bodies lying there, for they had gone there on his command.

The RSM had hit the ground as the shells fell, but he didn't realize that he had been wounded himself until a man noticed blood on his hand. He was persuaded to go to the Regimental Aid Post where he expected to be just bandaged up. The medical officer thought he might have shrapnel in the arm. "Just clean it up and I'll stay here overnight on a cot," Duffy said. The M.O. disagreed:

"I'm sending you down to the field dressing station. They have beds there. They can fix you up and send you back."

The idea of a bed sounded good to Duffy. The Regiment was expecting a few days' rest after the epic battle just ended and so he went to the FDS where he was given a bed. When he awoke, a doctor asked him how he felt. He stood up — and immediately collapsed. Within minutes he was in an ambulance heading for a British hospital in Syracuse.

On that day, July 24, the Regiment was ordered to turn its

positions over to the Seaforths and prepare to move toward the next objective. The war diary said that esprit de corps was at its highest level since mobilization. General Simonds was quoted as saying that the seizure of Assoro had forced the enemy to withdraw from extremely strong positions in great disorder, thereby causing collapse of the entire front and hastening the retreat of the Leonforte garrison. Such a spectacularly successful action, speeding the advance in a whole sector, would ordinarily qualify some participants for decorations. But not Assoro.

Tweedsmuir was recommended for the Distinguished Service Order. Simonds refused to approve it with words to the effect that Assoro was a good show for a first time in command, but there would be lots of future chances to win a DSO. Duffy was recommended shortly after Assoro for the Canada Medal, but this new decoration wasn't awarded to him or to anyone else, it turned out. Stockloser got a promotion to major. Padre Lane could never understand why Alex Campbell, already a hero at Valguarnera, was still not decorated after Assoro. Officers and men of other regiments seemed to get more recognition.

After an operation in Syracuse to remove shrapnel, Duffy was feeling much better in two or three days. A Corporal Duffy of the RCR arrived in the ward and they got talking. The corporal told of heavy action at Nissoria involving both the 48th and the RCR, as well as the Hasty Ps, whose C.O. had been wounded. Duffy declared that he must return to the Regiment as quickly as possible.

Corporal Duffy wanted to go too and they agreed that the easiest time to slip away would be about 10 o'clock that night. A side door was easily reached by way of the bathroom.

The two Duffys ducked out without difficulty, but they paused long enough to avoid running into the arms of the military police. Doubling back behind the hospital they soon found a route across two fields to the road. Out of the darkness came an NCO of the Royal 22nd Regiment to join them. The idea was to hitch-hike south, right down the coast to the Pachino beaches. There they could catch some 1st Division vehicle heading for the front. At one stop they saw a train being prepared for its first run under Allied military auspices. A British soldier persuaded them to wait for a ride.

Duffy, who was wearing no rank badges, switched jackets and paybooks with his taller namesake who seemed more believable as an RSM and the trio had no difficulty getting aboard the train. The two Duffys switched paybooks and jackets again after they were moving. The RSM was sure that the train would go right to the invasion beaches where supplies were still being landed and he stayed on when the other two left the train. He was right. The train stopped within sight of the sea.

Many vehicles with 1st Division markings were in the vicinity. Duffy headed quickly towards one truck with 1st Brigade markings and the driver agreed to take him along. They didn't get far before they came to No. 1 Canadian Base Reinforcement Depot. Duffy got out, went to the orderly room and identified himself, stating that he had been wounded and reporting where he had been in hospital. A medical officer asked who had discharged him and Duffy replied that he didn't know because there were both British and Canadian MOs there. He had no intention of staying around No. 1 CBRD either. He saw a vehicle that was to leave immediately for 1st Brigade and got aboard. With no difficulty he got another ride from there right to the Regiment.

Outside Battalion Headquarters Art Cornish of the Provost Section was directing traffic. On hearing that the Regiment might be moving soon, Duffy hurried to report to Kennedy. It was July 29. Monty had sent a message to the troops that day rejoicing in the fact that Mussolini had been driven from office and declaring: "We will now drive the Germans out of Sicily."

In the few days of Duffy's absence, the Regiment, and

indeed the whole 1st Brigade, had met reverses. A rapid westward push toward Agira had priority as soon as Assoro had fallen, but the town of Nissoria, half way along the route, was an obstacle of devastating proportions. On July 24 the RCR had tank, artillery and air support, but an attack through Nissoria ground to a halt and the gallant Colonel Crowe was killed. The Hastings made a pre-dawn attack over ground Tweedsmuir had not seen by day and ran into highly concentrated forces on high ground beyond Nissoria. With ammunition running low a withdrawal was necessary.

Four mortar bombs fell near Tweedsmuir, wounding him severely. Tommy Waitt, Eddie King and Pat O'Neil helped him down a hill despite heavy shelling. "Is the Colonel dead?" someone shouted. "No," Waitt replied, "but he's so full of lead that he wouldn't float in molasses."

Many more of the Hastings were wounded — indeed there were more casualties than any other Canadian battalion had suffered on a single day in Sicily.

Kennedy took command, although wounded and ill. The 48th had no better luck. Finally on the night of July 26 the Princess Patricias, with a squadron of tanks and tremendous artillery support, pushed the enemy back toward Agira in a bloody battle. The Seaforths exploited this success and the Edmontons finished the job. Agira fell on July 28.

The next major objective east of Agira was Regalbuto where tough men of the Herman Goering Division were ensconced in positions that conferred all the advantages on the defenders. The 1st Canadian Brigade and the 231st Malta Brigade got the job of dislodging them. By nightfall on July 30 the Regiment was in position about six miles west of Regalbuto. The inability of the British battalions to take the town on July 30 and 31, and the very limited success of the RCR and the 48th without supporting arms, convinced Kennedy that on August 1 the Hastings must make a wide flanking move to the right with as much fire power as possible.

Salmon Lake on a summer day.

I'm a sailor boy.

On the Bay of Quinte in the 1950s.

Just home from the Coronation,
1937.

Regimental officers listen in on camp lecture by Major Salmon.

Major Graham leads his company.

Bill Graydon goes to camp as a mess steward in 1936.

Duffy photographs Royal Sussex NCOs, 1937.

On their way from the Picton Armoury....

George Ponsford comes back with the battle flag.

Sergeant-major's on parade.

For an auto expert like Ron Church, wheels were important.

Plough-Jockeys, literally.

Canadian RSMs on square-bashing course at Guards' depot.

'A' Company, just back from France, made the Daily Sketch on June 18, 1940.

Marksmanship on the beaches.

The Colonel had a striking resemblance to His Majesty.

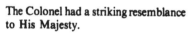

(Jack Morgan)

'D' Company tug-of-war team at 1st Division sports day.

(Gordon Way)

CSM 'Friday' Dainard and Duffy.

(Gordon Way)

Accompanied by Brigadier Rod Keller, Prime Minister Mackenzie King chats with Lt.-Col. H.D. Graham.

Hasty Ps guarded the Churchill family at Chartwell for periods in 1941.

(Courtesy of the British Travel Association)

Inveraray Castle overlooks peaceful Loch Fyne where the Regiment did assault landing training.

(Photo by the kind permission of Country Life)

Graham inspects Duffy's NCO class at Castropignano.

Armourer-sergeant John MacDonald and Pte. J.D. Flynn repair and adjust Bren guns.

Regiment parades in front of the village of Castropignano in a rest area before moving to the Adriatic coast.
(Public Archives of Canada 26,521)

Don Cameron, DSO, a cool commander in many actions, who went on to a lengthy postwar career.
(Public Archives of Canada, File 261)

Major Frank Hammond, MC, company commander of distinction.
(Public Archives of Canada 30353)

"Ack-Ack" Kennedy, daring escaper and quiet-spoken commander, receives his DSO for holding the Moro River bridgehead from Lieut.-General Sir Oliver Leese.
(Public Archives of Canada 30738)

'B' Company captured this farmhouse after a fierce fight on December 23, 1943.
(Frank Hammond photo)

In the farming area north and west of Ortona the big stone houses were all German strong points.
(Frank Hammond photo)

CWAC Privates H. Ashworth of Toronto and F. Shaddock of Winnipeg lined up with the men at the first mess call after 2nd Echelon established its camp in France.

(Canadian Army Photo in York University Archives)

Left to right, Sgt. Madder, RSM Duffy, Warrant Officer Simmons and Quarter-master Sgt. Grant.

(Pat O'Donnell)

Rocket causes terrible damage to building near 2nd Echelon in the heart of Antwerp.

(Rosaline Madder)

Duffy gives CWAC the place of honour on the right of the line on parade in the Antwerp financial district not far from the harbour.

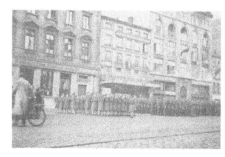

Large crowds greet Regiment on return to Belleville, October 4, 1945.

(Archives of Ontario)

RSM Duffy with Regimental mascot, Chief Petawawa-much at Camp Petawawa in 1949.

(Public Archives of Canada CC-3178)

Scout Commissioner Duffy.

Duffy passes RSM's badges of rank to his successor, Stan Down.

Lord Tweedsmuir (centre) on his first visit to Belleville in 1951.

The Regimental Association presents a Regimental Colour with battle honours to the Militia battalion and Lieutenant John Fullerton of the colour party receives it from Duffy.

Colonel Duffy and his officers at the height of postwar strength.
(Willian E. Riley photo)

General Graham accompanies Duffy as he
inspects the band on his last day as C.O.
(Intelligencer photo)

Duffy greets Major-General Sparling at camp.

Joan Goforth unveils a window in a chapel at Camp Borden in memory of Padre Fred Goforth. Tony Basciano represents the Regimental Association.

Lord Tweedsmuir goes to the House of Lords in uniform to make an important speech in 1963.

(Canapress Photo Service)

Floyd Marlin, Angus Duffy and Gordon Way visit Colonel Sutcliffe's grave at Agira in Sicily, 1975.

(Department of Veterans Affairs)

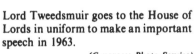

CN chief Donald Gordon wishes conductor Ernest Duffy well on his retirement.

Duffy signs documents as his period of command ends.

(Intelligencer photo)

Hasty Ps who fought in Holland returned for another welcome to Amsterdam in May, 1980.

(Canapress Photo Service)

A spring day finds Duffy tending the flower beds in front of the Regimental Memorial.

Duffy visits all the displays in the Bridge Street Armoury on his last day as Honorary Colonel, which the City of Belleville designated Militia Day.

(Intelligencer photo)

Governor General Schreyer presents the badge of the Order of Canada and congratulates Colonel Duffy.

(Photo by John Evans, Ottawa)

Governor General Schreyer greets Helena Duffy.

(Photo by John Evans, Ottawa)

Duffy stands at attention as his citation is read.

(Photo by John Evans, Ottawa)

Artillery FOOs were on the march and the mortar platoon manhandled its weapons and ammunition. George Baldwin took a patrol of 27 men in the lightest possible kit to within a mile of Regalbuto and sent information back by radio. The night approach march to Mount Tiglio, overlooking the objective lacked the nerve-wracking suspense of the Assoro climb. At 3 o'clock in the morning of August 2, atop Mount Tiglio, Kennedy's men found that the enemy had gone.

Graham ordered an attack on a ridge east of Regalbuto for 2 o'clock in the afternoon. By 10 that morning Duffy somehow got two carriers up Mount Tiglio with rations and water, and after a good meal the men were eager to go. 'D' Company drew enemy fire into the valley between Mount San Georgio and Regalbuto, while 'B' and 'C' moved to the left with fire support from 'A' and 'D' Companies, the battalion mortars and the 2nd Field Regiment, Royal Canadian Artillery. Two companies of the 4th Parachute Regiment, dislodged by the determined and beautifully planned Hastings attack, had held up the Malta Brigade and the rest of the 1st Canadian Brigade for four days.

Once again on the morning of August 3 two carriers caught up to the forward companies with rations, after spending 16 hours fixing roads in some places and forcing a passage along past marching troops in others. A captain in the Devon Regiment was amazed that such a feat could be achieved, even by "cockeyed Canadians."

Cockeyed or not, the Hasty Ps had fought their last Sicilian battle. They had certainly made their mark. Correspondent Ralph Allen's despatch on the front page of The Globe and Mail on August 18 left no doubt about it:

"When the folks around Belleville, Trenton, Picton and Madoc are preparing their welcome for the Hasty Petes, they'll do well to note that the town hall steps are strictly out. The Hasty Petes have already done enough climbing to put a mountain goat on full retirement pension. They've done a lot of fighting too. While the brigade and divisional staff officers sort out the triumphs and lessons of the Canadians' first major campaign in this war, no single group earns higher marks than the hard young warriors from the farms, hills and factories of Eastern Ontario. . . . There's a story for every mile of the Hastings' grimy journey."

The 1st Canadian Division had marched farther in Sicily than any other division in the 8th Army and had earned a rest.

On August 4 Graham visited the Regiment and spent time with all the companies. He had every reason to be proud of his old comrades. The Regiment paraded on August 8 and Padre Lane conducted a service of thanksgiving; reinforcements arrived on each of the next two days and it was time to move to a rest area. It was located on a plateau near the town of Militello on the edge of the Catania plain. Olive trees provided the only shade and daytime heat was extreme. A mountain stream nearby was dammed to make a swimming pool.

Training took place only in the early mornings and in the evenings. A rigidly enforced siesta covered the hours from 10 in the morning to 4 in the afternoon. One day Kennedy was angered by men who wouldn't be quiet during siesta. He grabbed a Bren gun and fired a long burst over their heads.

The troops found it difficult to take formal soldiering seriously. A special guard was called for on one occasion and when Duffy went to inspect it the corporal in charge fell down dead drunk. He had much better success drilling newly arrived reinforcement officers and organizing a platoon competition in night patrolling.

On August 20 a formal parade welcomed Monty who was visiting the 1st Division. He declared that the division had performed magnificently in Sicily. Two days later General McNaughton arrived to say how proud Canadians were of their fighting men.

While the fighting soldiers rested the paper war churned on at higher levels. On August 26 Lt.-Col. Preston Gilbride, assistant adjutant and quartermaster general of the 1st Division, sent a message to 1st Brigade:

R.S.M. Duffy — H. & P.E.R.

1. The m/n WO was taken on strength, 4 Bn, 1 CBRD while on the beach at Pachino having been discharged from hospital.

2. While at 4 Bn, 1 CBRD, RSM Duffy disappeared, apparently went AWL and has been shown as AWL from 4 Bn since that time.

3. As 21 days have elapsed, court of inquiry has now become necessary, but before convening same, in the event that this WO has returned to his unit, it is not desired to embarrass him and therefore may infm be received, please, as to date of his return.

4. In the event that RSM Duffy returned to unit within a reasonable time after disappearing from 4 Bn, on receipt of infm records at 4 Bn . . . will be amended to show him posted to unit.

And so it was that the 1st Division's most famous RSM wasn't charged with being absent without leave because of his zeal to get back to the fighting.

Duffy wasn't the only one to make his own way back to the Regiment after being wounded. For a fighting man who had been away from Canada for three years or longer, the Regiment was home. Other units, or formations, depots, transit camps or convalescent centres were places to escape from. After Nissoria Sergeant Keith Sharpe of the mortar platoon had the distinct impression that someone outside the Regiment had written him off. In hospital in North Africa he learned that his family had received official word that he had been killed in action. He was soon able to get around, but it was a long journey to get back to the Regiment.

A North African convalescent centre was a former German camp. Quarters were in a garage and beds were stretchers resting on empty German gasoline containers called jerrycans. There was nothing to do all day but drink cheap gin. His next stop was under canvas 50 miles further into the desert. Baseball was the main activity, with frequent games at a U.S. base where food was luxurious. But Sharpe hadn't come to the Mediterranean to play ball. He heard that a convoy was coming through from Algiers heading for Philippeville, where there was a Canadian base. He decided to be in that convoy, even without any papers. He managed

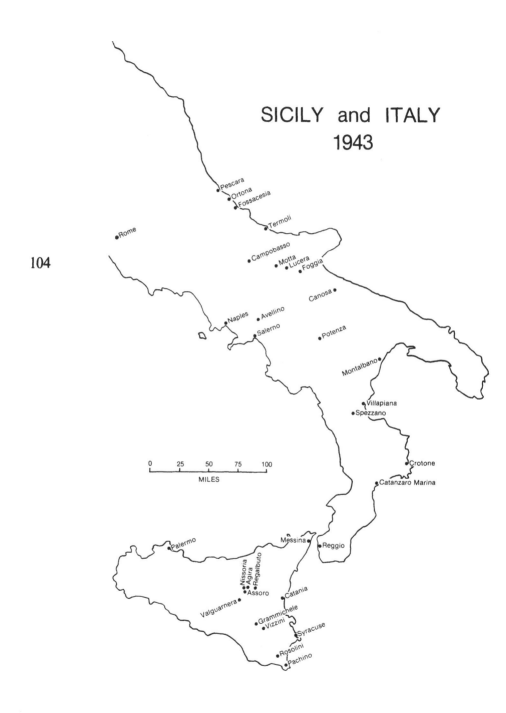

SICILY and ITALY
1943

104

Rome

Pescara
Ortona
Fossacesia
Termoli
Campobasso
Motta
Lucera
Foggia
Canosa
Naples
Avellino
Salerno
Potenza
Montalbano
Villapiana
Spezzano
Crotone
Catanzaro Marina
Messina
Reggio
Palermo
Nissoria
Agira
Regalbuto
Assoro
Catania
Valguarnera
Grammichele
Vizzini
Syracuse
Rosolini
Pachino

0   25   50   75   100
MILES

to find a place in one of the 100 or more jeeps of the convoy that went racing across the desert, sometimes 15 abreast.

Sharpe reported in at Philippeville. Lacking papers didn't bar him from sleeping accommodation. He was there for two weeks, hiding most of the time. By then it was November. He heard that a ship was leaving for Italy. A man he knew in the camp had been assigned to drive a truckload of kit bags to the ship. Sharpe was in that truck and walked aboard unchallenged. Once in Italy it was easy to hitch-hike and he got rides right to battalion headquarters.

The Regiment had received orders for the invasion of Italy on September 2, the fourth anniversary of mobilization. The landing next day was virtually unopposed, and the assaulting 3rd Brigade had all its objectives by 9 o'clock in the morning. Rifle companies of the Hastings, designated reserve battalion of the Brigade, were just marching to their landing craft to cross the Strait of Messina. There were 18 German divisions south of the Po, but only four in the foot of Italy. Canadians could tramp on the Italian toe with impunity.

Amid rumours that Italy would soon be out of the war, Italian coastal troops were offering no opposition. All the Hastings were aboard landing craft before noon. As they landed they saw hundreds of Italian troops, with white handkerchiefs in their breast pockets, lined up near the shore, waiting to surrender. Their rifles were stacked neatly nearby.

By 4:30 the Hasty Ps were marching inland into the mountains. An hour before midnight they were on top of Mount Callea, 3,300 feet above sea level. Because of road demolitions battalion transport did not catch up until September 5. It was cold and rainy in the mountains — shivery in khaki drill shirts and shorts in the daytime and downright cold and miserable at night.

Prisoners coming in during the next two days said Italian resistance had ceased. On September 8 Italy's unconditional surrender was announced. It was time to come out of the mountains and seek a speedier route to action.

💠

Chapter Nine
Mist and mountains

On the morning of September 9, the Regiment was aboard
trucks that wound their way down towards Reggio to start
moving eastward along the south coast. Before first light the
U.S. 5th Army, composed of the 10th British Corps and the
6th U.S. Corps, had begun its assault on Salerno, and part
of the 1st British Airborne Division landed at Taranto,
inside the Italian heel. Road and bridge demolitions and a
shortage of transport made Canadian progress along the
bottom of the Italian toe painfully slow.

Troops heading toward Catanzaro Marina on the bottom
of the Italian instep didn't reach it until September 10 after
a 10-mile march across country, but still arrived ahead of
their vehicles. From there they advanced inland to Catanzaro
aboard Italian trucks, recently surrendered. On September
11 Alex Campbell's 'A' Company, in troop-carrying
vehicles, joined a squadron of Princess Louise Dragoon
Guards heading for Crotone, 40 miles up the coast. Allan
Park's platoon occupied the port for a few days.

It was much different from the early days of the Sicilian
campaign to be resting for several days at this stage, instead
of being among the leading elements of the Eighth Army
which were then moving as quickly as possible to make
contact with the U.S. Fifth Army in the Salerno region. The
link-up was achieved by patrols from the British 5th

Division on the evening of September 16. That day the Regiment was aboard trucks once again and covered about 150 miles. By the night of September 17 the 1st Canadian Division was on a plain on the northwest corner of the Gulf of Taranto — the 1st Brigade around Spezzano, the 2nd Brigade at Cassano and the 3rd Brigade at Villapiana.

Jim Buckley, a tall and powerfully built young corporal who had joined the battalion in the Sicilian rest area, was to remember not only the exhiliration of his first days in action but the inspirational role of the RSM, as the companies wound their way up the mountain roads. Duffy would go up and down the column as men plodded along on a night march, offering an encouraging word, a slap on the back or a joke — and suddenly he would be gone. Buckley had never met a sergeant-major like this one before. He didn't remain distant from the men. Newcomers received encouragement and had a sense of being welcomed into a Regiment with a special quality. On the other hand, the jocular abuse Duffy tossed at old friends was a greeting they understood and cherished, for they had been through much together in four years.

Buckley found that a newcomer shouldn't try to take advantage of Duffy's friendliness. The corporal had bought a trench coat from an officer leaving for hospital and in a soaking rainstorm in the mountains he put it on. Other ranks just didn't wear officers' kit.

"Where did you get that coat?" Duffy demanded.

"I bought it from an officer."

"Why don't you take it off now? Wear it when you go to bed."

The coat would go back into a pack for a while and then it would come out again. In one rainstorm Duffy watched the column from a point where he could not be seen and pounced out roaring at Buckley so fiercely that the corporal switched back to his ground sheet for two wet weeks.

The Canadians' next objective was Potenza in the middle

of the southern Apennines. The 3rd Brigade led the advance with the 1st Brigade guarding the right flank, and in this role a relatively fast convoy carried the Regiment northeastward along the Gulf of Taranto into the Italian instep, stopping at Montalbano. There was a stand-to at dawn the next day. The PLDG had made contact with the 1st German Parachute Regiment about 30 miles to the north, and the Hastings medical officer was sent forward to treat the PLDG wounded. Patrols from the 1st Brigade, ranging widely toward Taranto, made contact with the British Airborne Division.

Potenza had fallen to the 3rd Brigade on September 20 in an attack that began on the night of September 19. Troops of the 2nd Brigade were soon patrolling further northward aggressively, helping to convince the Germans that the Allies' Salerno bridgehead could never be dislodged.

The Regiment remained near the Gulf of Taranto for another week. On September 22 Kennedy went to Crotone where he met some of the men who had been wounded in Sicily and they were among the 47 reinforcements reaching BHQ that afternoon. A move northward began in stages on September 22. The next day athletes and some supporters headed for Potenza where a 1st Division sports meet took place on the 29th. The 2nd Brigade dominated the event, and the same day its Brigadier, Chris Vokes, took command of the Division when Guy Simonds went out with a severe case of jaundice.

Tweedsmuir was on the way back from a convalescent camp on the Algerian sand dunes, east of Philippeville. A series of short hops by air brought him to Taranto on September 29, via Palermo, Syracuse and Catania. After a day of hitch-hiking on blinding white dusty roads, he reached 13th British Corps Headquarters by nightfall, and it was the end of the next day before he found the 1st Canadian Brigade.

The Regiment had moved northeast to the vicinity of Canosa on the Foggia plain, and on October 1 Tweedsmuir arrived as a passenger in Graham's jeep, just as breakfast was cooking. He resumed command with a feeling of exhiliration, he wrote later:

> "It gave me a wonderful feeling of home-coming. There were a good many new faces, new officers and new reinforcements, but Waitt looked just the same. We lazed the rest of the day away. My 2 i/c and I sat in the pleasant sultry darkness drinking a bottle of vermouth — discussing all that had passed since I left and our plans for the morrow when we were to move forward and again assail the Hun. . . . We left just after first light. The enemy . . . had abandoned Foggia. It was wonderful to see the line of trucks, Bren-gun carriers and guns rolling along again. There was that great feeling of companionship that comes to everyone when they are moving up to battle and that glorious electric feeling that there is danger ahead."

After a frustrating month, beset by troubles of terrain, the 1st Brigade was moving westward on relatively level ground again, if only for one day. It was the main road to Campobasso. Calgary Regiment tanks and the RCR were leading. From the steep hills of Motta Montecorvina the Canadians were being closely watched by the Germans. Late in the day intense fire from 88s pounded the column to a halt. The RCR prepared for an all-night fight for Motta and the Hastings took up a position in reserve as darkness fell.

Jim Buckley's treasured trench coat had remained part of his kit despite harsh words from the RSM, but an incident just after Tweedsmuir's return to the Regiment resolved the somewhat light-hearted conflict. The night was wet as well as very dark. Buckley was on guard near the crest of a hill overlooking 'D' Company headquarters. Duffy was inside this small building. The rain got worse and Buckley put on the trench coat. From the shadows came a tall fair-haired man whom Buckley had never seen before, asking the way to company headquarters.

"Yes, sir, but you'd have to tell me who you are."

"I'm your commanding officer and I'm looking for 'D' Company."

"It's right down there, sir. Just knock on the door."

"Thank you. Carry on, Mr. . . ."

"I'm a corporal, sir."

Tweedsmuir went down the hill and into the building. In a few seconds the door burst open. Duffy charged up the hill as fast as his powerful legs would take him.

"Buckley, what did I tell you?" Duffy roared. "You've embarrassed me as well as the C.O. Come into the woods and bring a shovel."

In half a minute the offending trench coat had become just one more military artifact in the soil of Italy.

The fierce rain threatened to bog down the vehicles and the Regiment moved two miles forward to a stubble field and dug in. Transported to the edge of Motta next morning, the Hastings marched through the town and encountered some shellfire. Ordered by Graham to attack a wooded ridge about three miles ahead, Tweedsmuir was shelled out of two observation posts before finding a house with a long view of three steep gullies leading up to the ridge. In mist and heavy rain the rifle companies began to file down the middle one.

An open area at the end of the gully was as quiet as a park. There were 400 yards to cross before reaching the cover of an oak wood at the foot of Mount Sambuco. A heavy mist seemed as good as a smoke screen and two companies headed for the road near the crest of the ridge. The leading company was 200 yards from its objective when heavy machine gun fire ripped across the weary platoons from four directions. The advance stopped. There was nothing for it but to lie under dripping trees until dark, with eight wounded.

Patrols then moved forward and located some of the enemy in the upper part of the wood, but the Germans seemed to be avoiding a fire fight at close range. In the middle of the night the Hastings companies were all moving up in single file and two of them got safely astride the road. The men were shivering in their khaki drill uniforms and water was two or three inches deep on the ground, but some managed to sleep.

The warm clear morning of October 3 revealed signs of a hurried German withdrawal — an abandoned signal truck and odds and ends of equipment. There was time to enjoy two breakfasts before Graham arrived by jeep with congratulations. The rest of the sunny day was spent in total relaxation. A company of 48th Highlanders passed through, heading for Celenza, said to be strongly held by German paratroops. Supper was in progress when Graham appeared again with orders to push on through the mountains and take Celenza, cutting off the enemy in San Marco and Carlantino.

These orders meant crossing 15 miles of mountains, over a route no one in the Regiment had seen and avoiding German positions about which nothing was known in advance.

This seemed to be the pattern in the Apennines. It was impossible to predict how long it would take to locate and engage the enemy and how soon he would pull back to the next defended locality. Suddenly encountering heavy fire could mean that a major enemy concentration was just ahead, or this might be only a heavily armed rearguard left to harass the Canadians for a time while a new position was prepared further back.

Well after dark the column moved off in pouring rain to establish a position on Mount Miano and thus to dominate Celenza. As a direction indicator the artillery dropped a shell well ahead, every five minutes until midnight. Just walking through oak forest in the misty blackness wasn't easy. Going uphill was so tough that much of it was done on all fours. It was the worst night since Christmas Eve, 1942, in highland bogs near Inveraray.

After hours of stumbling through sodden forest those at the front of the column were suffering from acute eyestrain and even seeing things that weren't there. Whenever the advance stopped for a brief reconnaisance in the vicinity, some men had to be awakened before the platoons and sections could go on. But just as the rain was easing off, those in the lead caught a glimpse of a road that seemed to be going approximately in the right direction. This easier route seemed worth a try. Everyone got safely across a valley and had begun climbing around a spur of another mountain when both ends of the column came under heavy machine gun fire. The way the road was cut into the feature gave some protection from the bullets, but the Germans began rolling grenades down steep banks. A machine gun kept firing down the road until the leading company retaliated with mortars and silenced it. A sniper dispatched another German gun crew. The immediate danger was over, but this roadway was no place to be caught in daylight.

By first light a withdrawal of several hundred yards had been made successfully to a position on Mount Ingotto, the highest point of a ridge running parallel to Mount Miano and separated from it by a valley. Maps indicated that it might be possible to follow this ridge right around the north end of Mount Miano. There was no food, but after a morning's rest, the battalion started moving along the ridge. Progress was slow, but the weather was balmy.

As the companies dug in that night, Tweedsmuir approached a nearby farmhouse. He talked to the farmer in a hut by candlelight.

"German patrols, he told us, had been there two days before, and a German force was at this moment on Mount Miano ridge, three miles to the westward. The children crept in to look at us and sat wide-eyed watching us. When they grow up they will probably tell tales of the men in strange, tattered uniforms who crept in from the darkness. Strange men with fair skins and hard mouths, whose tired eyes twinkled often with laughter, but whose hands were at their pistols whenever a cow moved in its stall or a dog barked across the valley. Young men who looked as if they had never been young, who disappeared into the darkness as quickly as they came."

Bert Kennedy and a ration party arrived in the morning. After a day's rest the long march around the north end of Mount Miano resumed. Near daylight Tweedsmuir was convinced that the intelligence officer and scouts out in front of the column had lost their direction. A little man suddenly appeared to warn that a strong German patrol was on a hill overlooking the route the battalion was following.

With daylight approaching a quick change of route brought the companies to a more secure position where some mountaineers were encountered. An Italian doctor with them made five mules available and the I.O. and three Bren gunners rode off on a patrol to find out if it was possible to get close enough to harass the Germans, if they were still at their reported location.

The patrol had barely disappeared when an unexpected radio message said Mount Miano had been cleared of the enemy. Who could have accomplished that? The answer brought both embarrassment and delight to the rifle companies. A patrol of drivers, cooks and other battalion headquarters men under Capt. Lyall Carr had gone around the west side. It was their job to bring up food and ammunition, but they thought they would try a little fighting. After a brief exchange of fire with some Germans, they had taken Carlantino.

Duffy had spent most of the previous three days as a one-man fighting patrol, out in front or on a flank as a precaution against being ambushed. On one occasion he spotted movement on a hillside and stalked a small group of men until he had come close enough to them to identify them as 48th Highlanders.

When the main body joined the adventurers, they found a bivouac area set up overlooking the Fortore River, and a meal cooking. There were pup tents to keep some of the rain out. Best of all was a four-day rest for everyone but a few scouts who patrolled far beyond the river and brought in a prisoner.

The rain stopped on October 12, the day the footsloggers found their wheels again. The 1st Brigade had been given the task of taking Campobasso, with the Hastings in reserve.

The advance in trucks was slow, because of blown bridges

and their narrow makeshift replacements. Beyond the crossing of the Fortore the ground rose steeply. Before nightfall the convoy stopped just short of the town of Jelsi. By 1 o'clock the next morning it was a marching column again, under a starry sky, with cook truck following. Gildone was reached by daylight with plenty of time for a good breakfast before taking up a position at a road and river junction.

On the approach to Campobasso the Canadians saw clearly that the Italian peasants wanted badly to be rid of the Germans. They knew that towns and villages would be ransacked as the Germans fell back, food would be confiscated and buildings burned. Families were clearing their homes of fruit, vegetables and bread and storing this food in pits they dug along trails and footpaths.

When the Hastings column passed through villages, the troops would see that practically every building had been ransacked by the retreating Germans, drawers were emptied, simple belongings and holy pictures trampled into the dirt. But just beyond that village, they might also find a few shepherds, women and children, handing out fruit, chunks of bread, grapes, slices of melon and even small pots of spaghetti.

"They recognized that we were tired and that we were a different order of soldiers from the Germans," Jim Buckley reminisced. "They were giving away food they couldn't replace. We appreciated what they did for us and we were glad to be able to take their land back from the Germans so that the Italians could occupy it in peace. We understood why they loved their land as we loved our own."

The mountain city of Campobasso was visible, about eight miles away, at the end of a long valley along which the RCR and 48th were advancing. The advance was slowed by enemy shelling. The 48th were leading and the RCR were to pass through to make the attack. Kennedy went forward to maintain liaison with the RCR. In the late morning he was following the RCR route, accompanied by an RCR private carrying a wireless set and a 48th stretcher-bearer, carrying first aid equipment up to his comrades. When Kennedy caught up to the RCR they were dispersed along the road. When heavy shelling started an RCR officer advised him to take a more covered route along a row of trees some distance from the road. Unfortunately a German platoon was advancing along the same path to outflank the RCR. At high noon Kennedy and his companions were taken prisoner.

In the afternoon near Ferrazzano there had been no word from Kennedy, but there was a warning of a German counterattack on the battalions ahead. For the Hastings it meant only shelling. That night Tweedsmuir was called to Brigade and given orders to move up through Ferrazzano and push westward on high ground, as if intending to attack Campobasso from the south. In the early hours of the 14th, 'B' and 'C' Companies went through the town. An enemy force was coming the opposite way and a brief fire fight erupted. The Germans were the more surprised and they disappeared quickly.

Beyond Ferrazzano at about 5:30 a.m. the Hastings put on their requested demonstration of heavy firing to suggest to the enemy in Campobasso that this was the direction of the main attack. On the western edge of Ferrazzano, Tweedsmuir set up battalion headquarters in a small 16th century castle with walls four feet thick. He was relaxing in front of a roaring fire when local inhabitants sent in a deputation offering eggs, huge loaves of bread, apples, pears and grapes that added up to an unforgettable breakfast.

A message from Brigade said that Campobasso had fallen and the Hastings were to pass through the city and take up a position on the right flank.

"It was a tedious march of some seven miles. Going through Campobasso the population mobbed us and all but broke our marching formation. I just escaped being kissed by three pretty signorinas and a horrid old man. It was a very footsore battalion that arrived in its area, a bowl in a hill with a blown-up brickworks and railway station."

After Campobasso had been occupied Kennedy's web equipment and empty holster were found in a large house in the outskirts. Italian civilians said a Canadian major had been shot by the Germans and buried behind the house. Padre Roy Essex and a digging party located and opened the grave, but the dead major wasn't Kennedy. The search went on. The padre and his men opened three more graves in the next four days.

Resistance seemed very light north of Campobasso and the town of Montegano, overlooking the Biferno River, was occupied with no difficulty. The troops were mobbed by the inhabitants. However, it was soon made clear that the Germans were not going to evacuate all the positions east of the Biferno just yet. A Hastings carrier patrol sent out the next day to the village of San Stefano, four miles away, had to withdraw under heavy fire.

From daylight on, Italians crowded around battalion headquarters in the morning, offering information about the enemy. Tweedsmuir decided to deal with a Mr. Di Paolo who had prospered in the United States, and Giovanni, a guerrilla leader with a price on his head, who had been wounded seven times. Mr. Di Paolo accompanied a reconnaissance in force against San Stefano before first light on the 16th. He went forward for two hours from an observation post and brought back information on German positions. The artillery started shelling them.

Carriers, mortars and 13 platoon of 'C' Company were called up to put in an attack, but surprise was lost when a dispatch rider missed a turn and drove right into an enemy position. But by nightfall the attacking force had moved successfully to within a few hundred yards of a crest over which the road disappeared to enter the village.

When 13 platoon attacked after daylight its officer and four men were killed. Four others were wounded and the platoon had to withdraw under a smoke screen. By that time 14 platoon had come forward. The attack went in again with two platoons, but by then the enemy force was even stronger and the attackers had to make their way back, pursued by mortar fire.

Tweedsmuir's men wondered if the Germans would come over the ridge, but apparently they decided that the Canadians would be just as tough in a defensive position as they were themselves. The C.O. felt one man had made the difference:

> "Trapper Davis settled himself down comfortably on a bank half way back, with the clear eye that only those possess who have never read print. He lined his telescopic sight on the point of the ridge where the enemy would cross if they intended to follow us. We waited only a few minutes before a German officer came into view, sweeping the landscape with his field glasses. Davis gently squeezed his trigger and the officer pitched forward onto his face, nailed by that gnarled old frontiersman at 700 yards. That discouraged pursuit."

The next two days featured rest and reconnaissance and planning for a heavily supported assault on San Stefano. 'A' Company in Montegano underwent more shelling and aggressive German patrols were cutting signal lines.

On the way to Montegano, Roy Essex was ambushed by a sharpshooter from behind a hedge. The tough and courageous Baptist padre, who owned a pearl-handled revolver, knew how to use a gun and shot it out with his assailant until he ran out of ammunition. The German limped away wounded. It was said that church parades drew full attendance after that.

At 5 a.m. on October 20, 'B' and 'D' Companies moved on Stefano in fog, supported by artillery, machine guns, heavy mortars and tanks. The Germans had pulled out quickly, leaving their bedrolls behind. The next day word came that the Hastings were about to be relieved by another battalion, and the Royal 22nd took over on the following night. The

Regiment moved back to an oak forest southwest of Campobasso, far enough out of the line to relax completely.

On Sunday, October 24 Padre Essex conducted a service among the oak trees, but it wasn't entirely a peaceful day for the Roman Catholics. Their service was in Campobasso, still not out of range of enemy shelling. As the service was drawing to a close, Duffy was outside selecting an assembly area in which he could form up the troops for a march-past. Firing started and a shell smashed into a building near the church. One of his friends said he never went to church with Duffy after that.

From Oratino, Tweedsmuir and his company commanders studied the terrain across the Biferno — where the RCR would move on Castropignano, the 48th would attack Torella and the Hastings would advance to seize Molise. The RCR had no trouble, and the 48th had a hard time, before the Regiment finally crossed the river on top of a dam on October 26.

The 12 miles to Molise were crossed by rugged, wooded ravines where ambush was possible — indeed one large German patrol was spotted in a gully. To maintain surprise the advance was halted for the night and it was nearly noon on the 27th when the battalion reached the last ridge before Molise. The final push was made in rain and thick fog. All the Germans were gone, but soon their gunners had the range of every Hastings position in the dirty town, thanks to Fascist informers. Six men were killed and 14 wounded in the first shelling.

Graham ordered Tweedsmuir to send one company to occupy Frosolone, five miles away. The next day 'A' Company did so and found no enemy, but shelling was heavy. Signal lines were being cut just outside Molise until Tweedsmuir summoned the shifty looking mayor and told him that some townsmen were in danger of being shot.

The Regiment was relieved on the night of November 1-2. Tweedsmuir described the prevailing emotions movingly:

"There was an orange glow in the sky as we cleared the town, and silhouetted against it were the neat rows of wooden crosses that marked the graves of our dead. The resting place of six men who had come thousands of miles, endured hardship, faced and met with death, all for something that none of them could have put into words, but was worth all that to prove. Soon a ridge hid Molise from us. We never wanted to see it again."

120

Chapter Ten
Mud, blood and brotherhood

Duffy knew a few days before leaving Molise that the rest area would be the village of Castropignano and it would be his job to see that for a while at least some men would have little or no rest. He was ordered to prepare an intensive course of training for a number of corporals and a few sergeants who had been promoted in action. These NCOs were going to have to prove that they could show leadership and good judgment as clearly on the parade square as in taking their sections forward in an attack or in organizing a defensive position. But what could you call a parade square in that untidy village? There was nothing but muddy ground on which to drill and rain was frequent.

Duffy obtained the essentials for spit-and-polish soldiering from Ernie Grove, the auxiliary services officer, in the form of tins and tins of boot polish, brushes to apply it and irons for pressing uniforms. Unfortunately within a few minutes of beginning any drill session the uniforms with knife-edge creases were flecked with mud and so were the glistening boots. Duffy hated the whole exercise, but orders were orders.

The candidates thought the course had been Duffy's idea. He made it interesting with lectures on military law, leadership, Regimental history and traditions. The toughest part for him came as the course was ending. He could see that not all the candidates were really NCO material, in spite of having done well in action. Three or four failed to qualify and that decision was Duffy's. There was no joy in being RSM that day, he said.

All the rifle companies followed a training syllabus that helped newly arrived reinforcements to get to know their new comrades and to learn how things were done in the Regiment. Tweedsmuir lectured the junior officers in the evenings. Seven men per company went into Campobasso in rotation on 48-hour leaves.

Sunday, November 7, was enriched with a sense of the miraculous. Tweedsmuir lay in battalion headquarters seriously ill with jaundice, knowing that soon he would have to give up command and go to hospital. A thin figure in ragged civilian clothes appeared at the front door and walked right into Tweedsmuir's room. He was good news incarnate! Bert Kennedy was back from one of the great escape adventures of the war.

Four days after his capture he and other prisoners were in a truck heading for Rome. As it got darker and rainier late in the afternoon, Kennedy kept moving ever so slowly towards the partly open back end of the vehicle. When a hairpin turn near Avezzano threw the guards off balance, he leaped out, dived into the ditch, then ran to a stream where he lay face down, undetected in tall grass and weeds. At dark he headed into the hills.

For the first few days of his southward journey he was alone. Pouring rain, fatigue and hunger eventually drove him to take refuge in a barn. Italian peasants found him and befriended him, and sheltered him. One man even accompanied him on a 40-mile train journey to within a few miles of Sora. Kennedy then was half way home, but the danger was greater the closer he got to the battle front. He knew he could trust the Italian peasants. His boots were worn out and his feet were in rags and cardboard. He met other escapers, one of whom would lend Kennedy his boots for nightly expeditions to scrounge food from the Italians.

Near the Sangro Valley Kennedy met Lieut. Fred Fisher of the Sherwood Foresters. The British officer, captured at Tobruk, had made his way from the north of Italy in spite of losing his spectacles without which his sight was severely limited. After crossing the last mountain obstacle and descending into the Sangro Valley, the pair took an hour to move across open ground near a busy road, eventually crossing that road between a German command vehicle and a sentry post.

The two escapers were in a battle zone. They heard firing all around them and kept low. At dark they entered Venafro and surrendered to an American patrol. Next day, in a borrowed jeep, Kennedy arrived at the battalion area. Duffy was just dismissing his NCO school. The RSM shouted and ran to the jeep and the others crowded around, but Kennedy was determined to speak to Tweedsmuir first.

When Tweedsmuir went to hospital the next day, Kennedy once more assumed command of the Regiment. When he lectured on escaping you could hear a pin drop.

Smartening-up drill was the rule for all, not just NCO candidates. Graham paid two visits that week, once to inspect Duffy's NCO class and once for a battalion parade. Graham also inspected battalion transport and found everything in good shape. Defence Minister Colonel J.L. Ralston paid a visit and promised to do something about the problem of slow mail.

Kennedy's determination to fight on with the Regiment whatever lay ahead, instead of taking a leave to England, inspired all ranks. He had shown that Hasty Ps could do the impossible. Certainly there were going to be more tough situations ahead. Duffy had done his best to inspire the NCOs because he knew that the Regiment's success in battle depended so much on their performance.

Much heroism had been displayed already at every rank from private to lieutenant-colonel, but there were few rewards in the form of decorations. Ross McKnight's DCM and the MMs awarded to Ivan Gunter and Huron Brant reflected only a fraction of the valour expended. Bruce Sutcliffe's DSO and Bob Waugh's MC represented only faintly the gallantry of the officers.

Duffy often wondered in Italy why men in other regiments seemed to receive more decorations for heroism. Perhaps writing recommendations was the key. He discussed this one day with the RSM of the 48th Highlanders. "We have a committee of two school teachers and a lawyer," the other RSM told him. "When we stop fighting, they start writing."

It may not have occurred to the Hasty Ps that they needed what we would call today a public relations approach. Perhaps they thought naively that if the Regiment did a

particularly outstanding job, it was mainly the responsibility of higher authority to recognize it and to see that individuals were rewarded, without the Regiment having to make a special effort to get the message to the top. To this point their exploits had brought headlines back home, but little else. Ironically the Hastings were about to enter perhaps their greatest battle where they would get a better share of the decorations, but relatively little newspaper ink.

All of that, however, lay some desperate days ahead.

On the last Sunday in November the RCs paraded to a service in the Campobasso cathedral and the Protestant service in Castropignano was conducted by the newly arrived padre, Fred Goforth. Word had been received that the 1st Division was moving soon to the Adriatic. Kennedy left the next day for a reconnaissance of coastal areas.

The Canadian landing on the toe of Italy three months earlier had been a piece of cake, but progress from there had been slow. The grim reality as winter approached was that things were going to get worse before they got better.

The Quebec Conference decided that Overlord, the coming Normandy invasion, was to have priority in equipment over Italy. By November most of the available landing craft and assault craft had been withdrawn from the Mediterranean.

It was impossible, therefore, to leap-frog a strong force up either coast to shorten the distance to future objectives. The Allied High Command hoped that the U.S. Fifth Army could advance rapidly and take Rome and that Monty's Eighth Army could reach Pescara on the Adriatic. The Germans were determined to deny these objectives to the Allies by holding an 85-mile line across the narrowest part of Italy, with its eastern anchor the town of Ortona.

On December 1 the Regiment left Castropignano in vehicles and spent that long, wet day and most of the next moving eastward to Termoli and then north to the Sangro River. The British 78th Division had smashed through the Germans' Bernhard Line there in late November. The 1st Canadian Division's task would be to relieve the tiring 78th and restore momentum to the advance by getting across the next river, the Moro, as quickly as possible.

In the afternoon of December 5 the 1st Canadian Brigade relieved the Irish Brigade. The Hastings took over from the Royal Irish Fusiliers on the bank of the Moro near the coast road. Enemy forces were presumed to be about 900 yards ahead. They were fresh troops. The 90th Panzer Grenadier Division had moved into the coastal sector only two days before.

General Vokes saw the 1st Brigade role near the coast as diversionary, while crossings in strength would be made upstream on the night of the 5th/6th by the Seaforths near San Leonardo and the Patricias at Villa Rogatti. Graham gave the 1st Brigade assignment to the Hastings. It was late in the day before the companies were in position, with a night attack to make over ground they hadn't seen properly in daylight. The valley was about 500 yards wide and near the coast the valley floor beyond the Moro terminated against an abrupt embankment.

Around 10 o'clock one platoon of 'A' Company crossed the river about 200 yards from the sea. When the other platoons of the company followed, the leading platoon had swung left to take advantage of a more gradual slope, but at about the same time all platoons encountered vicious machine gun and rifle grenade fire. The 'A' Company position was held until about 1 o'clock in the morning, but with the radio not working it was impossible to call down supporting fire. Capt. Paul O'Gorman brought 'A' Company back, having suffered some casualties, but the toll could have been much worse.

The Seaforths and the Patricias were beyond the river, but they faced determined counter-attacks from early morning on. By the evening of the 6th came the grim decision to give up the Seaforth bridgehead in favor of exploiting the Pats' hold on Rogatti. But down near the mouth of the Moro an epic was in the making.

Soft-spoken Kennedy was tough and inspirational. Sharing Graham's confidence in the fighting qualities of his Regiment, he was able to convince Vokes that with the right kind of supporting fire, the Hastings could get a permanent foothold beyond the Moro and he wanted to get going without too much delay. At about 2 o'clock on the 6th, after a 20-minute artillery barrage, Capt. Les Yates was leading 'C' Company across, supported by the heavy mortars of the Sask. L.I. It was a grim introduction to combat for newly arrived officers like Ian Dearness who was commanding 13 platoon. When enemy fire increased on the left flank of the attacking company, 'D' Company was quickly committed, but the situation worsened.

At 3:40 p.m. Kennedy ordered the withdrawal of 'C' and 'D' Companies under smoke from the carrier and mortar platoons, but radio trouble prevented 'D' Company from hearing the message. 'D' Company fought on and in less than an hour the three platoons commanded by Dean Seaton, Hub Vallery and Tom Davis had pushed the enemy back and had moved onto higher ground.

As light began to fade in the late afternoon, Kennedy sent the carrier platoon across on foot and then he led 'A' and 'B' Companies over. They waded waist-deep through the very cold water, carrying rations, equipment and ammunition, heading for the steep bank where the valley bottom ended. 'C' Company made its second crossing under the command of Lyall Carr who had succeeded the mortally wounded Les Yates. By dark Kennedy had the Hastings on top of the enemy in battalion strength and determined to stay, despite 28 casualties, including five killed.

Irv Chambers, a tall confident corporal in Frank Hammond's 'B' Company, had been through everything since the Sicilian landing, but he shuddered as he scrambled over German bodies, particularly one lying in rigor mortis with arms stretched upward in a ghastly silhouette. 'B' Company went 50 yards beyond the crest of the bank and dug in as heavy shelling began. The bridgehead was now 500 yards wide and 600 yards deep.

Deadly rockets, known to the Canadians as Moaning Minnies, came screaming down in the blackness. Some landed right in slit trenches with gruesome results. German tanks could be heard in the distance. The dreaded prospect for the morning was even deadlier fire.

No tanks were able to get forward to support the Regiment in the bridgehead. Anti-tank guns were the next best. Although the Regiment's own guns weighed over a ton each, members of the anti-tank platoon and 'C' Company, inspired by CSM George Ponsford, manhandled two of them across the river and into place. Enemy attempts to infiltrate the bridgehead during the night were repulsed. By morning many enemy dead lay close to the Hastings positions and one prisoner had been taken.

Strangely, Duffy had been left out of battle. Kennedy had ordered him to dig in a defensive position on the south side of the river in case the rifle companies were driven back by a counterattack. All available BHQ men, including Paymaster Winston Wensley, wielded shovels. As darkness fell Duffy became more and more anxious about how the battle was going, and wondered how he could get across the river in spite of the order to stay where he was and dig. He questioned closely anyone who had been as far as the river. A water truck came back badly shot up. A little later a wounded dispatch rider arrived.

Truck driver 'Pie' Conlin told Duffy he knew how to get across the river. Rum would surely be appreciated on that grim December night. Why not take some over? Duffy greeted the idea as inspirational. With an ammunition truck driver and eight bottles of rum he headed for the Moro. In the darkness he met Graham who asked where he was going.

"I'm hunting for the colonel," Duffy replied.

Graham had just come back from the Hastings bridgehead where he had been right up with the leading platoons.

"Colonel Kennedy has the battalion across the river in an extremely difficult position," he told Duffy.

"I'm not supposed to be there."

"He needs all the men he can get. Get across to Colonel Kennedy and tell him I sent you."

Duffy crossed the river and found Kennedy. The C.O. said the battalion badly needed ammunition and food. Ammunition was the RSM's main responsibility in action, and so he went back to the rear headquarters where the ammunition could be obtained and a mule train assembled. It took the rest of the night to get back and load the mules.

Duffy wanted to return to Kennedy before daylight, but the sky was bright when the mule train approached the river. The Moro was only a foot deep at the crossing point, but shelling was heavy at times. The approach to the near bank was exposed and so was the route from the river to the battalion.

Duffy found himself against a bank on the enemy side of the river, exhausted and shivering, and wondering if he could make it the rest of the way. Machine gun fire was heavy.

Charlie Hildreith, better known as 'Maw' Hildreith, was one of the muleteers with Duffy. There were also some Indian Army muleteers attached to the Hastings.

"You know what, sir?" he asked the RSM.

"What?"

"I'll bet those Indians think we've lost our nerve and we're too frightened to go ahead with this stuff for the troops."

Duffy was instantly aware of what Hildreith was trying to say in a roundabout way. It was Hildreith, not the Indians, who thought it was time for Duffy to get the show on the road again and quit hesitating for mere shelling or machine gun fire. And so they started out across the last few hundred yards, hooking both arms through the reins and crawling on their bellies between the mules. They made it.

By this time in his career, Duffy had long been a father figure to the men of the Regiment, and back in Canada a teletype operator made it official. A delayed Canadian Press story appearing in the Toronto Star on December 27 said that "mule trains were led across the valley under heavy fire, in charge of Rev. Angus Duffy of Trenton, and the battalion during its battle was never short of ammunition and food."

More than 35 years later Jim Buckley remembered Duffy as the spiritual father of the NCOs and the men in the ranks.

"He respected and valued the human qualities of every man serving in the Regiment. He didn't waste words. He spoke to us directly, sometimes bluntly. He could get very excited sometimes, but his presence was comforting to the rest of us who were young and a bit bewildered. He gave us courage and a sense of belonging, although we weren't originals. The task to which he gave himself was inspiring us and making soldiers of us. Those are the actions of a hero. In his opinion we were more important than commissioned officers. That comforted us. He made us feel pride because he took pride in us. Even a C.O. must have felt sometimes that it was Duffy's Regiment."

Early on December 7 the Corps Commander ordered the 8th Indian Division to take over the Rogatti area so that the 1st Canadian Division front could be shortened. By the end of the day the Patricias were back where they had started and the Hastings were alone on the enemy's side of the river. However, the Germans exerted less pressure during the day than expected.

After dark a platoon of 'A' Company and a platoon of 'B' had pushed forward beyond the crest of the river bank to positions commanding not only the coast road but a lateral road running parallel to the river towards San Leonardo. The enemy kept up pressure during the night and forced the 'A' Company platoon to pull back. The Germans moved quickly and confidently into what they took to be undefended territory, but it was really a trap between the two Hastings companies. They were within 25 yards of the waiting Canadians when heavy fire suddenly ripped into them from both flanks and sent them fleeing, leaving behind about 40 dead and 20 prisoners.

On the morning of the 8th, Sergeant Bill Nolan of 11 platoon, 'B' Company, who had won confirmation of his rank at Duffy's NCO school in Castropignano, won a place of honour in the Regiment's history.

At first light Nolan discovered that the Germans had occupied a house 300 yards to his left that could control the route along which the RCR were to come forward. Nolan didn't know that the intruders were men of the 1st Paratroop Division — cream of the German Army. He decided to remove the German strong point and was joined by 10 experienced 'B' Company NCOs and men, including Irv Chambers, Ivan Ellis, Fred Forshee, Les Richardson and 'Zeke' Thompson. With Hastings mortar detachments pouring in their bombs to keep German heads down, the Nolan attack was spectacularly successful. In hand-to-hand fighting the patrol took 18 paratroops prisoner, including one officer.

Nolan and his men held their house till an 'A' Company platoon could go forward and reoccupy it. The Germans shelled the bridgehead fiercely and frequently that day which was to see the other two battalions of the 1st Brigade get across the river at last. Both advanced at about 4:30 in the afternoon. The plan was to get the 48th across to bring pressure to bear on San Leonardo from the northwest, as the RCR swung left from the Hastings bridgehead to attack from the east. The 48th made their objective with little difficulty. The RCR crossed and moved up the left flank of the Hastings positions, but when the leading companies began to swing towards San Leonardo, they were stopped by devastating fire. An attempt to leap-frog the RCR companies forward in turn had to be abandoned.

About 1 o'clock in the morning of December 9 the Germans launched a vicious counter attack between the RCR and the Hastings, whose 'A' and 'B' Companies took the brunt of it. Hastings mortars had a key role in stopping this thrust. Thirty Germans were taken prisoner and numerous dead were left behind.

The RCR continued to have the worst possible luck when they tried to get moving again on the afternoon of December 9, just as a determined German counterattack was coming in. 'A' Company platoons on the Hastings' left flank held their fire until the Germans were 200 yards away in a vineyard. Mortar fire and small arms then carved up a German company, and on the 'B' Company front another German company was allowed into a ravine and cut to pieces with crossfire. By the evening the German attack was over. It had cost 170 casualties and about 50 prisoners. In the meantime the Seaforths and the Calgary Tanks gained control of San Leonardo.

By the early hours of December 10, the RCR had withdrawn across the river to reorganize, leaving the Hastings alone between San Leonardo and the sea, fiercely determined not only to hold on, but to push ahead. Graham sent congratulations to the Plough Jockeys and so did Monty. Kennedy, who had been so ill with jaundice that he could barely stand, went back to the rear BHQ.

From December 8 through the 10th, it had seemed that the Germans were counterattacking every few hours, although they didn't appear to be very certain about the actual limits of the bridgehead. Each time they attacked, there were dozens of enemy dead left for Padre Goforth to bury and scores of prisoners taken. The Hastings BHQ was in a gravel pit and prisoners were held there until they could be taken to the other side of the river.

Duffy and signaller Tommy Cunnell were in the gravel pit when one of the counterattacks bounced off a forward company. Cunnell had just stood up when he spun around suddenly and sat down. Duffy thought his old comrade was hit. The bullet had gone through the radio set on his back and only the radio was out of action. Cunnell pointed over Duffy's shoulder. A German leaning against the wall of a building near the lip of the gravel pit was calmly firing down on BHQ.

There were no rifles near Duffy and when he tried to crawl out of the gravel pit to get one, more bullets whistled just above his head. Duffy replied with four or five revolver shots and just at that moment the sniper disappeared and the attack ended.

The rifle companies needed every man they could get. Sometimes battalion truck drivers came up to BHQ to stand guard or keep an eye on prisoners. But with the bridgehead under frequent attack, it was neither safe nor easy to move around in the dark and the drizzle. Duffy was standing guard beside a path near BHQ late one night when he heard a peculiar noise. It was the sound of leather creaking. He knew there was no Hastings patrol out in that sector and was convinced that it must be a German patrol. He decided to let the first man get up very close to him. Just as he was about to squeeze the trigger of his tommy gun, he saw the outline of a truck driver's gauntlet. It was his own brother, Avon, leading a mule.

"You damned fool! What are you doing prowling around up here at night?"

"Don't get your shirt in an uproar. I'm just hunting for 'A' Company."

"What do you want to find them for?"

"I've got their mail and a bottle of rum. Now don't be an RSM. Just tell me where they are and I'll get on about my business."

"You can't go looking for any company in the middle of the night without getting shot."

"I'll give it a damn good try," Avon replied and he was off. He made it to 'A' Company with the mail and rum, checked in with the RSM on the way back and took five prisoners down the line for him.

On the afternoon of December 11, as the 2nd Brigade moved across to establish a second bridgehead at San Leonardo, the Hastings were ordered forward beyond the junction of the coast road and the San Leonardo lateral, and with tank support the companies easily reached high ground overlooking Ortona. Nightfall brought heavy shelling, including five-barreled rocket mortars. In the darkness detachments of anti-tank artillery moved up, and so did the carrier platoon and 30 reinforcements. Kennedy, informed that he was now a lieutenant-colonel, remained at BHQ, determined to stay in command, and refusing to be evacuated with jaundice.

The next day saw little enemy activity. A Saskatoon Light Infantry mortar platoon took up a position behind BHQ, the rest of the Hastings' own mortars moved up and so did the anti-tank guns. The bridgehead by the sea was a week old.

The reputation of a great Division had been on the line at the Moro and the Hastings' daring and determination kept it bright, while sometimes others failed to accomplish what they set out to do. Despite losses, morale among the Plough Jockeys was high. Heavy mortars and machine guns, tanks, artillery and aircraft laid down supporting fire for them that shook the ground, but sometimes the effectiveness of the Regiment's own Support Company was even more appreciated.

Stan Down of the mortar platoon went forward to an observation post in the upper part of a battered farmhouse with a signaller whose set was barely working. Through a small hole in the roof Down could see a German mortar position and he called for two ranging shots with smoke bombs. The next two smoke bombs landed close to the target. The fifth shot was high explosive. It landed right on the German position in a small building which must have contained a store of ammunition. A series of explosions followed demolishing the building completely. An enemy mortar crew and an ammunition dump with five bombs was good shooting.

On December 13 Graham ordered an attack against a ridge strongly held by the Germans. 'D' Company reached the ridge by late afternoon, but the company commander and leading platoon commander were among the many casualties. Capt. George Dinwiddie died of wounds the next day. By that time 'A' Company managed to reach the ridge, but more help was needed. Al Park took his platoon across the valley and was just moving into a position when he heard a German weapon click. He dived face-down into the mud. His wounds were terrible, but his helmet saved his life.

The Patricias, trying to come in from the left along the ridge, were unable to reach the Hastings companies which had to move back a little in the darkness. Positions changed again on the 15th and 'B' Company dug in quickly beside the coast road. German shelling became heavy, but jeeps and mule trains brought up supplies.

The situation was basically the same for the next two days, except for a change in command of the 1st Brigade. A great Hasty P had fought his last battle. Howard Graham had to relinquish command because of illness and Dan Spry, commanding the RCR, took over.

About this time a group of war correspondents and photographers descended on BHQ one day. Stockloser, acting C.O., called Duffy back from a forward position to meet them. They wanted the story of the Moro River crossing in the most dramatic form possible.

Duffy was about to sit down and tell them the story when one of the brasher correspondents interrupted with a request for about 80 men to re-enact the crossing for the photographers. Duffy was aghast at the suggestion.

"As far as I'm concerned, those men are going to rest," he said. "The only way they are going to get on their feet is to repel a counterattack; if I asked them to re-enact a battle just for you, they'd probably shoot you and me too. In future, if you want to write about a battle, come up when we're fighting it."

"Listen, wise guy," replied an aggressive correspondent towering over Duffy, "we're the ones who are going to tell the story to the folks back home. You'll never get any credit for this battle." And except for stories by William Stewart of the Canadian Press, they got precious little. The battle for Ortona got the big play, but if the Hastings hadn't held onto their bridgehead, Ortona mightn't have fallen until the spring.

Late on December 18 the Hastings came under the command of the 2nd Brigade in preparation for switching positions with the Seaforths who were north of San Leonardo.

As the 2nd Brigade began closing in on Ortona, high above the Adriatic, 1st Brigade was to push forward roughly parallel to the coast, but about two miles inland, bypassing Ortona and then swinging back towards the sea. The idea was to draw enemy support away from the isolated town which was soon to be fought for, room by room.

Farmhouses in the rolling country around Ortona were mostly large and substantial, of stone and brick construction, with tile roofs. Nearly every building became a strong point which had to be taken out by combined infantry and tank attack. But rain was turning the light soil to heavy gumbo, bogging the tanks down, while tangled wire and grapevines slowed down the infantry.

In the area of La Torre, inland from San Leonardo, the Regiment rested for two days. On the morning of December 22, the companies began moving up to relieve the Royal 22nd Regiment beyond the hard-won stronghold of Casa Berardi. By noon an attack had been ordered for the next morning, and support laid on from four field regiments of artillery and one medium regiment. Tanks were to follow.

Against the Hastings were men of the crack 1st Parachute Regiment. Their machine gun, mortar and artillery fire was so intense that it threatened to confine success to the intermediate objectives taken by 'A' and 'C' Companies. On December 23 'B' Company was awaiting the tanks for a push beyond 'C' Company and had to make a try without them which was driven back. But late in the day a determined 'B' Company thrust cut deeply into the German position, seizing a large farmhouse, taking a heavy toll in dead and wounded and capturing many prisoners. The carrier platoon came forward to help counter enemy infiltration.

Enemy shelling and machine gun fire kept Canadian heads down next morning and discouraged attempts to clear mines. In the late afternoon of December 24 the 48th passed through the Hastings and after dark the Germans managed to get between the two battalions. The tanks, hemmed in by mines, were needed worst by the Highlanders who were isolated and unable to get needed ammunition and rations. The RCR were unable to get through the 48th, but it was another 48 hours before the Germans realized that the Canadians had an extra battalion a mile out in front.

During the 24th about 138 reinforcements arrived, including several officers. Alex Campbell was back from hospital to command 'A' Company once again, Stan Ketcheson took over 'C' Company. Don Cameron arrived from the Stormont, Dundas and Glengarry Highlanders and was given 'D' Company with Allen Ross, from the Black Watch, as second-in-command. Bill Graydon and George Baldwin went to 'A' Company and Walt Exley to Battalion Headquarters.

On Christmas Eve 'A' Company moved forward, bumped the enemy and after a fire fight dug in and sent out patrols. Engineers came up to remove mines in preparation for the next day, but heavy machine gun fire ended that activity when it had barely begun.

After some shelling ahead of 'A' Company, Alex

Campbell led his company in a Christmas morning attack on well dug-in German positions in an olive grove on slightly rising ground. He was closing with the enemy when a burst from a Schmeisser cut him down, and a great Hasty P was gone. His father had died in action on a Christmas Day in the 1st World War.

All companies were shelled and enemy patrols were active during the rest of the day.

The next day Don Cameron moved far to the right with a fighting patrol and then cut back behind a German strong point that had resisted 'A' Company, killing several and taking two prisoners. A future commanding officer, Cameron had made his mark early.

A troop of Ontario Tanks got their Shermans up to the 48th by Boxing Day and the Highlanders were able to take the offensive, pushing the Germans across the Riccio River toward the hamlets of San Nicola and San Tommaso which they seized in the dying hours of the old year. The Hastings position changed little in the meantime. Shelling, patrolling, and sniping continued.

So did the rain. By the night of the 30th slit trenches were full. The last day of the year brought a delayed celebration of Christmas and planners of the feasting at BHQ decided that it was clear and mild enough to set the tables up outside the big square house. White tablecloths adorned a row of improvised tables. About noon, out came mounds of pork chops, potatoes and other vegetables, followed by mince pie and as many of the other seasonal delicacies as the quarter-master had managed to scrounge.

New Year's Day began just over a week of rebuilding. Rifle companies, shrunk to little more than large platoons, were assigned officers, NCOs and men from the 215 who arrived between December 30 and January 4, but the Regiment was to lose as well as gain. Some of the new arrivals, it turned out, had come in exchange for leaders who were going back to England as instructors.

On January 9 the rifle companies went into the line again,

in and around shell-battered San Nicola and San Tommaso
with some officers and men who had never been in action.
But that wasn't the whole story.

A new RSM was in the wings and Angus Duffy would be
gone in only five days.

Chapter Eleven
Frustration and flying bombs

December, 1943, was clearly the end of a chapter in the
Allied push towards victory. Early in January, 1944,
General Dwight Eisenhower was on his way to the United
Kingdom, having been designated Supreme Commander of
the Allied Expeditionary Force which would invade North-
west Europe. On New Year's Day General Montgomery
had turned over command of the Eighth Army to Lieut.-
General Oliver Leese and departed to command the 21st
Army Group under Eisenhower.

December had been a grim month for the under-strength
1st Division. On January 3 General Vokes reported to
Lieut.-General H.D. Crerar that during December all nine
infantry battalions had suffered losses that materially
affected fighting efficiency. Opposition they should have
taken in stride and easily overcome kept causing delays
because the troops were very tired.*

In December 35 officers in the 1st Division were killed in
action and 467 other ranks. In the same period 127 officers
and 1,544 other ranks were wounded, while 14 officers and
152 men were reported missing. In addition 77 officers and
1,540 other ranks went out sick. In spite of receiving 150
officers and 2,258 other ranks as reinforcements in December, Vokes had to report that he was still 60 officers and 990

* *Crerar Papers,* Public Archives.

other ranks under-strength when the advance stopped just beyond Ortona.

In retrospect it is possible now to see reasons why it might have been best for the whole 1st Division and the 1st Armoured Brigade to have gone back to Britain when Monty did, for they would undoubtedly have contributed significant power and experience to the 1st Canadian Army. "I could have done anything with that division," Vokes said 35 years later. "We had a marvellous spirit."

It had been understood, when the 1st Division and the Armoured Brigade joined the Eighth Army for the invasion of Sicily that they would be returning for the cross-Channel invasion. However, it didn't work out that way. By late October, 1943, the 5th Canadian Division and the 1st Canadian Corps Headquarters had sailed for Italy before Monty knew they were coming. He hadn't even been asked if he wanted more Canadians.*

Certainly more Canadians were needed to reinforce the 1st Division battalions which had been slugging it out with crack German units all through December. In the first few days of January recently arrived reinforcements were being absorbed by under-strength platoons.

On January 4 word came through that Kennedy's inspirational leadership at the Moro had been recognized with the Distinguished Service Order. Padre Fred Goforth and 'B' Company Commander Frank Hammond had won Military Crosses. Acting CSM Bill Nolan's spectacular raid had won him the Military Medal which also went to CSM Cece Yearwood, Sgt. Gordon Pemberton, Acting Sgt. H.A. Maxwell, Sgt. Harold Dracup and Cpl. K.C. Close.

Some Canadians were going back to England for various instructional jobs and some Hasty P officers were among them. Kennedy called Duffy in to tell him: "I've good news for you. You're going back to England till the spring." Instructors with battle experience were needed in England,

* See R.S. Malone, *Missing From The Record,* Chapter VI, and G.W.L. Nicholson, *The Canadian Army in Italy,* Chapter XII.

he said, and nothing much would be happening in Italy. Some other RSMs were going to England for various reasons, and he should go too. Duffy didn't like the idea. The Regiment had been his home since September, 1939. "I'll stay here as a corporal," was his immediate response. But the colonel's plan prevailed.

Did Kennedy really intend that Duffy should return in the spring? If the RSM was to be in England for only a short period, George Ponsford or Ray Huycke could have become acting RSM, but both of them had been sent to Avellino on December 27 as possible candidates for commissions. Before then Duffy's successor had already reached Italy from England and he was in Avellino too.

In late September, 1943, the Queen's Own Rifles of the 3rd Canadian Division had just completed assault training at Inveraray in Scotland and were heading south. Officers and NCOs were invited to sign up for a period in the Mediterranean theatre to get battle experience. RSM Harry Fox volunteered and soon found himself on draft with four officers, another warrant officer and four sergeants. The group of about 200 officers and 200 NCOs they joined in Aldershot was called 'Pooch draft'.*

Only three men in that draft wore the badges of a Regimental Sergeant-Major and Harry Fox was the only infantryman. He had been a prewar Militia soldier, having joined the Queen's Own in Toronto in 1932 at the age of 18. He worked at Eaton's College Street store, not far from the University Avenue Armouries where he spent much of his spare time. When the war began he was a sergeant and when the Queen's Own mobilized in June, 1940, a company sergeant-major. By November, 1941, this regiment was overseas with other 3rd Division units and located at Pippingford Park near East Grinstead.

It was a complete surprise to Fox when his C.O. told him in the spring of 1942 that he was to be Regimental Sergeant-

---

* See C.E. Corrigan, *Tales of a Forgotten Theatre.*

Major. He was one of the best shots in the battalion and had taken commando training, but he wasn't a classic parade square sergeant-major. He had never formed up a battalion parade and didn't complain when there were only three of them in the next 18 months.

The men of Pooch sailed from the Clyde in a large convoy that included 1st Division reinforcements, 5th Division units and reinforcements and 1st Corps troops. They landed at Philippeville on the Algerian coast and found that no one was expecting them. After a period in tents in the Cork Forest, they moved to Bizerte on the Tunisian coast. A rough 36-hour sea trip brought them to Naples and a truck convoy completed the journey inland to the Canadian base at Avellino. By then it was close to Christmas.

Fox and his companions found after arriving at Avellino that there was no apparent rush to send them to the front. Had any Regiment specifically requested an RSM? He didn't know. Weeks went by. Then on short notice he was detailed to go up to the 1st Division with a small group on January 12. Wherever the destination, he would arrive there accompanied by two ushers — Major Harold Usher of the Lincoln and Welland Regiment, and Company Sergeant-Major H.C. Usher.

Their vehicle went directly to a personnel depot near San Vito, high above the Adriatic and overlooking the Moro River. There Fox and Major Usher were met by Bert Kennedy who took them to his headquarters northwest of Ortona. Major Usher was to take command of Support Company and Fox found that he was to replace a famous RSM with only one day to look around. There wouldn't even be time to visit all the companies.

January 13 was a day of heavy shelling in the San Nicola-San Tommaso area and Duffy felt that it was all concentrating on the house where the mortar platoon was located. Stan Down had invited him to have lunch there. On the upper floor of the big stone house they sat down at a table with a white cloth on it and sparkling glasses for the wine. During the meal mortar shells came whining over the village and shaking the already battered buildings as they landed. The mortar platoon's house shook and the glasses kept tinkling. Duffy was scared but he couldn't admit it.

Duffy and Fox weren't able to tour the whole Regimental area in the one day they had together, but they went everywhere that was reasonably safe in daylight. Fox soon learned to choose routes that included stream beds or other depressions in the ground, into which he could dive for cover.

By noon on January 14 an era had ended.

The war diary described the event in a very offhand way: "In the afternoon RSM Angus Duffy left the battalion for England to take over duties as pre-arranged on the exchange of personnel program. RSM H. Fox took over the duties of RSM upon his leaving Bn. HQ."

But an unofficial diarist caught the significance of what was happening. Company quartermaster sergeant Basil Smith wrote:

"RSM Duffy left us today, returning to England on an exchange scheme. . . . We are all going to miss him like hell, because he is a great guy, a 100 per cent soldier, and perhaps more than any of us he seems to be the personification of the unit and its spirit."

A few weeks later near Ortona, Fox met an RCR officer who had been RSM of that battalion in England. He was surprised to learn that Duffy had gone. "Were you sent out from England to replace him?" the major asked.

Fox remained RSM of the Hasty Ps through the rest of the war and did a good job. But the Queen's Own didn't have permanent appointments in mind when they sent men to the Mediterranean for experience.

"The understanding was that, as in Africa, selected personnel were to be attached to units for a short time . . ." a Queen's

Own historian wrote later. "In the event, however, immediately after arrival in Italy, all were transferred to 1st Division units. This action rankled for a long time."*

A Canadian Press story from Italy in the Belleville Intelligencer of February 11, 1944, said that Duffy had returned to England on exchange. An officer was quoted as saying: "He earned the rest by his conscientious work out here, but left under protest and determined to return. The officer who said that Duffy was "wearing himself out" called him "the kingpin of the battalion."

Moving from the life Duffy had known in the Regiment from September, 1939, to the uninspiring surroundings of the Canadian base at Avellino would have eroded any active soldier's morale, but there was much more discouragement to come.

144

On January 27 Duffy embarked for England. On February 8 he was taken on strength at No. 5 Canadian Infantry Reinforcement Unit in Aldershot and in mid-March he was transferred to No. 4 CIRU. It was soon obvious that there had been no official arrangement to employ him as an instructor of invasion troops. "I'm a good instructor — put me to work," he urged his superior officers with almost no success. One Sunday he was called out to take charge of a parade of several hundred men and march them to the site of their day-long duties, shovelling coal. The warrant officer who gave him the assignment received a tongue-lashing from Duffy that must have left him shaking.

It has been said of those weeks leading up to the Normandy invasion that so many troops were being massed for the assault and for reinforcement roles that in the south of England it seemed to be standing room only. In the Aldershot area there were a dozen or so reinforcement battalions. Duffy was posted to No. 10 and then to No. 11.

* Lt. Col. W.T. Barnard, *The Queen's Own Rifles of Canada 1860-1960*, p. 184.

He was shocked to find how utterly untrained these thousands of young Canadians were. They seemed to have no awareness of basic infantry tactics. They were paraded three or four times a day, for roll calls, and little else.

Duffy did have one brief chance to instruct about 70 men from a battalion scheduled to reinforce a Highland unit about four hours after the landing. He quickly ordered them to follow him as he ran to a nearby woods. He told them to take off unnecessary equipment and informally he quickly explained the basics of fire and movement — how an advancing squad must always have "one leg on the ground" — a stationary group to give covering fire with rifles and automatic weapons to keep enemy heads down. He spent the next couple of days putting them through the drills for sections and platoons in attack and defence. They seized this new knowledge with enthusiasm. Ten years or so later at a Militia camp Duffy met an officer from the Stormont, Dundas and Glengarry Highlanders who thanked him for this brief training session which, he said, had ensured his own survival and that of his platoon in the hours right after being committed to battle.

The eager response of these reinforcements made Duffy feel that for at least some fleeting hours he was finding a useful role. Unfortunately, however, the syllabus called for a gas lecture, which to Duffy was absolute nonsense. Fighting troops in Sicily and Italy didn't carry gas masks. They had faced the toughest of German troops and had found no indication that the enemy was even thinking of chemical warfare.

After he had gathered the men around him, Duffy showed his contempt for this part of the training program in a few words. "This is a respirator," he said. "If there is a gas alarm or if you smell something awful, put it on. And leave it on until some idiot takes his off. If he doesn't drop dead, take yours off too. . . . End of gas lecture." A major approached just at that moment. He blasted Duffy for his light-hearted remarks. Duffy protested: "These men may be on their way tomorrow, sir. They'll need to know about more important things."

"You'll carry out the instruction as laid down. . . . What's more, you're improperly dressed."

"How's that, sir?"

"Your records show that you were wounded. You aren't wearing a wound stripe."

"In my Regiment, sir, if I ever put up a wound stripe, they'd laugh their heads off."

The major had had enough. Duffy was re-assigned.

As the days and weeks slipped by, Duffy's chances of returning to action seemed to be getting slimmer and slimmer. Reg Abraham, his company commander in the early weeks of the war, was commanding an infantry reinforcement unit, but unable to intervene on his behalf.

The Regiment left Ortona in April, moved westward and went into action in mid-May. Heavy fighting in the Liri Valley, west of Cassino, brought the Hastings more battle honours, helping to smash the Hitler Line in the drive for Rome. On June 4 the U.S. Fifth Army captured Rome and on June 6 Allied forces fought their way ashore in Normandy. Italy was soon to become a forgotten front and Duffy kept wondering how long the 1st Division would remain there. If he couldn't get a posting back to the Regiment, why couldn't he be assigned to some infantry battalion in France? Surely there would be an opening for a warrant officer with battle experience.

For a brief period in early summer Duffy had a chance to work with a group of battle-experienced officers and NCOs in establishing a campsite for 13 Battalion in the countryside between Aldershot and Crookham Crossroads. Tents to accommodate 1,200 soldiers had to be located, as well as men and materials for the construction of ablution huts at great speed. The deadline was met, thanks to a corporal who appeared periodically with truckloads of lumber from some undisclosed source. The troops arrived on schedule and their accommodation was ready, but they were hardly settled before they were on draft for the Continent.

Duffy wanted badly to go to France with this reinforcement battalion, but the officer in charge said he had strict orders to keep Duffy in Aldershot. However, a few miles away, there was a colonel looking for a good RSM.

The Canadian Section G.H.Q. 2nd Echelon which served with the 21st Army Group was a personnel records office for Canadians in Northwest Europe. Its Advance Reinforcement Control Officers (ARCOs), travelling in jeeps or on motorcycles close to the action, would be the links between the fighting troops and the reinforcement battalions, reporting casualties and reinforcement needs. Colonel V.S.C. McClenaghan, who had commanded a similar unit in the Sicilian campaign, took command of 2nd Echelon and set up headquarters in the pleasant town of Farnham. An advance group went to France shortly after the landing, but at Farnham the colonel had under his command hundreds of senior NCOs who had been in administrative work so long that they were distinctly unsoldierly in appearance. Even the arrival in their midst of members of the Canadian Women's Army Corps didn't have the smartening-up effect that might have been expected. The unit had an RSM, but he was no disciplinarian and certainly no parade square soldier. The colonel knew that he had to take the unit to France — in fact a location had been chosen — and he wanted someone who could help him to maintain the standards necessary for successful operation in the field.

One July night in Aldershot Duffy received orders to be ready to leave early the next morning. A driver met him at his quarters at the appointed time and they drove the few miles to Farnham. When they reached their destination Duffy could scarcely believe his eyes when he saw how many of the troops were members of the CWAC. This was 2nd Echelon, he was told, and he had better report to the Camp

Commandant. That officer told him that he was to be assistant RSM, a terrible come-down from being RSM of a 1st Division infantry battalion.

Duffy couldn't see how he could fit in with about 30 warrant officers and 400 senior NCOs who were all paperwork specialists. Clearly it was some time since many had polished their cap badges or made their beds properly or appeared on a parade. When paraded before Colonel McClenaghan he got a courteous hearing but no sympathy. "I want you for discipline, Mr. Duffy," he said, "and you know what that means — you'll do what you're told."

The thoughts of such an unsoldierly unit going to France in the condition he found it spurred Duffy to action. He made it known why he was there and that a new regime would begin with PT the next morning. Only a few NCOs fell in for PT. Duffy went into the barracks, confronted a warrant officer twice his size and backed him into a corner. "I'm an RSM, sir to you, and we're going to straighten this unit up. You won't be going to your office this morning; you're going to show me through your lines." The deplorable state of these quarters seemed serious enough to confine everyone to barracks until everything was clean and tidy, but the officers insisted that these NCOs must be at their desks. Basically, however, he had the colonel's support for his disciplinary efforts, and better still, a promise that he could transfer to the infantry as soon as 2nd Echelon was well established under canvas in France.

On August 13 the unit left Farnham by train, spent a night in tents in a marshalling area near the south coast and embarked the next day at Portsmouth in U.S. landing craft. A zig-zag course in the Channel brought 2nd Echelon to Mulberry Harbour at Arromanches on the 15th. The next day the unit occupied large technical school and other buildings in the village of La Delivrande, about a mile inland from Luc-sur-Mer. Senior officers' quarters were in a chateau. Other male officers, warrant officers and NCOs were in tents in a walled apple orchard at Clos du Coq, less than half a mile from the main office building in La Delivrande. The three CWAC officers and 91 other ranks were in marquee tents.

This camp was only seven miles from the front the first night. Enemy anti-aircraft guns could be heard and the sky was striped with tracers. A Canadian advance soon opened up considerable distance between 2nd Echelon and the front, but the fighting seemed close at times. Spent shells from air battles often dropped on La Delivrande. The Germans tried to drop sea mines on the Channel at night and came under fire from artillery near the front and in the Mulberry Harbour area. One night a German airman, trying to drop mines near a warship in the Channel, was attacked by the RAF and let his mines go over land. They landed close to the apple orchard. The shock waves brought apples pounding down on the tents.

"The top of my head seemed to be blown off by the explosion," CWAC Sergeant Rosaline Madder recalled many years later. "But I heard a voice that sounded miles away telling everyone to get fully dressed, with greatcoat, steel helmet and rubber boots and to take a blanket and get into a slit trench. We stayed there in two inches of water until it was discovered what had caused the commotion and it was certain that we weren't in any danger."

Soon the men and women of this administrative unit were busy with the mass of detail they were trained to handle — first and foremost the reinforcement flow, but also casualty figures, tracing lost mail, straightening out currency problems, dealing with the locations for mobile baths, tracing missing identity discs and even hospital patients' lost dentures. In September the war diary told of sorting out the problems of a reinforcement private who had no identification and had been put into a prisoner-of-war cage for transfer to England.

Duffy had worked at a fierce pace setting up the camp and soon requested the promised transfer to the infantry. The colonel kept his part of the bargain and provided him with transportation to the nearest infantry reinforcement battalion. But the longed-for return to infantry action was not to be.

Within a few hours the driver returned with a message from Colonel McClenaghan. The RSM left in charge had departed very suddenly and the C.O. wanted Duffy to take over. There was nothing to do but to return and soldier on. Duffy wasn't happy.

By mid-September CMHQ in London was pressing 2nd Echelon to move closer to the action. Antwerp was mentioned, although it was still under shellfire. This greatest port in Northwest Europe had been liberated by the 11th Armoured Division of the British Second Army on September 4 with dock installations mainly intact, but its capacity to receive 40,000 tons of cargo daily couldn't be used, because approaches from the sea were still in German hands. Indeed the Germans still held the northern fringes of Antwerp when the 2nd Canadian Division moved in on September 16. As October began, the 1st Canadian Army took on the task of clearing the Scheldt Estuary of Germans. The battle began on October 2, the day a 2nd Echelon convoy arrived from France.

Offices were set up in the Caisse Hypothecaire Anversoise building at 24 Meir Plaza. During the German occupation it had housed a section of the Gestapo. Some walls were bullet-scarred and bloodstained. Torture devices were found in the basement. CWAC quarters were set up on the top floor.

Immediately following the arrival in Antwerp Colonel McClenaghan issued orders requiring strict deportment by all ranks, correct dress, soldierly bearing and saluting. Unit parades were ordered for 8:25 every morning with markers falling in at 8:20. A major asked a memorably stupid question. Could the RSM form up a parade? (Could Winston Churchill make a speech? Could Douglas Bader fly?) For years Duffy often put the whole 1st Infantry Brigade on parade. He got back at the questioner by putting the CWAC in the place of honour on the right — mainly because they were so much smarter than the men.

The CWAC NCOs liked Duffy. "I gradually became aware of a stocky little man with a stentorian voice, ruddy complexion, bright hazel eyes, and when he allowed himself — a grin like a Cheshire cat," one of them recalled 37 years later. "He was humorous and polite and kept his language under control, but became highly flustered when certain subjects were discussed — such as a shortage of feminine necessities in the QM stores. Although he asked me repeatedly to call him Angus, I just couldn't force myself to do it. To me, anyone with the magic rank of RSM was a sort of demigod."

Duffy certainly admired the CWAC. "In a large metropolitan city, so recently occupied by the Germans, our girls were very much on show," he said looking back from the 1970s. "The obvious question from the Belgians was whether they were the same sort of girls as those who accompanied the Germans. They soon showed that they most certainly weren't. They were tremendously good soldiers and a credit to Canada."

Their families would have been desperately worried, had they known how close these young women were to the front line. Enemy forces in the Scheldt estuary were only a few miles away. A male officer who lived in an Antwerp apartment had Belgian neighbours who had two sons who were fighting the Germans and they came home to meals occasionally, travelling both ways by trolley.

The 2nd Echelon war diary noted on December 2 that a new location for the unit was being discussed. A week later a V-2 rocket landed 150 yards from the front door, half-destroying a building occupied by the Belgian police. Many of its occupants were killed or wounded. Many others were brought out by a 20-man rescue squad under Warrant Officer Pat O'Donnell. Other 2nd Echelon personnel helped the civilian firefighters.

The only damage to 24 Meir Plaza was broken glass, but

the splinters that flew around one CWAC typist shredded the paper in her machine and cut her hands badly. Four CWAC "battle injuries" were reported. Others working in the same area had their cuts bandaged up and they continued with their duties.

Colonel McClenaghan and Duffy continued to remind all ranks that soldierly deportment was required at all times. In a unit with good morale there are ways of showing the brass that sometimes things can be taken too seriously. This possibly accounted for the light-hearted message which appeared in the office one day:

NOTICE

DEPORTMENT

Personnel who indulge in the delightful pastime of "kissing their boy friends good-night" will find some dark secluded doorway, around any convenient corner, but will NOT put on their performance in front of the main office building for the benefit of the RSM, who is the jealous type, also a stickler for form, and would probably insist upon giving you a demonstration of how it should really be done.

In order to avoid this, as well as losing your best "Boy Friend", the only course left open for you is to obey the above order. That is all.

R. Madder, Sgt.

On December 16 the Germans began their desperate Ardennes offensive with which Hitler hoped to regain Brussels and Antwerp.*

Flying bombs and rockets increased in the Antwerp area. The Rex Cinema was hit during a Saturday afternoon matinee on the 16th and the bodies of two 2nd Echelon men were found. It became clear in a few days that enemy ground

* For background see C.P. Stacey, *The Victory Campaign*, Chapters XVI and XVII and R.S. Malone, *Missing From The Record*, Chapter XI.

forces were being contained, but it was still expected that paratroops might try to disrupt communications. On December 19 the CWAC left Antwerp for 2nd Echelon's new location in school buildings at Alost, 35 miles away between Brussels and Ghent. They highly resented having to leave the excitement of Antwerp.

Fog settled over Antwerp for several days, adding to the confusion about whether or not the area was being penetrated by the enemy. All remaining 2nd Echelon personnel were ordered to carry weapons and ammunition. The colonel had already ordered Duffy to prepare to defend the 10-storey building and at last the frustrated RSM had something like a fighting soldier's assignment. He was given 50 general duty men with small arms and grenades. But at the same time preparations to move went ahead quickly and the main body of the unit left Antwerp on Christmas Eve for Alost.

At Athaneum School, Alost, December 25 was a working day. The CWAC already had invitations to Christmas dinners in the town. Male members of the unit had stew and corned beef in the sergeants' mess.

On Boxing Day Duffy organized a defence squad of 21 to be assigned from a duty roster to guard the main building and to maintain guard posts at a nearby bridge over the Dendre River. Sentries were placed on the CWAC quarters, the officers' mess and the QM stores.

In the main school building there were no blackout curtains and on the night of the 26th everyone was working. The lights were on, and could be turned out quickly when an alarm sounded. But aircraft were over the building before any alarm sounded. Machine gun bullets ripped through a window and cut a metal leg off a table at which some CWAC were working. CWAC coats hanging in a row along one wall were riddled, but no person was hit.

On December 30 all Allied forces in the Alost sub-zone, consisting of Royal Marines, Royal Army Service Corps and 2nd Echelon, were placed under Colonel McClenaghan's command. For several days and nights Duffy never went to his billet. He kept his sleeping bag in the office and took only brief rests between inspections of the various posts. He was appalled sometimes to find men asleep or lacking ammunition. He longed to be with fighting soldiers again. In a Christmas letter to his sister, Nadine, he said that he had no enthusiasm for anything, even Christmas, adding: "I still miss the Regiment like hell."

Duffy concluded that he had little chance of being reassigned to the infantry from Alost. When a 30-day rotation leave to Canada became available he took it, convinced that it would be the best route back to the Regiment.

On February 14 he disembarked in Canada and proceeded to Kingston. After two weeks at home, he hastened to return to the Kingston depot, but received no encouragement there for the idea of a quick trip to any European battlefield. "Go home and finish your leave," he was told. "We aren't sending anybody over just now." By then the Hasty Ps had reached Northwest Europe.

At the end of his leave Duffy reported back to No. 3 District Depot in Kingston, but no one seemed interested in his desire to return to the Regiment. He spoke at Victory Loan rallies in Prince Edward County in April, and later that month he was posted to No. 2 Transit Camp, Debert, N.S. But there the journey ended. Assuming another name, he fell in with a draft going overseas under the command of a Hasty P officer, but unfortunately the camp RSM spotted him. A week after his arrival in Debert the war in Europe ended.

Missing the Regiment desperately, he departed dramatically from his usual form and set out to get drunk with another warrant officer whom he had known in England. After nightfall he went outside the sergeants' mess to identify himself in the only way he could with victorious comrades far away. In his superb parade ground voice he called on parade, drilled and dismissed every platoon of every company of the nine infantry battalions in the 1st Canadian Division . . . and keeled over.

Chapter Twelve
A legend works long hours

The Allies were still at war with Japan and it was anyone's guess how long hostilities would last. Duffy hoped to join one of the battalions in Canada's Pacific Force, but it was mid-June before he got a transfer from Debert back to No. 3 District Depot in Kingston. A Hastings battalion was being organized in Kingston, but there was no slot for Duffy. He needed an operation for a hernia resulting from extreme exertion setting up the 2nd Echelon camp in France the previous summer, so he entered the Kingston General Hospital. A month later he was transferred to No. 2 Conditioning Centre in Brampton and was still there when Japan was atomic-bombed into surrender.

Duffy and Sgt. Tom Madill celebrated VJ Day fairly quietly in the sergeants' mess, but it was a different story when they returned to their quarters that night. Madill was on crutches and Duffy on two canes. "We're Hasty Ps," Madill announced, "and my sergeant-major can lick anybody." Someone who objected to this rather belligerent awakening grabbed his cane and pulled Madill's crutches out from under him. Duffy came to the defence of his comrade but got a pounding for his trouble. The two Hasty Ps were on charge the next morning, but before they were called before the C.O., Bert Kennedy appeared as if by magic and interceded for them successfully. Duffy went on leave, reporting to the Depot in Kingston in late September.

His services had been requested in connection with the Regiment's return, expected in early October.

Hundreds of Hasty Ps who had served overseas were already home by early fall and a get-together was arranged for September 28 at the Picton Fair. A crowd of townspeople greeted the veterans enthusiastically when they marched by and the warmth of that welcome mellowed even the RSM. When called upon to speak, he said: "For the first time in six years I'm telling you fellows that you're good."

The Ile de France docked in Halifax on October 1 and Duffy was on his way to meet the troops before they reached Montreal aboard two trains. Those trains reached Belleville station about 9 o'clock on the perfect fall morning of October 4. The 530 officers and men were greeted by the younger and older soldiers of the 2nd Battalion who had not been able to serve overseas, and by wounded comrades who had arrived home earlier.

Families and other loved ones stood many rows deep around the edge of the station square as the returning troops formed up to march downtown. Some of the welcoming crowd who had shared their battles fell in too. The 1st Battalion turned the Colours over to the 2nd Battalion and the parade moved off.

Leading the column along the route narrowed by cheering crowds was Major Allen Ross DSO, of Montreal, a gallant officer who had been in command for months but had been denied his lieutenant-colonelcy by someone with more authority than sense.

The Regiment marched behind its prized battle flag, worked on beautiful blue silk by the soft hands of Italian nuns in a convent near Campobasso. "There goes the best fighting unit of them all," Telegram war correspondent Bert Wemp told local newsmen, for he had covered their exploits from the time they went into action.

The music of four bands swept the returning warriors and the crowd along toward the centre of the city. Brigadier

Graham took the salute near the courthouse. At the Armoury came the final 'Dismiss!' and the heroes of the hour rushed to a thousand embraces.

Only four of them had gone overseas with the Regiment in December, 1939 — Company Quartermaster Sergeant Lee Eames, Company Sergeant-Major A.J. Campbell, Sergeant Wilfred Hunter and Sergeant Stanley Scruby.

Duffy had been longing for almost 21 months to be back with the 1st Battalion, but its reappearance was fleeting and some of the men in the ranks were strangers who had come home with the Hastings only because they were from Eastern Ontario. He had discovered that for an RSM life without his Regiment was no life at all. He had never wanted to leave it. However, the lonely months did not dilute his enthusiasm for soldiering, but being shuffled from pillar to post by people who had never heard a shot fired led him to decline a peacetime career in the Regular Force.

Duffy refused to let a very natural resentment consume him. His love for his Regiment was as constant as his love of country and it was to be a guiding force for the rest of his days.

The two counties were at peace, but their great Regiment did not fade away. Duffy received his discharge from the Active Force in Kingston on October 13 and returned to Belleville by way of Picton where he enlisted as a private in the postwar reserve battalion. He was made a company sergeant-major almost immediately and was RSM by November.

For the youths and older men who had kept the 2nd Battalion alive in wartime and for the other veterans who joined up on returning, he was the old Duffy. However, it was soon clear that the reserve battalion was barely alive. Staff officers of Military District 3 in Kingston had found that training had ceased in Bancroft and the Madoc company had no training syllabus, one report noted. On a November visit to the Picton Armoury on a parade night, a staff officer found no one present but the caretaker and issued a blast about curtailing training without official approval. Duffy's long pent-up enthusiasm was to provide a strong stimulus for the battalion to become more active and attract more men.

But he did have to give some attention to finding his own feet in civvy street. In November he learned that a service station business on Front Street in Belleville was for sale. He managed to raise $3,000 and was soon in business under the Cities Service sign. Below it he hung a large 56 — the number that identified the Regiment in the 1st Division. No passing Hasty P could miss it.

The Belleville Intelligencer described him as having "relegated the glamor and bloodshed of war, with its parade grounds, route marches, blaring of bands . . . and dress parades to the limbo of memory." He was quoted as saying: "I should call it Duffy's tavern, but that would be stretching it too far. It's going to be sort of funny after all. Some of the boys of my old Regiment will probably get a great kick out of it.

"You can imagine one of my buck privates driving up and saying 'Fill 'er up, my man, and do it smartly.' And I'll have to say more or less meekly, 'Yes sir.' "

For the next 16 years from 7:00 a.m. to 11:00 p.m. six days a week, and occasionally on Sundays, the station was open and the proprietor dispensed a good deal of social service while assisting the travelling public. As RSM and soon president of Legion Branch 99, Duffy was an unofficial veterans' advocate in matters of pensions, medical treatment and the Veterans Land Act. In his memory was an invaluable file of information about hundreds of veterans, details about their service, disabilities, job situations and family circumstances. The station was recognized by Department of Veterans Affairs people in Kingston as the de facto Belleville office of DVA. Duffy not only identified problems for the DVA, but was often able to work out solutions. The problem-solving RSM didn't talk about his activities in this field, but in effect he was a marriage counsellor and financial counsellor to many a troubled veteran. He made many emergency loans that were never repaid.

In a speech to the Picton Legion he explained why he gave so much time to veterans: "I feel that we who have had the responsibility of giving orders have to make up for the harm done and the courage expended as a result of those orders."

The reserve battalion under the command of Lt.-Col. W.A. Davern of Wellington had one company in Picton and others in Bancroft, Madoc, Frankford, Trenton and Wellington, but accommodation in the distant places was poor and enthusiasm waning. A Belleville company was under consideration.

Duffy had much more than business and military matters on his mind — he was thinking of seeking public office later in the year. But before that came marriage to Helena Mary Bell with whom he went to high school in Trenton. The wedding was in St. James Chapel, St. Mary's Cathedral in Kingston on Wednesday, August 7, 1946. At the wedding breakfast the three-tiered cake was cut with an Italian dagger given to the bridegroom overseas by an Italian colonel. John Cote, a famed signal sergeant of the Hasty Ps, was the best man.

It was clear that the Regiment would have to be reorganized and revitalized if it was to carry on in peacetime in a way befitting a unit which could trace its origins to Loyalist battalions and had returned from overseas with such a distinguished record. Duffy felt that it had to be conspicuous in Belleville, the largest community in its sprawling territory. He saw Belleville as the natural hub of unit activity.

The 9th Anti-Tank Regiment, earlier known as the Argyll Light Infantry, held the Bridge Street Armoury, and although the Hasty Ps were supposed to have reasonable access to parts of it, the city unit gave the Plough Jockeys little encouragement. A small old building on Church Street, immediately east of the Armoury had been occupied by the 34th Battery which the 9th Anti-Tank had absorbed, and it would serve as headquarters for a Belleville company of Hasty Ps. District Headquarters in Kingston liked the idea. A staff officer visited Duffy who agreed to act as company sergeant-major as well as RSM. Max Porritt who had won the Military Cross in Italy would command the company.

Regimental headquarters were in Picton where The Times kept the public well informed about military matters. In a letter to the editor about recruiting Duffy said the reserve unit expressed the willingness of a free people to fight if their freedom is threatened. Recalling the struggles of the Militia to survive in the 1930s, he wrote in a spirit of total commitment:

"Again the people of Canada have forgotten their defences. Again like wanton children they have thrown away their army that was produced with so much blood and sweat. Again some stout-hearted men must fall in and hold that very thin line, so that the spirit that saved us from Hitler and our own apathy will not die. Suppose that we cannot find these stout-hearted fellows. Suppose that the old fire is dead. Then I say to you that Canada will die."

In December, 1946, Duffy was elected a Belleville alderman on a platform of expediting housing for veterans. His message was blunt. Ex-servicemen should have priority, he said, but they were being outbid by civilians who had stayed home and made money. Congratulations on his election came from Lord Tweedsmuir who wrote:

"I only wish more people like yourself would go into municipal and national politics in every country. I remember you mentioning it to me in a talk we had by candlelight at Castropignano, and you said that you thought you might try your hand at politics when the war was over. In those days we used to talk rather hazily about the end of the war, because, although we knew it must inevitably end one day, we had no reason to suppose that either you or I would be there to see it."

Duffy told one church group after the election that a housing registry had 250 applications which meant that about 750 people lacked accommodation. There were 100 houses in Belleville that had been condemned by medical authorities but were still being occupied. Because of selfishness and blindness home building in Belleville was 20 years behind the times, he declared.

Getting land opened up for housing required a bitter battle at City Hall. The Belleville Property Owners Association, Belleville Industrial Commission and the directors of the Chamber of Commerce were all against it and it was the spring of 1949 before Council voted 8 to 7 to approve development of the former County Home property on the eastern edge of the city. Duffy's aldermanic influence wasn't great enough to see that a group of contiguous streets were named Hastings, Prince Edward and Regiment, but a new residential area did contain a Hastings Drive and the Duffys built a home on it.

The RSM was a leading spirit in the Regimental Association which organized annual reunions on October weekends. They attracted several hundred Hasty Ps on each occasion. Some of these events were rowdier than others, but on the Sunday memorial parade the marching was impeccable. Wartime padres conducted the memorial services and wreaths were laid on cenotaphs. There was great concern for the Regiment's progress and concern for the families of whose who did not return from battle. The Regimental Association established a Scholarship Fund to assist the education of several young people whose fathers had given their lives. The Association raised $6,000 and in the next decade 11 students benefitted.

Hasty Ps living beyond the Regimental area organized social clubs as branches of the Association. Some were named after battles, such as the Assoro Club in Toronto and the Naviglio Club in Kingston. In Oshawa they formed the Ack-Ack Kennedy Club and in Peterborough it was the Duffy Club. Duffy asked why the club hadn't chosen the name of a battle. Paddy Gahagan replied: "If you don't think you were one long battle so far as the rest of us are concerned, you're crazy."

From November, 1946 to March, 1948, Lt. Col. W.K. Stockloser who had been second in command in Italy, was in command of the Regiment, succeeding W.A. Davern. At the same time two other wartime officers were commanding reserve units — A.A. Kennedy, the Grey and Simcoe Foresters in Owen Sound; and Lyall Carr, the Midland Regiment in Port Hope. Don Cameron, in the Regular Force, was in command of Fort Churchill.

By October, 1948, three years after the reserve battalion accepted the Colours from the wartime battalion, there were clear signs that the unit had regained the spirit it needed to become great again. A reunion in Belleville greeted CSM George Ponsford who had come from South Africa; Don Cameron who had taken command of the PPCLI and Major-General Howard Graham who had returned from a two-year posting in London to become Deputy Chief of the General Staff.

The new commanding officer, appointed that month, was clearly the man to bring back the smartness of wartime years.

Lt.-Col. R.W.K. Abraham, OBE, who had served overseas in the First World War, joined the Regiment in 1923 as a lieutenant, went overseas as quartermaster in 1939 and later became a staff officer. By 1948 he was District Administrator of the Department of Veterans Affairs in Kingston. He managed to spend much of his time in the next 12 months in the Regimental area. He was a great organizer and his high standards attracted good people.

Facilities in the Armouries in Picton, Belleville, Trenton and Frankford were improved. Imaginative training exercises were carried out, such as a river crossing at Foxboro and a large number of wartime officers and NCOs were taken on strength. Bill Graydon, who had won the Military Cross in Italy and had been severely wounded, was given command of 'C' Company in his home town of Picton.

Max Porritt's Headquarters Company in Belleville grew

in strength. Wartime quartermaster George Hepburn was back, with Kippy McAlpin as RQMS. Joe Nayler took over 'B' Company in Madoc with Percy Gray as one of his officers. Support Company was in Trenton; 'A' Company was in Frankford but moved to Bancroft in the spring of 1948 where car dealer Cliff Broad and newspaper editor Stan Walker were officer stalwarts and Jack Milne a key NCO. Bancroft, nearly 100 miles north of the unit's most southerly Armoury at Picton, didn't remain a strongpoint for many years. Training took place in a community centre beside a church. The floor above ground provided drill space and in the basement was a canteen which was sometimes a little noisy. Some neighbours expressed their objections to federal authorities.

In mid-September, 1949, Reg Abraham retired and Max Porritt began three eventful years in command of a battalion moving steadily toward a standard of performance that was in keeping with the wartime record of the Hasty Ps. This period brought not a few surprises — particularly for Duffy.

It was almost 10 years since he had become RSM and he was planning to retire and give younger men an opportunity to hold this uniquely important post. His obvious successor was Stan Down of Trenton, CSM of a company and before that an outstanding mortar sergeant in action.

The idea of losing Duffy by retirement didn't sit well with Max Porritt and his second in command, Bill Graydon. Duffy hadn't exactly said that he was going to leave the Regiment. They wondered if he would stay on as an officer and concluded that he would. Getting approval to commission him after 10 years as an RSM seemed to be an unlikely prospect, but Porritt and Graydon thought it was an idea worth pursuing. They went to see Major-General Chris Vokes, a tough 1st Division commander who was familiar with Duffy's record in action. Vokes liked the idea and successfully recommended it to Lieut.-General Charles Foulkes, Chief of the General Staff in Ottawa. Porritt and

Graydon kept their plan to themselves and told Duffy they agreed it was time for him to step down as RSM.

On December 14 companies from Belleville, Picton, Madoc, Marmora, Bancroft and Trenton were on parade in the Bridge Street Armoury. Many of the 260 men wore Second World War medals. History was to be made.

Duffy formed up the battalion for the annual inspection by the Area Commander, Brigadier Geoffrey Walsh, who was accompanied on this occasion by the former C.O., Colonel Abraham. After the inspection Duffy performed his last act as RSM — presenting his badges of rank to Stan Down. He took up a position in the ranks. Then came the surprise.

Duffy was immediately called to the front and the adjutant, Capt. Len Hyslop, read the official order that made him a lieutenant. "If ever a man deserved a commissioned rank in the Canadian Army, it is Mr. Duffy." Colonel Porritt told the cheering Regiment and the applauding crowd in the balcony.

Brig. Walsh placed the symbols of his new rank on Duffy's shoulders during a post-parade reception. Colonel Abraham was given a silver tray as a token of appreciation for revitalizing the Regiment during his period of command. The colonel replied: "I am glad to see Duffy get his commission. In fact, I had it in mind in 1941. . . . Now, like me, he is growing old and is no longer the rip-roaring sergeant-major of old, although he was in good voice tonight. I am glad that he accepted the commission, something he should have done years ago. Seeing Angus Duffy get his commission is the highlight of my Army career."

Duffy felt that he owed it to the Regiment in gratitude for the commission, to stay on as an officer for a year or two. Later when he discussed with Porritt the tradition of Hasty P officers always being qualified for the next higher rank, the C.O. suggested that the best way to lead was by example. Duffy had no comeback for that and soon found himself taking courses and more courses.

Life in the 1950s turned out to be even more complicated than in the late 1940s. Alderman Duffy, businessman Duffy, Boy Scout Commissioner Duffy and Lieut. Duffy had to become accustomed to 20-hour work days.

In the deep midwinter Saturday of January 20, 1951, Lord and Lady Tweedsmuir paid their first visit to Belleville, after spending an evening with the Assoro Club in Toronto. Lord Tweedsmuir inspected the Regiment on parade, praised all ranks for their smartness and declared: "You are often in my thoughts and you will never do better than I wish for you." He apologized for not instantly recognizing old comrades whom he had never seen in civilian clothes before.

A Canadian Press story in The Globe and Mail on the following Monday said: "It was a day replete with wisecracks and reminiscences, like the corporal's advice to Angus Duffy at the dinner. Mr. Duffy apologized because there was no microphone and asked if he could be heard at the back of the room — he who could put an entire brigade through its paces by voice, unaided. 'Don't worry sir,' cracked a corporal, 'just speak in a regimental whisper.' "

Just eight days later the Regiment won praise from Brig. Walsh at the annual inspection. About 280 all ranks marched with precision behind the band of the Royal Canadian Corps of Signals, from Kingston. On parade were members of 'A' Company from Bancroft, 'B' Company from Madoc, 'C' and 'D' Companies from Picton, Support Company from Trenton and Headquarters Company from Belleville. Veterans seemed to be increasing and wartime officers were more conspicuous than ever. Howard Reid, Jim Bird, Fred Burtt, R.F. (Dude) Dafoe, Fred Lazier, Joe Johnson and Bob Scott brought the total to 14. Duffy was about to go on full-time service.

On April 1, 1951, it was announced that he had been called out for three months' administration and training duty to improve communications among the companies scattered between Picton and Bancroft, but within a month he was busy with an entirely new task.

A Canadian Brigade was to be recruited for North Atlantic Treaty Organization forces in Western Europe, consisting of an infantry battalion, a rifle battalion and a highland battalion. An all-star lineup of reserve units from across Canada would raise one company each for one of the NATO battalions and one for reinforcement purposes.

Contributors to the 1st Canadian Infantry Battalion were the Hasty Ps, Les Fusiliers Mont-Royal, the Carleton and York Regiment, the Algonquin Regiment and the Loyal Edmonton Regiment. Officers, NCOs and men for the 1st Canadian Rifle Battalion were to come from the Queen's Own Rifles, the Victoria Rifles, the Royal Hamilton Light Infantry, the Royal Winnipeg Rifles and the Regina Rifle Regiment. The 1st Canadian Highland Battalion would include detachments from the Black Watch, the North Nova Scotia Highlanders, the 48th Highlanders, the Seaforth Highlanders and the Canadian Scottish Regiment.

Recruiting for the Hastings 'E' Company for the NATO Brigade and 'F' Company as reinforcements began in Belleville in May and demanded much of Duffy's time. He resigned from his post as Scout Commissioner.

The 9th Anti-Tank C.O. didn't take kindly to one of Duffy's recruiting ideas, which was to park military vehicles on the Armoury driveway bearing signs — MEN WANTED TO DRIVE THESE. Duffy defended his methods, insisting that his own C.O., Colonel Porritt, had instructed him to recruit men. Area Headquarters was consulted and ruled in Duffy's favour.

Major Bill Seamark, signals officer with the Regiment in England in 1940 and later a staff officer, was named commander of the Hastings company for NATO. A large proportion of those recruited were already members of the Regiment. An inspiring send-off from the Bridge Street Armoury on a Sunday in June was attended by former C.O.s, civic officials and members of the public. It featured a drumhead service conducted by the Regimental padre, Capt. A.S. McConnell, MBE. General Graham read the lesson and later inspected the company and took the salute.

With the company departing for final training at Valcartier, went Capt. Joe Johnson MC and Lieuts. George Hepburn, Bob Fisher and Barry Lind, CSMs P.V. Fitz-patrick and J.W. Hamilton, Sergeants Bill Sarley, Percy Kelly, Bob Wigmore, Clarence Whitman, D.F. Green, Eddie King and Harry Jones. Colonel Porritt presented a replica of the wartime battalion's battle flag and Little Chief, a four-foot wooden Indian of the same lineage as the Regiment's famous eight-foot Chief Petawawa-much, survivor of great battles in Europe.

Canada's NATO force became known as the 27th Brigade. Training proceeded at Valcartier throughout the summer and well into the fall. In mid-September Major George Baldwin, who had seen much action with the Regiment in Sicily and Italy, took command of the Hastings company. Brig. Geoffrey Walsh commanded the brigade.

In October, Princess Elizabeth, on her first Royal tour of Canada, inspected the Brigade in a colourful ceremony on the Plains of Abraham. The infantry battalion wore red berets, the rifle battalion green and the highlanders their traditional head-dress. A small number from the Hastings company attended the Regimental reunion in Belleville just before the Brigade sailed for Europe. By November all units were in place in Germany.

The return of Hasty Ps to Europe stirred many memories of the 1940s. Padre Fred Goforth and his wife, Joan, had sailed for Europe in late April, returning to Canada a few weeks later with an excellent array of colour slides of Britain, Italy and Holland. The padre's reunion account of his travels and the views of scores of familiar places made such an impression on the 200 men who looked and listened that the story of their own Regiment struck them more power-fully than ever before. The English landscape, the village pubs, the battlefields and the military cemeteries were such powerful reminders of events which shaped their lives that all agreed that it was a story for all Canadians to share.

The annual meeting of the Regimental Association the next morning eagerly approved Gordon Way's motion that an editorial board should begin collecting material for a Regimental history. A popular choice for chairman was Art Norrington of Calgary, a former journalist and teacher who had been adjutant of the Regiment in 1939 and with DVA since the war. A fund for this work was established and members began sending in donations. Farley Mowat's first book, People of the Deer, appeared in February, 1952, and there was little doubt that he was the man to write the story.

Duffy gave up the presidency of the Regimental Association at the 1951 reunion and was succeeded by Cam Wallbridge — not that Duffy would be any less involved in association affairs, but there was something else on the horizon. An Ontario election was called for November 22 and Alderman Duffy would be the Liberal candidate in the riding of Hastings West. He ran hard but finished second. Leslie Frost's Conservatives were returned in a landslide.

In 1952 Max Porritt was succeeded in command of the Regiment by Lt.-Col. R.H. Widdifield, a native of the Parry Sound district and a 1932 graduate of the Royal Military College who had served overseas in the Royal Canadian Corps of Signals. After the war he was in an RCCS reserve unit in Ottawa and had come to Belleville as branch manager of the Borden Co. Ltd.

Colonel Widdifield told veterans attending the 1952 reunion in Peterborough that he was proud to take command of the unit and pledged to maintain its traditions. The Hastings, with the Midland Regiment of Port Hope and the Princess of Wales Own Regiment of Kingston formed the 6th Infantry Brigade. Lyall Carr had been promoted to Brigadier to head this formation.

No unit deserved more to have its story told, Padre Goforth declared to resounding cheers at the reunion banquet. Bill Graydon became president, determined to see the history published. At a December meeting in Belleville Farley Mowat agreed to be the author. He and the padre began touring the Regimental area with notebook and tape recorder. Veterans began sending in written reminiscences.

County councils of Hastings and Prince Edward each

donated $1,000 and so did the Regiment. By May, 1953, Mowat was in England preparing to trace the Regimental route through Italy. By fall he was starting to piece the story together and calling on veterans for more personal recollections.

The Hasty P spirit was on the rise. Training officer Duffy became a captain. The Regiment won the 6th Brigade shield in camp at Niagara-on-the-Lake, but Duffy and other officers wanted to see more recognition at home — and the Regimental crest over the entrance to the Bridge Street Armoury. It was coming.

In May, 1953, the Chief of the General Staff assembled a panel of senior officers under the chairmanship of Major-General Howard Kennedy to review the role of the reserves, and the report came down in 1954. One recommendation, acted upon quickly, was the restoration of the name Militia. The Militia's primary role was defined as providing a partly trained and equipped nucleus for units that would be mobilized in an emergency.

The number of Militia units was reduced and one result was a conspicuous strengthening of the Hasty Ps. The Regiment absorbed the 9th Anti-Tank Regiment, formerly the Argyll Light Infantry, a unit with its roots deep in local history. Lt.-Col. E.S. Fairman, commissioned in the Argylls in 1937, an artillery officer overseas and in the 9th Anti-Tank after the war, became the new commanding officer of the Hastings. His friendliness and diplomacy had much to do with strengthening the union of the two old rivals.

Half of the Midland Regiment of Port Hope became part of the Hastings while half went to the Ontario Regiment and its colours were laid up in St. Mark's Church. It would soon be no problem at all to put 400 men on parade from Belleville, Madoc, Picton, Trenton, Port Hope, Millbrook and Norwood. Clearly the Regiment was one of the biggest and one of the best in the country. Duffy was becoming more involved in Militia matters than ever and he didn't seek re-election to City Council at the end of 1954.

Another veteran was directing much energy toward building up 'C' Company in Picton and he got the unit some good publicity in the process. "If the army is having trouble getting young Canadians into its chowline," said a Toronto Telegram story on December 30, "the military can make Major W.L. Graydon a general and let him solve recruiting."

About three months earlier Graydon had promised regular attenders a trip to an NHL hockey game in Toronto. He made good his promise by chartering a bus and taking 45 of his men to the Gardens. They saw a thrilling game and afterwards presented pewter steins to Conn Smythe and Gardens director John Bassett. The happy recruits included Private John Inrig who in 20 years would be a lieutenant-colonel commanding the Regiment.

In 1955 the Regiment continued to flourish. In that year Canadian Militia units had more people in camp than at any time since the war. Led by an excellent bugle band, 47 officers and 200 other ranks marched into Camp Niagara after crossing from Toronto aboard the SS. Cayuga. Duffy was a major by this time.

Hasty Ps were in the news that year. George Henderson of Burlington, who had served with distinction in Italy, completed four years as commanding officer of the Royal Hamilton Light Infantry and was promoted to colonel to head No. 17 Militia Group. In late summer came the announcement of Howard Graham's promotion to Lieut.-General to become Chief of the General Staff. Serving Militia officers and wartime officers gathered in Cobourg on August 27 to extend their personal congratulations. On the same occasion Don Cameron was congratulated on his promotion to Brigadier to command the 4th Infantry Brigade in Camp Borden.

The fall publication of Mowat's powerful history, simply titled The Regiment, was a literary landmark and an inspirational theme for the annual reunion.

As wartime Hasty Ps were gathering in Belleville on Saturday, October 15, Queen's University conferred an honorary Doctor of Laws degree on Lord Tweedsmuir . . .

"explorer, soldier, author whose interest in and knowledge of our northern frontiers is equalled by few Canadians, under whose command the Hastings and Prince Edward Regiment achieved great distinction in Italy. . . ." On the previous day 4,000 volumes and private papers of John Buchan, the first Lord Tweedsmuir, had been presented to Queen's as the gift of Colonel and Mrs. R.S. McLaughlin of Oshawa. Lord Tweedsmuir told Queen's students:

> "All human beings collect something. My collection is of people and places. It includes a good deal of wandering about this vast country, nearly 3,000 miles of it by dog team . . . a year in a Hudson's Bay post on Baffin Island . . . dust flying from the hooves of ponies in the cattle roundups of the West and grim-faced Ontario farmers shooting bitterly straight under the burning sun of Sicily and Italy."

Ceremonies marking the official dedication of the Regimental history took place in the Belleville Collegiate on the Sunday and afterwards Lord Tweedsmuir received thunderous applause from his old comrades when Colonel Fairman conferred on him the rank of Honorary Colonel.

"You've done me a very great honour I will remember all my life," he said. "We've probably the finest Regimental history in the world. The days of obscurity are long past. We started as a group of citizens, grafted onto a small nucleus. But the forces that left Britain to fight on the Continent were more professional than those of Haig and Wellington."

The great battles in Europe had ended a decade before, but the Regiment would not be resting on those laurels. Duffy, now second-in-command, was confident that its profile could be higher yet.

Chapter Thirteen
Who did this dreadful thing?

In May, 1957, Second World War battle honours were awarded and no unit got more than the Hastings & Prince Edward Regiment's 31. These honours commemorated the following battles in which the Regiment had distinguished itself:

Landing in Sicily
Grammichele
Valguarnera
Assoro
Agira
Adrano
Regalbuto
Sicily 1943
Landing at Reggio
Motta Montecorvino
Campobasso
Torella
The Moro
San Leonardo
The Gully
Ortona

Cassino II
Gustav Line
Liri Valley
Hitler Line
Gothic Line
Lamone Crossing
Misano Ridge
Rimini Line
San Fortunato
Bulgaria Village
Naviglio Canal
Fosse Vecchio
Italy 1943-1945
Apeldoorn
Northwest Europe 1945

Although the Regiment was only 37 years old, its honours already included battles in which men of predecessor units from the Quinte region had participated before 1920. These 10 actions were:

Northwest Canada 1885, Mount Sorrel, Somme 1916, Arras 1917, Ypres 1917, Hill 70, Ypres 1918, Amiens, Hindenburg Line, Pursuit to Mons.

Duffy officially took command of his Regiment on the blizzardy Sunday afternoon of February 16, 1958. The hundreds of Hasty Ps on parade marched with pride and precision behind the bugles and drums of the Regimental band. The retiring C.O., Lt.-Col. E.S. Fairman, led the Regiment in a march-past and Brigadier Lyall Carr, commanding 13 Militia Group, took the salute. Later Colonel Fairman took a farewell salute from his men marching past under Colonel Duffy's command. Former C.O.s, Bert Kennedy and Bryson Donnan were present.

"I want the members of the Regiment to know that I am the least among you," Duffy said. "It is the young officers and men who are vitally important. If they learn discipline, patriotism and loyalty, the Regiment will fulfil the two reasons for its being: first, the prevention of war by being strong and resolute during the years of peace; second, the winning of battles by high morale and discipline in time of war."

The award of 31 battles honours to the wartime battalion should be not only a great source of pride among the men who served overseas, Duffy believed, but it should have great inspirational value for the Militia battalion. Soon after he became C.O. he began planning a ceremony to bring this about. He felt that the most appropriate way to do this would be to place the designated 10 Second World War honours on the existing Regimental colour which had been presented before the war. And when the work was done, the refurbished colour looked like new.

The 1958 Regimental reunion provided the setting for the ceremony Duffy planned. The Thanksgiving weekend gathering drew a large attendance from far beyond the Regimental area. George Ponsford, the legendary sergeant-major of 'C' Company, came the furthest, from Durban, South Africa. On the perfect Sunday afternoon of October 12, the veterans and the Militia battalion marched east from the Armoury to a large playground on Bridge Street which was surrounded by tall trees in every autumn hue. Here Padres A.S. McConnell and Fred Goforth conducted a memorial service, commemorating the men who had given their lives in the Second World War.

In the golden sunshine of the late afternoon Colonel Kennedy carried the Colour across the leaf-strewn lawn and presented it officially to Colonel Duffy, on behalf of the wartime battalion. Colonel Duffy thanked him on behalf of the Militia battalion and handed it to Lieutenant Jack Fullerton who marched to his place in the colour party. The parade moved out to Bridge Street and back to the Armoury behind the Militia battalion's superb bugle band.

The colourful event received extensive coverage by the news media of the region. The Belleville Intelligencer said it was the first time in the history of the Canadian Army that a regimental association had ever presented a Colour emblazoned with battle honours to a Militia battalion. The Hasty Ps were accustomed to making history, but Ottawa officialdom was unimpressed and angry.

A senior officer at National Defence Headquarters in Ottawa telephoned Duffy, declaring that the Regimental Association and the Militia battalion had had no permission to do what they did. "By what authority was it done?" the Ottawa official demanded, "by what authority?" Duffy said that it had been done for the good of the Regiment, on his authority as commanding officer.

It had been done and there was no way it could be undone, Duffy declared without hesitation. As we shall see, that controversial Colour was to cast some strange shadows.

The 10 battle honours on the Colour were signposts on a rugged road between two worlds. Canadians took up arms in 1939, not because this would automatically make the world better, but because it was the only way to prevent the world situation from becoming unbelievably worse. Canadian soldiers helped to save the world from decades of darkness. They could not create Utopia, but they made possible the continuity of hope. Their sacrifices helped keep alive an awareness of individual worth. The men who fought to hold back barbarism had as their greatest resource the very thing that Naziism was trying to kill — individual freedom and initiative. And yet there was an even greater consideration — one that makes names like the Moro live in our nation's story. While defending their freedom men saw that there were times when the individual must risk everything or sacrifice everything for the Regiment. Duffy was determined to see those ideals passed to a new generation of Canadians as the Colour passed to eager young men's hands.

The war had been over for 13 years, but many veterans were following their commanding officer's example and were still serving in the Militia battalion. Stan Down, who had succeeded Duffy as RSM in 1949, completed 10 years in that rank and was promoted to captain. The new RSM was Lawrence Vernon Aubrey (Blackie) Simpson, who had served overseas and like Stan Down and been a member of the signal platoon before the war.

On Saturday, April 30, 1960, General Graham ended the last day of his service as Chief of the General Staff with officers of his Regiment. At a mess dinner in the Belleville Armoury he was greeted by many who had served with him before the war, as well as in the United Kingdom, Sicily and Italy. In October of that year the General was appointed Honorary Colonel of the Regiment, continuing in that advisory and ceremonial role for five years.

The Regiment had continued to flourish through the 1950s in spite of public uncertainty about the Militia's role. Major-General F.F. Worthington, Civil Defence Co-ordinator for Canada since 1949, suggested in 1954 to Lieut.-Gen. Guy Simonds, Chief of the General Staff, that in the event of hostilities, rural Militia battalions might form mobile civil defence columns. Simonds didn't want to publicize such a role, but acknowledged the feasibility of Regular Force and Militia assisting civil defence authorities in the event of a disaster.*

In 1955 Militia camps attracted more men and women than in any previous postwar summer, but the Conference of Defence Associations wanted stronger government action to mobilize community support for the reservists.

Major-General W.H.S. Macklin, a former Adjutant General of the Canadian Army, wrote in Saturday Night magazine on June 9, 1956, that "again this year as formerly, the Militia is going to camp in a state of chronic emaciation. Renowned infantry units were training at strengths far below their establishments." The Militia, in his view, was lower than 1939's total which exceeded 51,000. General Macklin blamed the Militia's weak support on 'air-power extremists' whose concepts of thermonuclear war made armies and navies obsolete.

The General cited a White Paper issued by Defence Minister Ralph Campney for 1955-56, stating that for the first time North America faced the possibility of an attack that could cripple the military and industrial potential of Canada and the United States.

If we were ever attacked with the thermonuclear weapons, the document added, our immediate problem would be national survival, and everyone not directly involved in an urgent military role would immediately be caught up in the problem of rescue, rehabilitation and the maintenance of essential services.

If North America's air defence still left the United States and Canada open to the kind of catastrophe the White Paper envisaged, what was the sense of creating it, General Macklin asked. "I reach the conclusion that it is not the Militia which is obsolete." The Militia had been organized,

* Uncertainties about the Militia's role in the late 1950s are described by G.W.L. Nicholson in *The Canadian Militia's Introduction to Civil Defence Training,* one of a collection of essays under the title, *Policy By Other Means.*

reorganized and tinkered with, times without number, General Macklin wrote. It was not obsolete but neglected by government and the public.

On June 20, 1956, Defence Minister Campney told the House of Commons that the Militia was operating at new levels of efficiency and interest. As an important part of Canada's defence organization, it deserved the whole-hearted support of every citizen. The General Staff's training directive for 1956-57 praised both the Regular Force and the Militia, but customary summer camps for Militia units ended with 1957. The new system was to attach selected personnel to Regular Force units for a week's training.

On May 18, the Minister had announced that the Canadian Army was carrying out special training to increase the effectiveness of aid to the civil defence organization in the event of an attack on Canada. The October, 1956, annual training directive from the General Staff covering the period April 1, 1957 to March 31, 1958, broadened the scope of Militia training to provide a nucleus in Militia units capable of assisting civil defence organizations. Vacancies in the Civil Defence College at Arnprior would be allotted to the Militia.

General Graham, as Chief of the General Staff, insisted that the primary role of the Militia was as a military force. The situation remained fairly quiet until the fall of 1957. Strong opposition to the civil defence role was expressed at a meeting of the Royal Canadian Armoured Corps Association in Ottawa. The training directive for 1957-58 said the aim of Militia training was to prepare units for a role in assisting any future mobilization for active service and for civil defence. Emphasis would be given to civil defence. A Canadian Press report in the Globe and Mail on October 11 called the directive "a first step in what may be eventual elimination of Canada's reserve forces."

The first reaction of senior Militia commanders was said to be one of dismay. One view reported, but not attributed to anyone, was that the Militia might well be done away with.

The agenda for that day's session of the Armoured Corps Association was abandoned in order to concentrate on the dire prospects foreseen in the wire story. General Worthington, father of the Armoured Corps, who had just retired from the post of civil defence co-ordinator, warned that it would kill the Militia to say that it was going to take over a civil defence role. General Macklin said the Militia couldn't serve two masters. If efforts were going to be diverted to civil defence, Armoured Corps reservists might as well turn in their tanks.

General Graham told the Armoured Corps Association that the decision to cut out Militia camps and reduce authorized training to 40 hours from 60 hours a year was necessary to make more funds available for expensive equipment for the Regular Force.

Graham felt that the defence associations weren't being very realistic. They seemed to be thinking entirely in terms of going back to Europe and getting into slit trenches. A few days later he told the Military Engineers Association it was essential that the Militia continue training both to reinforce the regular army and to assist in civil defence. "If you don't get your military training, you won't be worth a damn in civil defence, because one of the great strengths of the armed forces in assistance to civil defence will be the fact that they are a disciplined group of people, operating under trained non-commissioned officers and officers. . . .

"I wish that all Militia personnel would be patient enough to wait until they get their orders before they begin to comment and act upon the orders emanating from the press, because while the press may have all the good intentions in the world, they are sometimes prone to get things a little mixed up."

On retirement from the post of Chief of the General Staff in August, 1958, General Graham undertook a review of the state of civil defence programs. His report early in 1959 recommended that the federal government assume sole responsibility for civil defence which would be transferred to the Army. Senior government and civil defence officials reviewed and modified the report, and further work by a cabinet committee and finally a federal-provincial conference produced a Civil Defence Order, tabled in the House of Commons on July 2, 1959. The Army would become responsible for most technical functions, including attack warnings, location and monitoring of explosions and fallout, re-entry, rescue and decontamination and support to local governments in maintaining order. The new name for all this was National Survival.

Bureaucrats who came up with a document setting out the National Survival organization in June, 1959, were so carried away with the prospect of thermonuclear destruction that they listed Halifax, Saint John, Quebec City, Montreal, Ottawa-Hull, Toronto, Hamilton, Windsor, Niagara Falls, Winnipeg, Edmonton, Vancouver and Victoria as 13 probable targets. At least St. John's, Regina and Calgary would be spared.

Uncertainty about the civil defence role, if there was any in the Militia, didn't faze the Hasty Ps.

Civil defence did become a major part of the Regiment's training and it was taken in stride. First aid was covered extensively and much time was spent lowering 'casualties' from the Armoury balcony or from buildings, on ropes. Men went on parade in blue coveralls with ropes tied around their waists. As one officer of the early 1960s put it, it seemed sometimes that rescue was everything and traditional infantry tasks were pushed into the background.

Plans were prepared for the reception and billeting of people who would leave the Toronto area in the event of nuclear attack and for the handling of traffic. Potential fallout patterns were studied. Men became familiar with equipment for measuring levels of radiation and emergency radio networks were established. When it came to the Civil Defence College, Duffy and his officers were convinced that their troops could perform civil defence tasks well enough to attend as a unit.

From July 23 to 29, 1960, there were 111 Hasty Ps in camp at Arnprior with their own vehicles, kitchens and communications, their own drivers, cooks and signallers. The unit received three days of concentrated training in rescue work, leading to a night rescue exercise in which all ranks moved in convoy and rescued about 60 'casualties' from designated sites.

Favourable comment came from Area Headquarters, noting that junior officers and junior NCOs were of exceptionally high calibre, supporting their company commanders and the C.O. to the utmost. The greatest credit for the success of the exercise should go to the unit's commanding officer, the critique concluded.

> "The personal example, enthusiasm and drive that the C.O. set was of the highest order. By continuously holding in front of the men the fine traditions of the Hastings & Prince Edward Regiment, and by working them very hard, he has proved that teenage Militia soldiers have the ability and stamina to work hard and produce results under difficult conditions, providing they have good leadership."

In the period 1961-62 over 1,400 men in Belleville and Picton received special Militia training in civil defence tasks.

On Sunday, February 19, 1961, a tactical exercise was in progress and the Armoury was open in the afternoon. At 6:30 p.m., with the day's program completed, a mess steward and the caretaker checked to make sure that no unauthorized person had remained in the building and a second check was made an hour later. About 11:00 p.m. caretaker Wally Leavitt, whose quarters were on the third floor above the officers' mess, heard a radio playing. He found a door from the balcony to the mess area ajar and lights were on. There were people in the mess, but their voices were familiar and the caretaker did not go in. No other person was found in the building.

The next morning it was discovered that the Regimental Colour had been stolen from a locked case in the mess. The mess door had been forced open and locked again as the intruder or intruders left. The Colour's glass case had been forced open but left undamaged. Some officers thought that the removal of the Colour bearing the Regiment's battle honours was a prank and that it would soon be recovered.

After several days had passed without any real clues being found, Duffy felt that he must do something to dramatize the situation.

He must remind the public that nothing is more treasured by a regiment than its Colours. To make that point he must visibly bear the shame of such a grievous loss. He called a special parade. Standing before the Regiment, he said: "The circumstances of this loss indicate that the person or persons who did this dreadful thing are members, former members or closely associated with the Regiment. As the C.O. I am in disgrace."

Duffy then removed his cap, took off the badge he had worn for 31 years and handed it to the adjutant for safe keeping, pledging never to wear it again until the Colour was found.

The issue was dramatized alright. Newspapers across the country gave the story conspicuous play. The Belleville Intelligencer said editorially that removal of the Colour affected not just the Militia battalion but the men of all ranks who made the Regiment's great record in the Second World War.

The Regimental Association offered a reward for the return of the Colour — no questions asked. Duffy offered a reward and through newspaper ads sought information from anyone who might have knowledge of the Colour's location. Veterans in Legion halls were urged to keep their ears and eyes open when there was any mention of the Colour. But no clues were discovered.

Duffy received an anonymous note, written on the back of a mimeographed page of some notes on the history of the

Regiment. It took a form resembling an order for a military operation.

Aim — to take back Battle flag and regimental colour to the proper place.

Prep. — boldness, 3 keys

Obstacles — time element, janitor

Facts — officers and ladies having party in no way involved, had to wait till they left, thought they would never go, glass there too much noise, tried for battle flag Wed. night but janitor changed locks, almost made it Sun. night, but watchman up and down stairs too much to break glass — if Duffy would just go back a few years he will remember plan ahead and know what the hell your doing, he taught me and I will do it, need keys now.

Since the note referred to taking the Colour to its "proper place", this seemed to suggest that the location was Picton or Madoc, formerly Regimental headquarters. Another note indicated that the Colour belonged in "the Boot" in other words, in Italy. Still another note seemed to indicate that the Colour had been taken to a church in Ortona, but Hasty Ps on a veterans' pilgrimage in 1975 found no evidence of this.

The thief was apparently in the Armoury or its vicinity from time to time in the months following the theft, for notes were found taunting Duffy and others about their lack of success in solving the mystery. The notes mentioned events the writer could have known about only by being in the Armoury. They seemed to indicate that the writer wanted to be caught. One note said that he had watched the caretaker and his wife on an evening stroll and described their route and what they wore.

Notes received at the Armoury gave the impression that the writer travelled in the region and stopped at Belleville occasionally. Since he appeared to keep the Armoury under surveillance on these visits, police checked the register at the nearby Quinte Hotel periodically.

A note received just before the spring inspection of the

Regiment suggested the possibility of an attempt to steal the battle flag from the sergeants' mess:

"Now I have been thinking. Who knows, maybe with a little persuasion there will be no difficulty getting into the place Sunday night even for a neuresthenic case."

An empty flag staff was carried by a member of the colour party at the Regimental inspection on Sunday, May 14, and security officers mingled with the crowd in the Armoury, for the thief had warned that he would be there to hear Duffy's "sabre-rattling speech". Once again, no clues were discovered.

Apparently the same man was present at the Regimental reunion that October. A message in heavy black letters was left in a cubicle in the men's latrine on the main floor of the Armoury:

YOU SEEK IT HERE, YOU SEEK IT THERE
YOU SEEK THAT FLAG MOST EVERYWHERE.
IS IT HERE OR IS IT THERE?
A LOT OF PEOPLE JUST DON'T CARE.
PETAWAWA, BORDEN, KINGSTON SO
IT'S TAKEN SIX MONTHS — YOU STILL DON'T
    KNOW.

The trail has been cold since 1961.

Four members of the Ontario Provincial Police were in the Regiment during Duffy's period of command and they pursued the investigation in their spare time. RCMP officers were also called in. It seemed that the person who knew where the Colour was had been a wartime member of the Regiment or someone very closely associated with the Regiment. He apparently had a mental problem. Wartime nominal rolls were combed and investigations were carried out on men who had been discharged with indications of instability. Nothing significant was discovered.

Twenty years after the theft Duffy had not given up believing that the Colour could return. The thief's family might not find it or feel able to return it until he is gone. In the meantime an empty flag staff was waiting in a Picton church and Duffy's beret bore no badge.

Postwar Regimental parades were probably never better than in the Duffy era. The bugle band had already done much to keep the Regiment's profile high, not only in the Quinte region but far beyond it. Duffy decided correctly that it would be possible to attract even more attention by adopting a late 19th century style of uniform with scarlet tunics and dark blue trousers. He had been seeking appropriate helmets, not only in Canada but in Commonwealth countries when, in 1961, workmen demolishing a Belleville house found 40 white spiked helmets bearing the Maltese cross badges of the 49th Hastings Rifles. All but one of them were fit for rehabilitation and they were soon in use.

That year brought sadness too with the unexpected death at 54 of the beloved wartime padre, Fred Goforth. He had retired to Brantford only five months before as a lieutenant-colonel after serving as Deputy Chaplain-General of Canada's armed forces. He was the minister of Farringdon Church where a full military funeral took place with many members of the Regiment present. Later the Regimental Association held a memorial service in the Protestant chapel at the School of Infantry in Camp Borden where a memorial stained glass window was unveiled.

An editorial in the Kingston Whig-Standard paid this tribute:

"In many a desperate engagement during the campaign in Italy his unshaken faith and inspired devotion to his calling were bulwarks upon which officer and man alike could lean for comfort and reassurance. He was always a man who represented hope when all hope seemed lost; who brought to his work of battle padre a rare combination of spirituality, earthiness and a penetrating understanding of the strengths and frailties of his fellows. It mattered not to Fred Goforth what religious convictions a man held, or indeed, if he held none. But by example and a realistic tolerance he proved time and again the strength of his own strong belief. . . . The Rev. Mr. Goforth always maintained that the world had been good to him. Truly it can be said of him that he in turn was good for the world."

The Hastings & Prince Edward Regiment was probably the largest Militia infantry unit in Canada. Adapting it to a changing role, keeping an eye on widely scattered sub-units, doing things in unofficial ways, skating around strange rulings and unnecessary regulations from area headquarters, scrounging money from here and there, courageously developing his own interpretations of official policy, concentrating his energy on making the Regiment efficient and keeping its profile high would have been a tough assignment for a full-time soldier.

But Duffy had his own garage business to operate and he could never escape the father-confessor role old Hasty Ps thrust upon him, not to mention organizing Regimental reunions, Remembrance Day parades, Santa Claus parades and any number of other community events. It was a stress-producing package of responsibilities. The result was a severe heart attack in December, 1961.

On Sunday, May 6, 1962, about 500 Hasty Ps on parade and 3,000 spectators saw Duffy turn over his sword to his successor, Joe Black. Buttons and badges gleamed in the sunshine; the Regimental band never played more stirringly and 80 veterans of the wartime battalion joined the march-past. The next day the Intelligencer gave the event extensive coverage including front-page headlines, and the parade was described as the largest and most colourful since the war.

As he recalled the events of 32 years, the retiring C.O.'s remarks were vintage Duffy:

"In the Regiment I have learned that duty, discipline, courage, generosity, service and good friends are the important things of life. To many people of the unit whose guidance, instruction and inspiration helped me to be a better soldier, and therefore a better man, I say sincerely and humbly, thank you. To the present serving members of the Regiment, I say remember always that by keeping the unit strong and resolute, you are contributing in a very real way toward peace. In the event of war you will be the means of the country's survival. The role of the Militia is of vital importance to Canada. . . .

"Being your commanding officer has been a wonderfully rewarding experience. I am truly grateful for your loyal support and hard work. I wish also to thank your families. Your duties as a soldier call for sacrifice on their part. I know that without the loyal encouragement of the two Mrs. Duffys in my life, my duties would have been most difficult, if not impossible. May the star of your badge shine brightly. Good soldiering, good fortune to each and every one of you. God bless you."

A distinguished period of command was over, but it was far from time to fade away. Duffy left his successor a detailed appraisal of the state of the Regiment which he declared to be at a postwar peak of efficiency and morale, with a strength of 450. Continuing to carry out tough and realistic training seemed to be the surest way to guard its good health, he wrote, but every effort must be made to reduce administration required by sub-units.

In fact Duffy recommended that higher formations give serious study to the idea of cutting paper work in half. "Administration, controls, safety regulations etc. have reduced the Militia to where it is no longer an efficient organization, taking into consideration the total amount of time and money spent," Duffy reported. Clearly he was concerned about the vulnerability of the Regiment, with its seven armouries and many sub-units scattered across hundreds and hundreds of square miles.

The best way to protect and develop the outlying sub-units would be to divide the Regiment into two battalions. The First Battalion would cover Bancroft, Madoc, Picton and Napanee with headquarters in Belleville. The Second Battalion should have its headquarters in Cobourg and cover Trenton, Norwood, Millbrook and Port Hope. Taking in Cobourg and Napanee would involve absorbing local units, but Duffy saw this as feasible, for a significant number of men in both areas had served with the Regiment. In the event of a national emergency, this enlarged Regimental area would be capable of raising three battalions — an infantry brigade.

Duffy had worked hard in his four years as C.O. to strengthen the Regiment with notable success. To reinforce success should be axiomatic for the military, but events were to show that not even the best rural regiment in Canada could be sure that would happen. Times were changing.

Chapter Fourteen
The long battle for survival

The Regimental change of command was followed in three weeks by a change in Duffy's civilian occupation. Quinte Region Emergency Measures Organization needed a co-ordinator. Duffy was selected from 15 candidates.

EMO's emphasis in 1962 was on survival in the event of a nuclear attack. Duffy told one meeting at a Trenton high school that survival was a personal business. He urged homeowners to see that their families had protection. They should be preparing to shield themselves behind thick layers of earth, brick or concrete. Although it was not practical to build shelters for every Canadian, individuals should decide for themselves to provide protection against a nuclear blast and radiation. The disclosure that Soviet weapons were in Cuba in the fall of 1962 heightened the sense of danger, but after President John Kennedy's ultimatum forced Nikita Khrushchev to withdraw them, the crisis passed.

Duffy told the public that the function of EMO was not defence. It was to make it possible for Hastings and Prince Edward Counties to exist as an organized entity under an attack that might disrupt all the normal functions of government. He said EMO was mostly concerned with governments and people and their relationships. Quinte EMO was controlled by a committee headed by the Mayor of Belleville and composed of representatives of all municipalities in the two counties. In case of air attack the EMO office and the rest of the city government would move to the basement of Belleville city hall and the walls would be sandbagged. Each of the other municipal governments would have selected an appropriate location.

In an emergency, Duffy said, EMO would govern the area from the shelter until federal and provincial governments were able to resume their roles. EMO would supervise the billeting of refugees from major centres and each local municipality should be able to absorb about four times its own population. EMO would provide auxiliary firemen and police and other municipal services during an emergency. The Regiment would not be available to help, because plans called for it to be assigned to duties in Toronto. The Regiment had most of the vehicles required to outfit a rescue column.

If Toronto were hit with a nuclear weapon, the Regiment would take part in re-entry and rescue operations conducted by the Army. While Toronto was subject to attack, Belleville would be left without Militia forces.

"The surest way of provoking war is to be unprepared for it." Duffy said in one public speech. "Two giant nations are locked in an ideological battle. Occasionally tension erupts and we get a situation like Korea or Cuba last week. Our government has decided that it's worthwhile spending a lot of money on civil defence. And if they think it is worthwhile, surely you should. It would be ridiculous to build shelters for everyone in Canada, but each individual should decide for himself to prepare for it."

His municipal council experience told Duffy that an organization such as EMO could be of great assistance to local authorities in handling natural or man-made disasters that had nothing to do with warfare at all.

The threat of serious flooding on the Moira River in the spring of 1963 found Duffy working closely with the Moira River Conservation Authority, the mayor, city clerk and city engineer of Belleville. If the river rose enough to cover

Front Street, it would flood City Hall, and so preparation was made to set up emergency flood control headquarters on much higher ground in a gymnasium at Belleville Collegiate.

As an old soldier Duffy could see the need for good communications when mobilizing people and equipment to deal with disasters. He soon organized courses for men, women and students in radio communications and first aid. Police, firemen, hospital administrators and key municipal officials in the two counties were encouraged to plan together how best to deal with natural or man-made disasters. Duffy discovered that the fire chiefs of Trenton and Belleville had never met and he made it his business to end that kind of isolation.

It was Duffy's aim to bring all communities in the region to a high state preparedness for any kind of peacetime emergency — on the Bay of Quinte, on Lake Ontario, on the Moira River or the Trent, at Trenton airport, on Highway 401 or the busy Montreal-Toronto rail line that cut through his territory. Training schemes were held regularly to dramatize the need for preparedness. Institutions that could be affected by a real disaster sometimes became involved without much warning.

One day a large number of people acting as 'casualties' were brought on stretchers to the Belleville General Hospital where preparedness was not very evident. One of the 'casualties' was Helena Duffy, an experienced senior hospital nurse. The EMO co-ordinator's report to the hospital, reflecting her observations, fairly rattled the windows. The state of preparedness at BGH was upgraded rapidly.

Duffy's EMO activity made it plain to the public that it was practical good sense to be prepared to handle the kind of emergency that could cripple a community. As a regional resource, EMO was like a second Militia battalion.

Busy as he was, constantly travelling through the two counties, planning and conducting training exercises and filling many speaking engagements every month, Duffy still had time for the Regiment. He had long hoped to see a Regimental museum established, and with the co-operation of serving officers and others, the work had begun when he was C.O. In 1960, thanks to a generous donation from Major Hubert Campbell, the first display case had been placed along one wall of the games room in the officers' mess. Major Ken Willcocks designed and built it. After his retirement from command, Duffy encouraged further development of the museum and in the subsequent years the Regimental Association, Officers Association and Senior NCOs Association, the Ack Ack Kennedy Club and the Argyll Chapter of the I.O.D.E. made additional improvements possible.

A large collection of cap badges was presented to the museum in memory of Corporal Ray Denike. Unit Support Officer Capt. Dennis Shanks of the PPCLI presented a display of about 25 weapons. Sergeant Jack Milne donated his large collection of wartime photos. Sergeant Orval Berry did important work on the badge collection and other displays and Sergeant Major Wally Leavitt provided many hours of labour in addition to generous contributions.

Later it would be suggested that the artifacts be transferred to the Hastings County Museum, but that wasn't feasible because much of the material was for the use of the Regiment only, and if not so used, would have had to be returned to the donors. Since this was the only military museum between Toronto and Kingston, it was considered too useful to be abandoned and Duffy gradually assumed a larger role in its administration and care.

Three thousand miles away an important public occasion was also to highlight the Regiment's historical background. On November 12, 1963, the House of Lords in Westminster would hear an address of thanks to Her Majesty the Queen for the speech delivered on the opening of Parliament. It is customary for the person moving this address to wear a military uniform if entitled to do so, and for probably the first time it was to be a Commonwealth uniform. Lord Tweedsmuir arrived at the House of Lords in the uniform of the Hastings & Prince Edward Regiment, and in moving the address he noted that it was the second successive year in which the honour had been entrusted to a Scot.

"We Scots, or most of us, are a far-wandering people, which I think is perhaps sufficient excuse and reason to explain why I appear before your Lordships today wearing the uniform of the Army of Her Majesty the Queen of Canada. . . . My Lords, I welcome the mention in the gracious speech of the continued affirmation of faith in the Commonwealth. These newer nations are the work of many hands, of many men of many races over many years. They are no accident. They are to my mind the greatest achievement of the British race. . . . The uniform that I wear today is that of the Hastings and Prince Edward Regiment of Canada. That regiment was founded from among those who had fought at the British side against George Washington. They, being citizens of the country which became the United States, and having lost, were determined to stay under the British Crown and live under British institutions. So they made their way northwards to Canada and they called Hastings County after that very brilliant general of the British side, Rawdon Hastings. Rawdon Hastings went on to gain many distinctions and eventually as the Marquess of Hastings, he became the Governor-General of India."

Replying later to congratulations from Ken Willcocks, Lord Tweedsmuir wrote:

"There is only room in a man's life for a very few great loyalties and the Battalion is one of my greatest. Just before I was going into the Chamber to make my speech Field Marshal Montgomery came up to me, looked at my badges and said, 'the old Hastings and Prince Edward Regiment. Jolly good fighting troops.' "

Few if any members of the Regiment could describe its historical context in such a dramatic way, but in the areas of early Loyalist settlement around the Bay of Quinte the sense of history was strong. Indeed the Regiment was living history. The City of Belleville was about to give that concept official recognition. Lord Tweedsmuir would be present and so would many of his wartime comrades, some of whom had never made it to a reunion.

Sunday, May 17, 1964, was a perfect late spring day in Eastern Ontario. The highlands of Hastings County were clad in a soft green and apple blossoms in profusion almost hid the farmhouses of Prince Edward. The Bay of Quinte was a sparkling blue.

Since the formation of the 1st Regiment of Prince Edward Militia in 1800 and the 1st Regiment of Hastings Militia in 1804, the citizen-soldier had been a familiar figure in the countryside and in the towns. On this shining day the City of Belleville was about to pay tribute to the generations of men from the two counties who had served as soldiers from the War of 1812 through the Second World War. Lieutenant-Governor Earl Rowe would be presenting new Colours and Mayor Jack Ellis would be granting the Regiment the Freedom of the City.

As a memorial to all who had served in the Regiment or its predecessors, Belleville was granting in perpetuity the right "as long as the waters of Quinte Bay embrace the shore of the said City, to enter therein and march throughout its streets, thoroughfares and highways without hindrance or trespass, on any and all occasions, with Colours and Battle Honours flying, bayonets fixed and bands playing."

The Church of St. Thomas, a handsome stone building on a hill overlooking the Armoury, was crowded that Whitsunday morning. Second World War veterans joined with people of the parish and the community to mark the historic day. Words were warm and comfortable. But halfway through the service one petition startled the kneeling congregation. "Let us pray," said a padre, "for the defence of Confederation."

The phrase struck like an electric shock there in one of the oldest Loyalist settlements in Ontario where the continuity of Canada had never been questioned. The enemy to be

Freedom of the City of Belleville

to

The Hastings and Prince Edward Regiment

THIS DAY AND HENCEFORTH MAY IT BE KNOWN THAT, *on this occasion of the Presentation of Colours and in honour of the history and tradition of The Hastings and Prince Edward Regiment and its predecessor units, that the Corporation of the City of Belleville in the realm of Canada of her Gracious Majesty, Queen Elizabeth, the Second, by virtue of the authority of a resolution passed unanimously by the Council of the said Corporation on the sixth day of January, One Thousand, Nine Hundred and Sixty-Four.*

HEREBY PROCLAIMS AND GRANTS TO
THE HASTINGS AND PRINCE EDWARD REGIMENT

The Freedom of the said City of Belleville and all rights and privileges pertaining thereto, as long as the waters of Quinte Bay embrace the shores of the said City, to enter therein and march throughout its streets, thoroughfares and highways, without hindrance or trespass on any and all occasions with Colours and Battle Honours flying, bayonets fixed and bands playing.

This Freedom is granted and confirmed in grateful acknowledgement and recognition of services rendered and duty bravely performed since the formation of the Regiment's parent units, the first Regiment of Prince Edward Militia in the year One Thousand Eight Hundred and the first Regiment of Hastings Militia in the year One Thousand Eight Hundred and Four and continuing throughout a distinguished record of service in the wars of 1812, the rebellion of 1837, the Fenian Raid of 1865, the World War of 1914 to 1918; the unit formally became the Hastings and Prince Edward Regiment in 1920, and this grant is particularly to perpetuate its feats of bravery, devotion and glory from 1939 to 1945 from North Africa to Sicily, to Italy and to the European Theatre, to witness the capitulation of its enemies and thereafter, in causes dear to the hearts of the said City, and all its citizens.

In particular and without limiting the foregoing, This Freedom is granted and to be recognized as a memorial to all ranks from said Regiment and its predecessors contributing to its distinguished history, who have given their lives on the altar of freedom in the performance of their duty and earned for their comrades and all who came after them the honours now recognized and being secured to them in perpetuity by their fellow citizens hereby recorded.

SIGNED AND SEALED *on behalf of the* CORPORATION OF THE CITY OF BELLEVILLE *on this seventeenth day of May, in the Year of Our Lord, One Thousand, Nine Hundred and Sixty-Four.*

CITY CLERK

MAYOR

defeated was not any attacking force but complacency. The prayer was a reminder that national strength and survival depend on more than military action.

The role of the citizen soldier can be more demanding in the days of peace and prosperity because greater dedication is required to serve when there is no overt threat to national security. Day in and day out, Militia activity sets an example for the whole community. Its quiet but telling message is that the community or country can survive only as long as men and women are willing to make great sacrifices to see that it does.

The principal task of the infantry battalion is survival — staying alive despite public apathy, poor planning by higher formations or a lack of appreciation by governments. The Militia maintains a readiness to risk all in the event of an emergency and its presence perpetuates the deeds of those who met such a challenge in the past.

The Freedom of the City was given to the Regiment that day in grateful acknowledgement of services rendered and duty bravely done since the earliest days of the two counties, but it was primarily a tribute to the Regiment's great record in the Second World War. It was a memorial to all ranks who had given their lives. The award was received by a basically young battalion, but there were still some men on parade who had seen service overseas.

Granting the Regiment the Freedom of the City was in keeping with local tradition. But Canadian attitudes generally were moving away from that tradition. Although Canadians were soon to celebrate a Centennial and there would be great emphasis on history, many of them were unwilling to admit that tradition mattered.

They were thinking more about the prosperous present and their own comfortable, three-bedroom suburban future than about the men and women who had brought the country through times of trial and testing. Canadians saw happy days ahead in terms of jobs, big pay and prosperity. But this wasn't the prospect for the Militia. In 1963 Paul

Hellyer became Minister of National Defence and by the fall of 1964 he would be ready to open fire on his own troops.

The Minister had appointed a commission under Brigadier-General E.R. Suttie to recommend organizational changes in the reserves. Their role was to be revised. It was no longer to emphasize national survival. The new purpose was to be support for the Regular Force, but the drastic changes to come would reduce the Militia's capability, both in recruiting and training.

There were rumours in Militia circles about where changes would be made. Hasty P old-timers felt that the Regiment was vulnerable because of its large number of armouries across a sprawling territory. Lyall Carr in Port Hope arranged through his MP to meet the Minister in Ottawa — accompanied by Duffy and General Graham. The Minister couldn't refuse to see a group that included a former Chief of Staff. They had 20 minutes to make their case.

Duffy expected Graham to be the spokesman, but after the opening pleasantries, the ball was passed to him as a recent C.O. He went right to the main point — the Minister's apparent determination to close armouries in outlying areas. Duffy said that would be a mistake, because armouries were links between government and people. The discussion went something like this:

"I can't prove their value to their communities today in dollars and cents, but over time they have proved their worth. Armouries are part of the Canadian fabric. They are centres of community activities. If they are closed, what other service might be cut off next because of cost? Closing armouries means cutting strength."

"But city units are stronger."

"In peacetime, yes, because of the social life, but not in wartime."

"My people tell me that it costs too much to keep the Madoc Armoury open. You could bus people down to Belleville at less cost."

"Who are your staff people, sir? Are they Navy or Air Force? No infantryman would say that. I speak as an infantryman from away back. You can't bring people in by bus. The minute you cut off an outlying area you're starting to destroy our Regiment. We'll need those outlying armouries some day."

But the die was cast.

In the summer of 1964 a new C.O. succeeded Joe Black. Kenneth D'Arcy Huxley Willcocks, a mechanical engineer, was born and educated in England. Commissioned in 1951 in the Royal Electrical and Mechanical Engineers, he served in the British Army on the Rhine before coming to Canada in 1954. He served in the 6th Technical Regiment RCEME in Windsor and commanded the 27th Technical Squadron RCEME in Belleville, becoming a Hasty P when the Regiment absorbed that unit. He was a commanding officer with conspicuous organizational and communications skills, who knew how to keep the Regiment in the news and morale up.

On Sunday, October 4, 1964, the Regiment laid up its 30-year-old Queen's Colour at the Anglican Church of St. Mary Magdalene in Picton, and with it an empty staff on which the old Regimental Colour would have been, if it had not been stolen in 1961. That afternoon a change-of-command parade in Belleville made the turnover from Black to Willcocks official.

Defence Minister Hellyer was about to attack. The Telegram quoted him as saying that he wanted to cut the Militia from 44,000 people to 30,000 and save $15-million a year.

On November 4 newspapers carried the grim news — 72 Militia units were disbanded, including six armoured regiments, 18 artillery regiments and seven infantry battalions. The 25 Militia group headquarters set up 10 years earlier were wiped out. The blitz closed six of the Regiment's armouries:

'A' Company in Trenton
'B' Company in Madoc
'C' Company in Port Hope
No. 5 platoon of 'B' Company in Norwood
No. 7 platoon of 'C' Company in Millbrook
'D' Company in Picton.

The Telegram said "one of Canada's most famous World War II infantry regiments suffered a fate almost as bad as disbandment — dismemberment."

About 70 per cent of unit strength resided in the areas where armouries were closed. Willcocks argued that if this meant training must be "relocated" to Belleville, the Army had to provide transportation for those who wanted to carry on. Buses could have been provided, but for some of the distances it just wasn't practical to do so for only a night's training. The ever-innovative C.O. saw weekend training at Camp Picton as the answer.

Willcocks made contact with an RCAF Auxiliary Squadron in Montreal whose pilots were mostly airline pilots. The squadron would pick up the Hasty Ps on a small air strip just east of Belleville and fly them to Picton for weekend training once a month. The Regiment got good co-operation from the Regular Force troops — the Canadian Guards — stationed in Picton. In training schemes the RCAF squadron provided air reconnaissance information about the 'enemy' and dropped equipment and rations. Air-to-ground communication was established, so the training schemes had a high degree of realism.

Only a year after slashing the Militia, the Defence Minister integrated the three services and did away with the Army's geographic command structure. The Militia was reshaped into three groups:

The ready reserve — individuals with sufficient trade training to cover deficiencies in Regular Force establishments.

The regional reserve — units and individuals to reinforce

units committed to the defence of Canada or needed to deal with civil emergency operations.

The Mobile Command reserve — units to assume a training role to reinforce fighting formations of infantry, armour and artillery.

This also meant no more summer camp training as units. In future sub-units would be grouped in ad hoc battalions for training under Regular Force officers. This was potentially a devastating blow to unit esprit de corps.

Willcocks' strategy was to carry on regardless. He knew the importance of ceremony to mark special occasions. In 1965 the Regiment trained for Trooping the Colour for the first time and after weeks of rehearsal did it well, attracting a large crowd to the Belleville fairground.

On the reviewing stand, General Graham marked his last occasion as Honorary Colonel, commending the Regiment on its performance and taking a farewell salute. Don Cameron became the new Honorary Colonel shortly afterwards.

Willcocks regularly distributed newsletters to all ranks, reviewing events, complimenting those who had done particularly good jobs, describing new activities planned and generally projecting a contagious enthusiasm for the Regiment. Two of the hardest workers and best morale builders in the Regiment were husband and wife. Howard Kokesh was RSM and Kaye Kokesh was adjutant.

At the annual inspection on May 2, 1966, Colonel Tom de Faye, commander of the Eastern Ontario District, had some encouraging words for the Regiment: "You have a more important place in the Armed Forces than you have had in the past," he declared. "Your primary role has been changed to that of soldiering."

Centennial celebrations in 1967 provided many occasions on which to show the flag. The Regiment marched through city streets during Victoria Day celebrations; a drill team put on displays and the transport section showed how quickly a jeep could be taken apart and put together again.

Willcocks was determined to show that although the rural armouries were closed, the Regiment was very much alive. Lord Tweedsmuir paid a visit during the weekend of July 22-23, read the lesson at St. Thomas Church on the Sunday morning and was inspecting officer at a well performed Trooping the Colour in the afternoon.

The Regimental Association's project to mark Centennial Year was the construction of a memorial on the Armoury lawn, facing northwest toward the corner of Bridge and Pinnacle Streets. Angus Duffy was chairman of the Memorial Committee and with the dedicated assistance of Helena Duffy, information about the project and requests for donations were circulated to every Hasty P with a known address. Money to meet the cost of the memorial came from many parts of the country and from outside of Canada.

The simple but strong design featured a large bronze Regimental badge and shoulder title near the top of the 14-foot central column of white granite, below them the words LEST WE FORGET 1939-1945 and then the 31 battle honours. Bronze plaques on each wing of the structure bear the names of 364 men who died on active service. Access to the concrete walk leading to the base of the memorial is through an attractive pair of iron gates on which Regimental collar badges were subsequently placed.

The memorial was unveiled on Sunday afternoon, September 10, 1967, by General Graham and Colonel Allen Ross. Wartime padres Reg Lane and Roy Essex participated in the dedication. Colonel Willcocks led a strong detachments from the Militia battalion and at least 180 members of the wartime battalion and 70 next-of-kin were present. Brigadier-General Don Cameron, president of the Officers Association, and Rollie Fleming, president of the Regimental Association, placed wreaths.

Willcocks' period of command was nearly complete. He had done much to maintain morale by refusing to concede that anything had changed the Regiment's objectives or diminished its spirit. In a speech on relinquishing command on February 25, 1968, he discussed the challenge that was faced when rural companies were cut off late in 1964. By the fall of 1966 numbers had increased sharply and he had received "a wonderful warning" from higher authority that the unit was close to being over-strength.

Ross Allan, the new C.O., was a Belleville high school teacher who had joined the Regiment in 1960 after serving with a Royal Canadian Army Service Corps unit in London, Ontario. He would have challenges to meet.

By 1968 Paul Hellyer was touring Canada as housing minister seeking public views on housing. Pierre Trudeau, the new Prime Minister who was the right age but did not serve in what he considered an imperialistic war, was starting to weaken the military by talking about disarmament and drastically cutting the number serving abroad with NATO forces.

In April, 1969, the government announced that the defence budget would be frozen for three years at $1.815-billion and new tasks would be assigned to give greater emphasis to the defence of Canadian sovereignty. Within a few months it was apparent that budgetary restraints would bring further cuts in Militia strength.

In the fall of 1969 rumours were circulating in Belleville about the possibility that the Hastings & Prince Edward Regiment was in danger of being wiped out completely as a victim of government austerity.

Colonel Max Porritt sounded the alarm at the October reunion in Belleville, marking the 30th anniversary of mobilization. A resolution opposing any further cutback was prepared for dispatch to Ottawa. Fortunately one veteran to whom the disappearance of the Regiment was unthinkable was in a position to do something about it. Dr. Russell Scott, Mayor of Belleville, discussed the rumours with Colonel Allan and volunteered to do what he could to keep the Regiment alive. He wasn't a Hasty P, but he had known the Chief of Staff, General Frederick Sharpe, since school days and had served with him overseas. General Sharpe and Mrs. Sharpe (whose home town was Trenton) were invited to visit Belleville and be received officially at City Hall. They were given the key to the city and royally entertained. In the officers' mess they heard first-hand why the Regiment must stay alive. The C.O. could put more men on parade than would appear in many other units, the general was reminded.

On November 27, 1969, the Intelligencer quoted Mayor Scott as saying that he had been assured by Ottawa sources that the Regiment would not be affected by any reduction in the Militia establishment. Later Mayor Scott was officially appointed an honorary major.

Militia cuts did occur that fall. All armoured and infantry units survived, but six artillery units were reduced to no strength. The demise of the 50th Anti-Aircraft Battery in Peterborough involved its transformation into a company of the Hastings & Prince Edward Regiment!

The Regiment celebrated its 50th birthday on March 14, 1970, by receiving a new Queen's Colour from Governor-General Roland Michener. The new Colour was the red and white Canadian flag, replacing the Red Ensign. The Queen's representative had this to say:

> "The Queen's new Colour, which I have the honour to present to you on behalf of Her Majesty is thoroughly Canadian as you can see, and a fitting tribute to a Regiment which has such a fine record. . . . I salute you in the name of Her Majesty. Furthermore, I bring you the good wishes and appreciation of Canadians generally for whom it is my privilege to speak. We owe our security and freedom to men like yourselves who have been ready at all times to defend their country."

But did Canadians really care?

In the late 1960s it became increasingly difficult for Militia units, however distinguished their histories, to sustain anything like the community interest and support that most had enjoyed for about 15 years after the Second

World War. Authority, discipline and tradition were all scorned in a society pursuing individual pleasure. Neither the public nor the politicians saw much need for armed forces. Increasingly a sense of loneliness was descending on the Militia.

About the end of Duffy's term as C.O., Canada's reserve forces were at their peak, numbering more than 66,000, of which 60,000 were in the Militia, about 3,700 in the Naval Reserve and 2,300 in the RCAF Reserve. Like the 51,000-man Militia of 1939, the 60,000 of the early 1960s benefitted from the participation and leadership of men with experience in a major war.

Duffy's successor, Joe Black, was the last C.O. with service in the Second World War. Veterans began to retire during the 1960s and younger men and women donned the uniform. In Hastings and Prince Edward Counties love of the land had come down the generations, accompanied by a commitment to defend it. But the 1960s was a dark decade for traditions. The Militia could not flourish as it had, for it represented traditions with which Ottawa officialdom had begun to feel uncomfortable. A flag representing no particular historical tradition or symbolism replaced the Ensign. The tradition of three military services wearing British-style uniforms and insignia was swept away. The individuality which units had always treasured was shrouded in anonymous dark green. By 1972 the Militia had slipped to just above 15,000 and was still stuck there at the end of the 1970s, despite statements from a succession of defence ministers that the Militia had high priority. In the 1980s only Luxembourg among the NATO allies had a less impressive level of commitment.

In 1971 Ross Allan was succeeded as C.O. by Lt.-Col. Jack Richardson, vice-principal of a Peterborough secondary school, who had both Regular Force and Militia experience. Members and supporters of the Regiment were confident of its future with a C.O. who was a cousin of Defence Minister James Richardson. Training was carried on enthusiastically, but the 70 miles between 'A' Company in Belleville and 'B' Company in Peterborough made it difficult to generate real Regimental spirit.

Nevertheless, in the summer of 1973, just after the Regiment came under the jurisdiction of the Toronto Militia District, Hasty Ps were among the 75 Militiamen selected to participate with Regular Force troops in the 15-day Exercise Viking near Resolute Bay in the far north.

Major Carl Hubel, who had served for a time with an RCR company in the NATO force in Germany, commanded a company that included 38 Hasty Ps — 19 from Belleville and 19 from Peterborough. The Militia soldiers did well on the Arctic exercise. One feature was a voluntary 43-mile one-day march in full kit over shale slopes, led by Warrant Officer Dave Nichols. They had passed arduous tests at Petawawa and their standard of performance in the north was as good as the Regulars displayed.

But public support for the armed forces, particularly in urban centres, had declined rapidly through the 1960s and into the 1970s. Horrors of war-torn Vietnam were presented by news media which generally condemned everything that U.S. forces did and anti-war activists were given hero status. U.S. attitudes spread easily to Canada where fugitives from the draft were greeted by some young Canadians as saintly and all-wise. Expanding Canadian universities had draft evaders as students and teachers. Student unrest in Canada seemed to copy the U.S. pattern.

In the course of a reunion speech Duffy stated his views on student unrest with unhesitating anger. There should be a crackdown by university officials, he declared. "We are paying dearly for their education. But we aren't giving subsidies for their stupid, wanton waste of time, material and energy.

"We say to the immigration authorities that we do not want draft dodgers from the United States in this country. Further we say to our universities which we are subsidizing that there is no room for them in our universities, and above all we do not want these welchers as instructors for our young people."

The well attended 1973 reunion in Belleville marked the 30th anniversary of the early battles in Italy. Lord Tweedsmuir was on hand from Aberdeen, Scotland, and the Regiment greeted George and Joyce Ponsford of Durban, South Africa, and their son Barry. The 1974 reunion in Peterborough featured a change-of-command parade. Lt.-Col. Richardson was succeeded by a 39-year-old pharmacist, Lt.-Col. John Inrig of Picton, whose father, Major James Inrig, had served with the Regiment from 1927 to 1944. Inrig was the first C.O. from Picton since Sherman Young took command in the spring of 1939, about five months before mobilization.

While the Regiment carried on with two widely separated companies, the Quinte Emergency Measures Organization under Duffy's direction was building back into Hastings and Prince Edward Counties some of the human resources which were severely reduced when far outlying companies and platoons were disbanded.

But EMO was subject to the same hazard as the Militia — cost-cutting by politicians and bureaucrats who didn't really understand the whole picture. The bad news was contained in a brief passage in the Ontario budget on April 7, 1975. Treasurer Darcy McKeough said that "programs which have outlived their usefulness such as the Emergency Measures Organization" would be reviewed with a view to eliminating them. The federal government's 75 per cent support had been withdrawn and Ontario's 15 per cent was being cut off as a matter of routine. Local emergencies would be handled by various provincial agencies, but Duffy and others wondered how much provincial employees might be hampered by the bureaucracy in Toronto.

Probably no one in the Quinte region commanded more respect than Duffy and nobody else would be likely to achieve his degree of success in persuading people that unpublicized and even tedious work for the community is the essence of good citizenship.

"Civil Defence force faces dissolution brought on by peace", said the heading on one Toronto newspaper story that never got down to the main issue. In 1975 no EMO was a collection of tin-hatted bomb shelter builders. EMO had emphasized protection against blast and fallout until the early 1960s, but for a decade or more the emphasis had been on dealing with man-made or natural disasters. (A 1979 Mississauga train derailment was to remind Ontario how perilous the transportation of chemical cargo had become.)

Working days and nights and weekends, Duffy inspired people to plan together ways to protect their own communities or neighbouring communities when emergencies occur. In the early evening of July 13, 1973, a tornado roared through the lakeside town of Brighton, about 10 miles west of Trenton well outside the Quinte EMO area. Rows of maples along Main Street went down in tangles of utility wires, the Presbyterian church lost its steeple and the town hall collapsed. Only one person was injured, but the town looked like a battlefield. Duffy was far away on holidays, but members of Quinte EMO went to Brighton on their own initiative to take a leading role in the cleanup.

Officials of the Belleville General Hospital, the St. John Ambulance Association and municipal councils throughout the Quinte region were appalled by the 1975 Queen's Park decision to scrap EMO. They made their protests, but to no avail. Duffy would be retired at 61.

There wasn't much time to think about that. Within two weeks Duffy and Basil Smith were in Rome as official representatives of the Regiment on a government-sponsored pilgrimage to Sicilian and Italian battlefields and war cemeteries. Other veterans and their wives accompanied the official tour at their own expense.

Between the landing in Sicily and the departure for Northwest Europe early in 1945, about 91,500 Canadians served in the Mediterranean theatre. After the Normandy landings Italy became a forgotten front. Killed and wounded totalled more than 25,000 and 5,900 Canadians were buried in 17 cemeteries from Sicily to the Po Valley.

The tour brought many highly emotional moments — travelling through familiar terrain and once-battered villages, walking where shells had screamed down and remembering those whose bright young lives ceased suddenly — or those like Captain Grover Dennis who survived fierce fighting in the Moro bridgehead only to die of wounds later in hospital. In the long, neat rows of headstones were shattering reminders of how very young some of their comrades had been. "Their young faces kept flashing across my mind," Duffy said.

Men on the pilgrimage may well have asked themselves: Why did we survive? What have we done with all the days they left to us? Wives, seeing Italy for the first time, could understand why their husbands were often silent, or sometimes wept, or sometimes drank too much or sometimes did both.

While some veterans were retracing their steps in Italy, others at home were appalled to learn on Monday morning, April 30, that fire had gutted St. Thomas Church in Belleville, totally destroying Regimental colours which had been laid up there.

At a mess dinner marking the Regimental birthday in March, 1976, Colonel Inrig announced that Angus Duffy had been appointed Honorary Colonel and Bill Graydon Honorary Lieutenant-Colonel. No stauncher Hasty Ps existed anywhere, it was agreed, and these popular appointments did much to raise the morale of the Militia battalion and the interest of the veterans of the wartime battalion. Honoraries with such good news sense as these two advising an enthusiastic C.O. would do much to keep the Regiment in the public eye. However, there just wasn't enough money available from official sources to enable Colonel Inrig to 'show the flag' as consistently as he would like.

In June, 1976, Inrig told the Officers Association executive that he had plans for Trooping the Colour during the weekend of the October reunion, but finding sufficient money would be difficult. Letters to charitable foundations and other organizations had drawn non-commital replies or outright refusals. Inrig expected to be $1,500 short and the Officers Association executive agreed to provide that amount which they didn't have either, but they were prepared to borrow it.

This stimulated discussion of how to establish a trust fund from which the C.O. could obtain financial support for projects and events not covered by Militia funding: a band, special parades, period uniforms, sub-unit competitions, support for cadets. Gordon Way undertook to consult experts at Revenue Canada on how to establish a charitable foundation with the right to issue receipts to donors for income tax purposes.

The Trooping went off well, in spite of huge pools of water on Zwick's Island Park following a heavy snowfall the night before. All costs were met, but plans for a trust fund went ahead. The Senior NCOs Association and the all-ranks Regimental Association joined wholeheartedly with the Officers Association to form the Hastings & Prince Edward Regimental Associations Trust Fund in 1977.

The objective was a large capital fund of at least $50,000 which would yield investment income. It was agreed that the Trustees would be the presidents of the three associations, the Honorary Colonel, the Honorary Lieutenant-Colonel and an Honorary Secretary-Treasurer. Major-General Chris Vokes was the first donor. Hasty Ps of all ranks contributed — some more than once. Growth of the capital fund was greatly accelerated through the initiative of Captain Leitch Scott who had seen action overseas. A donation of $40,000 from Kenscott Ltd., when reinvested in that company, meant that significant revenue could be provided for the Regiment by 1980.

In the year ended March 31, 1982, more than $9,000 was directed to the Regiment from the proceeds of investments and by then the total capital fund was approaching $55,000.

During the restoration of St. Thomas Church the Officers

Association, Senior NCOs Association and the Regimental Association decided to commemorate the Colours lost in the fire. Representatives joined in a Regimental church parade on Sunday, May 8, 1977. A bronze plaque, unveiled by Colonel Duffy, was consecrated as a memorial attesting to the long association between military units in the Belleville area and St. Thomas Church. It recalled that among the church's irreplaceable treasures, the fire destroyed Colours deposited there by the following:

15th Battalion A.L.I.	in 1906
39th Battalion C.E.F.	in 1915
80th Battalion C.E.F.	in 1916
155th Battalion C.E.F.	in 1916
Argyll Light Infantry	in 1951
Hastings & Prince Edward Regiment	in 1970

The City of Belleville marked its Centennial in 1978 and the Regiment was much in the public eye. A well trained Centennial guard in period uniforms participated in many events and the Honorary Colonel was present just as often. Having uniquely embodied the Regimental spirit in six years of war and 33 years of peace really meant that Duffy's loyalty had no limitations. Sixteen years after he had ceased to be commanding officer, he was still in the Armoury two or three or more times a week — showing a school class through the museum, preparing museum material for display, conferring with the C.O. on a parade night or offering an encouraging word to a junior officer or a rear-rank private. At 65 as Honorary Colonel, he went on field exercises and attended camp with his Regiment, providing encouragement to all ranks that went far beyond mere words. In addition he was giving much time to the Quinte Hastings Trail Association in the development of that important recreational resource.

The 1978 reunion marked the 35th anniversary of the start of the Italian campaign and Lord Tweedsmuir was present. Lt.-Col. John Inrig was succeeded in command by Lt.-Col.

Duncan Campbell, another second generation Hasty P. His father, Major Hubert Campbell served as a Militia officer in the Regiment, and as a wartime Can-Loan officer with a battalion of the Black Watch, he was the first 'British' officer across the Rhine in March, 1945.

The change of command took place on Front Street, right outside the doors of the Belleville City Hall. The Regiment paraded smartly and a good crowd watched the proceedings, but the commander of the Toronto Militia District wasn't quite prepared. Apparently the only person unaware of Inrig's bachelor status, he gave lavish praise to the C.O.'s wife for all the support given during Inrig's years in command.

Communication with TMD over a distance of more than 100 miles wasn't easy, but distance could also be advantageous. It enabled the Regiment to continue to wear red berets on home ground (commemorating the wartime 1st Division and the infantrymen of the 27th Brigade that went to Europe in 1951), but for parades in Toronto green headgear was imperative.

Regimental anniversaries closed out the 1970s. Two months after the 1979 reunion commemorating mobilization, Duffy marked the 40th anniversary of the Regiment's journey to Britain with a pacemaker operation. The spring of 1980 brought the 35th anniversary of the short, sharp campaign in the Netherlands and victory in Europe.

George Renison and Allen Ross who commanded the Regiment in the final months overseas led a Hasty P contingent to Amsterdam in May, not just for a reunion but to receive an emotional outpouring of thanks from the Dutch people for their liberation. Riding in restored Canadian vehicles through cheering throngs was an experience these Canadians would never forget. Many regiments were represented, but only the Hasty Ps had captured a palace. A plaque from the Regiment was presented to the City of Amsterdam commemorating the 1980 visit, but Colonel Renison wondered when he might see a plaque placed in the palace at Het Loo which a German officer surrendered to him.

In 1980 Duffy was named an Officer of the Order of St. John in recognition of his longtime work with the St. John Ambulance Association. That year was also the 60th anniversary of the founding of the Regiment and the 50th anniversary of his enlistment as a private in the signal platoon. The October reunion in Trenton was an enthusiastic gathering. On Thanksgiving Sunday morning, General Graham, a sprightly 82, led a half-mile march to the memorial service in a lakeside park. Near the end of the weekend's events the Regimental Association presented commemorative plaques to both Angus and Helena Duffy.

During the weekend of May 2 - 3, 1981, the Regiment and the City of Belleville officially recognized Angus Duffy's retirement as Honorary Colonel. But no one believed that he would ever lessen his commitment to the Regiment upon which his loyalty had been focused for 51 years.

On the Saturday evening the Officers Association honoured him at a mess dinner. Members recognized that in the previous 35 years his day-in-and-day-out determination that the Regiment must survive had been the most important reason for that survival. Bill Graydon, who was also stepping down as Honorary Lieutenant-Colonel, praised Duffy's inspirational qualities during his toast to the Regiment.

Special greetings were read from Generals Graham and Vokes in Oakville, General Walsh in Ottawa, Lt.-Col. Ian Dearness and Major Jim Fraser in Vancouver, Capt. Gordon Dainard in London, Ont., and RSM Harry Fox in Toronto.

Capt. Stan Down, Duffy's successor as RSM in 1949, presented an inscribed silver tray and four silver wine goblets on behalf of the Officers Association. On behalf of Premier William Davis, Hugh O'Neil, MPP for Quinte, presented a plaque congratulating Duffy on his long career of community service.

Major Gordon Way reminisced about the prewar Militia and Brig.-Gen. Bill Seamark recalled wartime days in rural Surrey and Sussex.

The next day had been declared Militia Day by Belleville City Council. The Militia battalion paraded to the Church of St. Thomas and was joined by representatives of the three associations. The large congregation heard Padre Michael Cole thank God "for the career of Your servant, Angus Duffy."

At an all-ranks luncheon in the Armoury, Colonel Campbell praised Duffy for the high standard he had set in every rank he had held and pledged that the Regiment would strive to meet these standards.

Duffy said he had been described as if he were the Angel Gabriel. He was all too well aware that he had done things that he should not have done and had failed to do many things that he ought to have done.

"But I'd rather have the praise of people in the Regiment than have won the VC or received any recognition that the world can give. I love my country and I serve it in the Regiment. To serve is to know discipline and be a leader and a good comrade. So that's what I am — a very ordinary person. Duty and honour and discipline give life a meaning. There's no greater honour I'd rather have than to be called a Hasty P.

"What pleases me is to see the young men and women of the Regiment. We think that we were wonderful, and we were, but you're as good or better. Serve your country because it's a good country, and if you serve it in the Regiment with purpose and duty, your life is fulfilled. I have had the honour of serving you for 50 years. I leave you in great pride."

For more than 50 years the traditions of the Regiment had inspired him. His ability to inspire others had enriched the very fabric of Canadian military history and he had become a legend.

On Sunday, October 11, 1981, Colonel Campbell announced the appointment of George Renison as Honorary Colonel, succeeding Duffy and Gordon Way as Honorary

Lieutenant-Colonel, succeeding Bill Graydon. In sparkling autumn sunshine Colonel Campbell passed his sword to Brian Milroy and marched alone along the front rank of the Regiment to the strains of Will Ye Nae Come Back Again? played by the Regimental Pipes and Drums.

There clearly was some community interest in the change-of-command parade in front of the City Hall, but the Regiment's place in the community had diminished somewhat in the 20 years since Duffy's term was drawing to a close. He could parade 400 men. Under Milroy the battalion had an authorized strength of 167. The new C.O. said in March, 1982, at the celebration of the Regimental birthday, that the paper strength was 145, but the real strength only 118. Authorized strength was about to be increased to 269, but there would be no increase in government financial support until 1983. In fact when he was officially informed about his budget for 1982 it was lower than in 1981. In spite of a 19 per cent increase in the defence budget, the Militia portion declined by about $1.5-million. Aircraft and frigates had priority.

Retired Major-General Bill Leonard, Colonel Commandant of the Infantry, urged senior Militia officers of Ontario infantry battalions at a Toronto conference in February, 1982, to begin a write-in or phone-in campaign and a public relations campaign to impress MPs and the public with the importance of strengthening our NATO land forces, our regular forces in Canada and the Militia. The Militia lacks vehicles, weapons and other equipment required to prepare its troops for the field. It needs a realistic mobilization plan, setting out clearly what tasks the Militia should be ready to assume, it was generally agreed.

The conference was reminded that recent government reports had described serious Militia problems. In December, 1981, Minutes and Proceedings and Evidence of the Standing Committee on External Affairs and National Defence appeared under the title, Action for Reserves. In January, 1982, came Manpower in Canada's Armed Forces, the First Report of the Subcommittee on National Defence of the Standing Senate Committee on Foreign Affairs.

In addition to recruiting 6,400 more regulars and increasing our troop levels in Europe, the Senate subcommittee recommended a complete overhaul of the Militia and the Supplementary Reserve and their dedication to specific tasks fitting their own characteristics.

> "The importance of the Militia regiments and other units should be recognized and the Militia should be assured that it will be employed mainly by units, so as to strengthen morale and guarantee that as many of its 16,000 members as possible can be utilized in an emergency. A major re-equipment program for the Militia should also be launched."

The Commons Subcommittee on Armed Forces Reserves published figures to show that while Canadian Reserve Forces were only a quarter the size of the Regular Force, in Norway there are more than four times as many reserves as regulars. The report, Action for the Reserves, said that increasing national tension made it necessary for Canada to pay more attention to improving the forces' state of readiness.

> "Canada's reserves are in serious need of strengthening. Although they constitute an integral and essential part of the total force, they are deficient in a number of vital respects."

The report declared that "a commitment to enhance the status, capability, and role of the Reserves should be publicly enunciated at the highest political level and supported by increased funding."

But is funding the heart of the problem? Old-timers like Duffy could recall that in the 1930s, when Militia morale was relatively high, there was little pay for anyone. Officers and often NCOs didn't take any.

In the late 1970s, T.C. Willett, a sociology professor at Queen's University and a former soldier, made a three-year study of the relationship of 28 infantry, armoured and artillery units with their communities and with the Regular

Force, by interviewing officers, warrant officers, mayors, police chiefs and citizens in various walks of life, comparing the 1955-1980 period with the decade right after the Second World War and the period between the wars. He talked with Duffy at great length about the prewar Militia.

Willett found that Militia units had lost the prominent civic role they had once had. He found no public hostility toward the Militia, but mainly a lack of knowledge and a lack of interest.

Writing in the Canadian Defence Quarterly, he said that the Militia appeared to be no longer the kind of citizen force it once was when all sections of the community were represented in its ranks. In his view there was too much emphasis on pay and too many people in the Militia seemed to view their service as a second job. Instead of being a pale copy of the Regular Force, the Militia could be more effective as dedicated amateurs, he suggested. Militia units might be more effective as irregulars, particularly units with easy access to rugged country for their training. Certainly the patrolling exploits of wartime Hasty Ps showed the same flair for the unusual as present-day special forces in the British Army.

As this is written the 40th anniversary of the 1st Canadian Division's march to fame in Sicily is approaching and those who were there may be wondering whether Canadians will ever see a force of its quality again. It took three years of training in Britain to produce it. It will soon be 45 years since the infantry battalions of that great division were mobilizing. There is unlikely to be time for traditional mobilization in the future. Indeed a 1983 Militia battalion would be hard pressed to provide much more than a trained platoon to a formation needed on the ground, say in Norway, within a few days. Methods are going to be different, but the spirit sustaining any combat force will be the spirit that inspired the men whose story has been told in these pages. Regimental tradition is vitally important. The Falklands campaign proved that. But Canadian policy of the past 20 years has done little to nurture tradition.

In those two decades Canadians in the Militia found themselves out of step with contemporary society. Many people seemed to consider Canadian history and tradition to be irrelevant. But the voice of history could not be stilled as long as living history — the Regiment — remained. And this was Duffy's cause, as it had always been since he first put on the uniform in 1930.

The uniqueness of his contribution to his community was the depth of his experience over decades in the classical role of the citizen-soldier. Members of his Regiment acknowledged him to be the living embodiment of its spirit, guardian of its traditions and eloquent advocate of the Militia's role in peace and war, as defender of community and country.

As businessman, alderman, emergency measures co-ordinator, conservationist, supporter of charitable causes, organizer of parades and public occasions, his influence for good found its way into every aspect of community life.

Late in 1982, Duffy was informed by Government House that he was to be appointed a Member of the Order of Canada. He was not aware that he had been recommended. The award was a complete surprise to him and a delight to the host of friends and acquaintances who heard about the official announcement on Christmas Eve.

When a Belleville reporter reached him by telephone in Florida, Duffy said that the appointment was "an official Christmas gift that kind of staggers me. I don't know what I did to earn it. It's a very great honour — but I don't look on myself as any particular hero. In anything I've done, I've had a lot of enjoyment, so I've been amply rewarded."

As he thought about it further, Duffy felt that he must have been given this honour as a representative of Militia-men in many communities who had performed leadership roles over many years. On the wintry April day that found him in Government House to be inducted formally into the Order of Canada, he heard more than 60 citations read as men and women went forward to receive their badges of the

Order from Governor General Edward Schreyer. Afterwards he described meeting and talking with these men and women as a powerful reminder of the rich human resources existing on a community level across Canada, giving greatness to the whole country. "I am more proud than ever to be a Canadian," he said.

Congratulated shortly afterward at the annual mess dinner of the Regimental Officers Association, he spoke of how honoured he was to represent those who had helped to build the Regiment over the previous 50 years, and he was optimistic about the prospects for future leadership. The only reward he had ever hoped for could be within the grasp of all in the next 50 years who share the same hopes and pursue them with dedication.

If any regiment in Canada has a future, surely Duffy's Regiment will live on.

Bibliography

Barnard, W.T., *The Queen's Own Rifles of Canada 1860–1960*, Ontario Publishing Co. Ltd., Don Mills, 1960.   219

Boyce, Gerald E., *Historic Hastings,* Hastings County Council, Belleville, 1967.

Comfort, Charles, *Artist At War*, Ryerson Press, Toronto, 1956.

Corrigan, C.E., *Tales Of A Forgotten Theatre*, Day Publishers, Winnipeg, 1969.

Douglas, W.A.B., and Greenhous, B., *Out Of The Shadows, Canada In The Second World War,* Oxford University Press, Toronto, 1977.

Galloway, Strome, *A Regiment At War, The Story of the Royal Canadian Regiment, 1939–1945,* 1979.

Goodspeed, D.J., *The Armed Forces of Canada 1867–1967,* Directorate of History, Ottawa, 1967.

Malone, R.S., *Missing From The Record,* Collins, Toronto, 1946.

Masefield, John, *The Twenty Five Days*, William Heinemann, London, 1972.

Mowat, Farley, *The Regiment,* McClelland & Stewart, Toronto, 1955.

Munro, Ross, *Gauntlet To Overlord*, Macmillan Co. of Canada, Toronto, 1946.

Nicholson, G.W.L., *Official History of the Canadian Army in the Second World War, Vol. II, The Canadians in Italy, 1943–1945,* Queen's Printer, Ottawa, 1955.

Nicholson, G.W.L., *The Canadian Militia's Introduction to Civil Defence Training,* in *Policy By Other Means,* edited by Michael Cross and Robert Bothwell, Clark Irwin, Toronto, 1972.

Pearson, Lester B., *Memoirs, Vol. I, 1897–1948,* New American Library, Scarborough, 1973.

Porter, Gerald, *In Retreat, The Canadian Forces In The Trudeau Years,* Deneau and Greenberg, Ottawa, 1978.

Shapiro, Lionel, *They Left The Back Door Open,* Ryerson, Toronto, 1944.

Simonds, Peter, *Maple Leaf Up, Maple Leaf Down,* Island Press, New York, 1946.

Stacey, C.P., *Official History of the Canadian Army in the Second World War:*
Vol. I, *Six Years Of War,* and
Vol. III, *The Victory Campaign,*
Queen's Printer, Ottawa, 1966.

Stanley, G.F.G., *Canada's Soldiers 1604–1954, The Military History Of An Unmilitary People*, Macmillan, Toronto, 1954.

Swettenham, John, *McNaughton,* Ryerson Press, Toronto, 1968–69.

Lord Tweedsmuir, *Always A Countryman,* Robert Hale, London, 1953.

Parliamentary Reports

Manpower In Canada's Armed Forces — First Report of the Subcommittee on National Defence of the Standing Senate Committee on Foreign Affairs, Ottawa, 1982.

Action For Reserves, Minutes of Proceedings and Evidence of the Standing Committee on External Affairs and National Defence, Ottawa, 1981.

Public Archives, Ottawa

Crerar Papers

Acknowledgements

Old soldiers from private to general have encouraged the writing of this book and it is likely that they will be able to recognize their contributions as they read. People having no direct links with the Regiment were as helpful as old friends in assembling some of the information.

Long conversations with Lieut.-General Howard Graham, Major-General Chris Vokes and Brigadier-General Bill Seamark and with wartime padres Walter Gilling, Reg Lane and Roy Essex helped to outline the shape of the story, to which Lieutenant-Colonels Gordon Way, Bill Graydon and Ken Willcocks added detail surrounding prewar, wartime and postwar events. The most important ingredient was the patient interest of Angus and Helena Duffy whose memories were reinforced with a great wealth of scrapbook material.

Among public sources the Directorate of History at National Defence Headquarters in Ottawa was outstandingly helpful. Special thanks must go to W.A.B. Douglas, W.A. MacIntosh and Philip Chaplin. Lord Tweedsmuir took a great interest in the project and his accounts of Sicilian and Italian action in the possession of the Directorate of History were invaluable.

Helpful staff at the Trenton Memorial Public Library, Belleville Public Library and Picton Public Library provided ready access to useful material and the same was true at the Royal Canadian Military Institute in Toronto, the Metro Toronto Reference Library, the Archives of Ontario and the Public Archives of Canada. Access to the Regimental Museum was of very great assistance.

Jim Buckley provided not only thoughtful reminiscences about events in Italy but helpful comment on part of the manuscript. Basil Smith's wartime Diary of a Quarterbloke shed new light on events, as did articles and letters in the Plough-Jockey, newsletter of the Regimental Association, which he had edited for many years.

For background on 2nd Echelon, 21st Army Group, the author is indebted to Rosaline Madder, Pat O'Donnell and Colonel F.N. Ovens, not forgetting what must be the most neatly typed war diary in the Public Archives.

To a patient and understanding family who saw little of the author during periods of the past few years, I must give special thanks. Nigel became involved in the project eventually and his design contributions were superb.